A LITTLE PHILOSOPHICAL LEXICON OF ANARCHISM FROM PROUDHON TO DELEUZE

Daniel Colson

Translated by Jesse Cohn

A Little Philosophical Lexicon of Anarchism from Proudhon to Deleuze
Daniel Colson
Translated by Jesse Cohn
ISBN 978-1-57027-341-4

Cover design by Haduhi Szukis
Interior layout by Margaret Killjoy

Released by Minor Compositions 2019
Colchester / New York / Port Watson

Minor Compositions is a series of interventions & provocations drawing from autonomous politics, avant-garde aesthetics, and the revolutions of everyday life.

Minor Compositions is an imprint of Autonomedia
www.minorcompositions.info | minorcompositions@gmail.com

Distributed by Autonomedia
PO Box 568 Williamsburgh Station
Brooklyn, NY 11211

www.autonomedia.org
info@autonomedia.org

CONTENTS

ACKNOWLEDGEMENTS

DANIEL COLSON THANKS J.-P. E., C.V., AND Y.C. IN MEMORY OF MARIE-Louise Marsella.

Jesse Cohn would like to thank Daniel Colson (for permission, but even more for an education), Ronald Creagh (the best mentor I could have asked for), other participants in the Lyon symposium (John Clark, Francis Dupuis-Déri, and our gentle host, Alain Thévenet), Nathan Jun (for helping me to learn Colsonian French), Corinne Dupont (for encouraging me to listen to more voices, to be a better *relais*), Mark Mellor and Arabella Bond (the best unwitting patrons of this enterprise), and not least, Stevphen Shukaitis (for his infinite patience), Margaret Killjoy (for her lovely design work), and Karen Alderfer (who is largely responsible for the readability of the book in your hands). Even what hurt ultimately helped.

PREFACE:
THE TRANSLATION MANUAL

> The way that the media and courts have framed the "Tarnac"
> events…and the State's efforts to criminalize the most radical
> currents and turn them into "terrorist organizations"…
> demonstrate their inability to understand movements that also
> radically escape their own logic.
> – Daniel Colson[1]

> Understanding anarchism in its own terms means that whenever
> we understand it in terms that look odd or irrational, it is our
> understanding that must first be questioned…We must indeed
> understand the language of anarchism. However, making sense
> of anarchism, as of any other movement, ultimately means
> interpreting it in terms that we understand. We need to find a
> translation manual.
> – Davide Turcato[2]

1.

IN ONE OF THE DARKEST MONTHS OF AN EXCEPTIONALLY DISMAL 2017, A
crowd of students, along with a group of "black-clad protesters wearing
masks," prevented a scheduled speaking engagement on UC Berkeley's campus
by Milo Yiannopoulos, a far-right troll best known for instigating campaigns

---

1   Colson, "Histoire et actualité du sujet révolutionnaire," *Réfractions* 25 (Fall 2010): 25-26.
2   Turcato, *Making Sense of Anarchism: Errico Malatesta's Experiments with Revolution, 1889-1900* (Basingstoke, UK: Palgrave Macmillan, 2012), 10.

of harassment against women. To defend the community against what they had identified as a fascist recruiting event, they broke windows and lit fires until the announcement came that Yiannopoulos had fled.[1] This Black Bloc action drew criticism not only from the media – who reliably described it as an irrational, violent assault on "free speech" – but also from renowned feminist theorist Judith Butler. While noting that "violence and nonviolence are terms that are already twisted by the frameworks in which they appear" (indeed, the Boycott, Divestment and Sanctions movement against Israel's treatment of the Palestinians, in which she has long participated, has been labeled violent[2]), she warned against thinking of violence in instrumental terms, as a mere means to an end:

> What might at first seem to be a mere instrument to be dis-carded when its goal is accomplished turns out to be a praxis, a means that posits an end at the moment it is actualized; the means of violence posits violence as its end. In other words, through making use of violence as a means, one makes the world into a more violent place, one brings more violence into the world.

Moreover, although she acknowledged that we face "a crisis in democratic politics" – an increasingly pervasive and well-founded belief that elections do not adequately reflect or translate the will of the people – Butler argued that the Black Bloc's action "only compounds the sense of hopelessness and skepticism about the possibility of practicing democracy, when that is precisely what we need most: the exercise of judgment, freedom, and power within the sphere of politics that can activate the true majority to drive Trump and his crew out of office." Finally, she underlined the irony of the fact that the smashed windows belonged to the Martin Luther King Jr. Student Union. Why hadn't the Black Bloc, "a group of mainly white men emphatically able-bodied…

---

1   Madison Park and Kyung Lah, "Berkeley Protests of Yiannopoulos Caused $100,000 in Damage," *CNN.com* (February 2, 2017). A year later, Mark Bray, author of *Antifa: The Anti-Fascist Handbook* (2017), concluded that the Black Bloc action largely achieved its goal. It not only denied a platform to Yiannopoulos in Berkeley but also made hosting him a far less palatable proposition to other venues, subsequently fearful of property damage and bad publicity. See Bray, "Antifa vs. Milo Yiannopoulos: Who Won?" *Salon.com* (January 31, 2018).

2   See, e.g., Cary Nelson's suggestion that "BDS and Hamas are conceptually and political-ly linked" ("The Problem with Judith Butler: The Political Philosophy of the Movement to Boycott Israel," *Los Angeles Review of Books*, March 16, 2014), or, more bluntly, Alan Dershowitz's *BDS: The Attempt to Strangle Israel* (Prager University, July 14, 2014).

[thought] in advance about how painful it would be for many people to witness an attack on the building on campus that symbolizes and honors the struggle for civil rights?"[1]

Months later, at a conference not far away in Oakland, Joshua Clover offered a pointed rejoinder to Butler. For Clover, the problem does not only lie in the fact that the act of breaking a window is represented as "violent," that our electoral systems do not (and cannot) represent "the people," or even that resistance to white supremacist fascism is being represented as somehow identical to what it resists. The problem is also that discourses like Butler's tend to reduce all action to representation, and that this reduction is *already* oppressive. Butler's discourse turns the Black Bloc into a signifier of whiteness and the building into a signifier of blackness. In this gesture, a material reality of glass, steel, and capital is transformed beyond recognition and the material practice of denying fascism a place in public life is rendered unintelligible.

For the span of a generation now, anarchism has been a widespread and visible form of radical politics in the U.S., but the same arguments around it have circulated in almost unchanging form ever since the Black Blocs' debut before the mediatized public gaze in Seattle '99. A number of scholars have tried to suggest, in various ways, that such representations carry a fundamental misunderstanding of anarchism – a misunderstanding that reproduces the prejudices of the liberal model challenged by anarchism.[2] In this liberal model, political life unfolds within a polis, a space within which only one thing must ever occur: civil discourse, the free exchange of words among citizens reasoning with one another about the common good. Force can only enter into this space either (illegitimately) as a menace to this unceasing circulation of signs or (legitimately) as the restoration of the order that permits this circulation. This model cannot account for the often violent operations by which the public sphere was constructed nor how the power exercising "legitimate" violence arrived at legitimacy in the first place.[3] It also fails to anticipate how fascism can gain a foothold in the liberal polis, representing its exercises of force as the legitimate exchange of signs ("free speech") and its opponents as the agents of illegitimate force ("violence"). In this way, liberals have been persuaded to

---

1 Judith Butler, "The Big Picture: Protest, Violent and Nonviolent," *Publicbooks.org* (Oct. 13, 2017).

2 See, for instance, Don Herzog, "Romantic Anarchism and Pedestrian Liberalism," *Political Theory* 35.3 (2007): 314-15.

3 See UTA Editorial Committee, "Behind the Mask: Violence and Representational Politics," *Upping The Anti* 11 (Nov. 2010); David Graeber, *Possibilities: Essays on Hierarchy, Rebellion, and Desire* (Oakland, CA: AK Press, 2007), 365-66; A.K. Thompson, *Black Bloc, White Riot: Anti-Globalization and the Genealogy of Dissent* (Edinburgh: AK Press, 2010), 113.

allow fascists access to the theaters of the U.S. polis *as their right* and to expel anarchists as invaders utterly alien to it.

Within this context, Daniel Colson's lexicon is especially welcome. Drawing inspiration from Deleuze's rejection of the dualism between "signification" and "force," linking this to Proudhon's proto-pragmatist insight that "the idea is born from action,"[1] Colson sets forth the elements of an understanding of the world that is thoroughly opposed to the liberal model that relentlessly severs ideas from actions, signs from forces, "the 'good' law-abiding protestor" from "the 'bad' terrorist element."[2] It is from this radically monist and immanentist perspective that the anarchist action can be understood and meaningfully evaluated. Here, then, is a "translation manual" such as has been called for.

2.

Released just days before the clash in Berkeley, Iwona Janicka's *Theorizing Contemporary Anarchism: Solidarity, Mimesis and Radical Social Change* makes a provocative and persuasive case for reading the work of Judith Butler (among others) as providing "a more suitable theoretical structure to understand contemporary anarchism in practice."[3] Indeed, Butler's critique of the Black Bloc action invokes a concept central to anarchist ethics: the rejection of the kind of utilitarian calculation in which an ideal, ultimate goal located in the future justifies any action, no matter how sordid, in the present. The positive corollary of this refusal is prefigurative practice, the attempt to enact the desired future in the very struggle to produce it: "For libertarian thought and practice," as Colson puts it, "the end is necessarily contained in the means."[4] Nor is Butler unacquainted with anarchists or anarchism. Many anarchists have praised Butler's contributions to queer theory[5] and she has attested an interest

---

1   See Colson's entry for "Manual/intellectual."

2   Thompson, *Black Bloc, White Riot*, 35.

3   Iwona Janicka, *Theorizing Contemporary Anarchism: Solidarity, Mimesis and Radical Social Change* (London: Bloomsbury, 2017), 161.

4   See the entry, "Ends/means." The general embrace of a prefigurative principle by anarchists does not make it a completely "decontested" concept for anarchists (Michael Freeden, *Ideologies and Political Theory: A Conceptual Approach* [Oxford: Clarendon Press, 1998], 5). For a contemporary anarchist interrogation of the concept, see Uri Gordon's "Prefigurative Politics Between Ethical Practice and Absent Promise" in *Political Studies* (22 June 2017): 1-17. However, Gordon's genealogy of "prefiguration" seems to render it a dubious concept only insofar as (in some conceptualizations) it appears to presuppose the kind of "mastery over time" that Colson's conceptualization explicitly rejects.

5   See, for instance, Lucy Nicholas, "Anarchism, Pedagogy, Queer Theory and Poststructuralism: Toward a Positive Ethical Theory, of Knowledge and the Self," *Anarchist Pedagogies: Collective*

in anarchism for several years now,[1] participating in a high-profile conference at the New School for Social Research in 2011, "The Anarchist Turn," at which she spoke on the questions raised by the pro-Palestinian Israeli organization Anarchists Against the Wall. Yet, as we can see from confrontations like the one at Berkeley, most anarchists do not regard property destruction as violent, nor do they interpret the principle of prefiguration as prohibiting violent resistance to oppression. Where, in this process of translation, has the misunderstanding arisen?

Butler's most concrete engagement with anarchism (as a movement and not as an abstract theme) also takes the form of a question about translation and translatability: while "there are anti-Zionist anarchists in Israel…[whose] work and contributions should be gratefully received," she suggests that "the lexicon for understanding the problem of Palestinian oppression may well differ in Palestine and in Israel."[2] In other words, even if Palestinians might well have reasons of their own to be suspicious of statist projects, the question of "whether anarchists can or should support the Palestinian national struggle if that struggle is for a state of their own" seems unavoidable, and this apparent "impasse" raises an even larger question about how distinct and disparate struggles can connect up with one another.[3] For Butler, this question can only be answered through an unending Hegelian labor of "cultural translation," a process for which the anarchists appear to be too impatient.[4] However, she does not stop to ask whether this question of intersectional struggle – the central question of post-1960s radical theory, in fact – might already have a place in the anarchist tradition.

Reading in the margins of this tradition, Colson draws considerable inspiration from a seemingly insignificant reference in the Eighth Study of Pierre-Joseph Proudhon's sprawling magnum opus, *De la Justice dans la Révolution et*

Actions, Theories, and Critical Reflections on Education, ed. Robert H. Haworth (Oakland, CA: PM Press, 2012), 242-259 and Lena Eckert, "Intersexualization and Queer-Anarchist Futures," *Queer Futures: Reconsidering Normativity, Activism and the Political*, ed. Elahe Haschemi Yekani, Beatrice Michaelis, and Eveline Kilian (Aldershot: Ashgate, 2013), 51-66.

1   See Butler, *Notes Toward a Performative Theory of Assembly* (Cambridge, MA: Harvard University Press, 2015), 160-63 and Jamie Heckert and Judith Butler, "On Anarchism: An Interview With Judith Butler," *Anarchism & Sexuality: Ethics, Relationships and Power*, ed. Jamie Heckert and Richard Cleminson (New York: Routledge, 2011), 103-130.

2   Butler, "Palestine, State Politics and the Anarchist Impasse," *The Anarchist Turn*, ed. Jacob Blumenfeld (London: Pluto Press, 2013), 208.

3   Ibid. 215-17.

4   Butler, "Restaging the Universal: Hegemony and the Limits of Formalism," *Contingency, Hegemony, Universality: Contemporary Dialogues on the Left*, ed. Judith Butler, Ernesto Laclau, and Slavoj Žižek (London: Verso, 2000), 20.

dans l'Église, which has yet to appear in a complete English translation. There, in a critique of the 17th-century rationalist philosophers, Proudhon suggests that, while the questions that preoccupied them (e.g. "whether or not matter is divisible ad infinitum" or "[w]hether or not there are truly souls") were merely speculative, their questions concerning free will and necessity could be rethought in practical, political terms.[1] Thus, even if we don't ascribe any literal reality to Gottfried Wilhelm Leibniz's notion of "monads" – infinitesimal, indivisible atoms of existence, each one incapable of being modified from the outside, which nonetheless move together in coordinated ways – we can take this as a model for thinking through questions of individuality and collectivity, autonomy and cooperation, or, in more contemporary parlance, agency and structure. This passing reference to Leibniz's monadology, Colson observes, is writ large in Deleuze (particularly in *The Fold*), where – as reformulated by the sociologist Gabriel Tarde – it is elaborated into a "neo-monadology."[2] Synthesizing Proudhon, Deleuze, and Tarde, Colson elaborates "[a] conception of a world based on the spontaneity of beings, a world in which everything comes from within," which is nonetheless a world where, as Tarde puts it, "*everything is a society…*every phenomenon is a social fact."[3]

At first, this might seem to be merely a strange embellishment on the more familiar notion that what we have taken to be unified, intact categories or entities (like "humanity," "women," or "self") are actually heterogeneous composites (in Deleuzian terms, "assemblages"). However, Colson is interested in the more seemingly mystical aspects of monadology: if a monad has "neither doors nor windows," no way of receiving or emitting signs, how does it communicate and coordinate its movements with all the other monads? In other words, Leibniz's strange ontology poses epistemological questions, questions "on the

---

1   Proudhon, *De la Justice dans la Révolution et dans l'Église*, vol. 3 (Paris: Rivière, 1930-5), 408, trans. my own.

2   Both Leibniz and Tarde are, in an irony Colson and Deleuze readily acknowledge, arch-authoritarians: as Deleuze remarked in his lectures on Leibniz, "He is the philosopher of order, even more, of order and policing…He only thinks in terms of order." And yet, Deleuze notes, it is this very rage or "scream" for order that propels Leibniz into "the most insane concept creation that we have ever witnessed in philosophy" (Deleuze, "Cours Vincennes" [April 15, 1980], trans. Charles J. Stivale, *Webdeleuze: Les cours de Gilles Deleuze*, accessed February 10, 2018.) Once monadology is freed from "the divine mortgage" of a God who guarantees harmony, Colson argues, "[i]t is transformed from a conservative justification of (divine) order into a subversive conception of this order, into an emancipatory necessity: the necessity of constructing, in a radically immanent manner, the best of all possible worlds that Leibniz believed to be already present" (Colson, *Trois essais de philosophie anarchiste: Islam, histoire, monadologie* [Paris: Léo Scheer, 2004], 91-92, trans. my own).

3   See the entry for "Focal point."

terrain of knowledge."[1] As Colson writes elsewhere, an anarchist neo-monadology proposes a different way of thinking, for instance, about how works of fiction may relate to a seemingly quite distinct reality, how events in the present may relate to a seemingly irretrievably lost past. It proposes a way of knowing that consists in "'finding' oneself in the other and finding the other in oneself as already there...being oneself and an other, or rather all the others."[2]

Colson's summary of his neo-monadology, in *Trois essais de philosophie anarchiste: Islam, histoire, monadologie* (2004), may be helpful here. Leibniz deduces that, while each monad is windowless, "this connexion or adaptation of all created things to each and of each to all, means that each simple substance has relations which express all the others, and, consequently, that it is a perpetual living mirror of the universe."[3] Similarly, in neo-monadological theory, each being is intrinsically connected to all the others:

> Every being possesses in itself the totality of that which exists, the totality of possibilities, but from a certain point of view, from a "perspective" that belongs to it. In other words, each being is at once radically singular, different from all the others in the singularity of its point of view and, at the same time, similar to them, "completely" similar to them, one might say, since like them it contains in itself the totality of possible perspectives, even if only from a certain point of view. To put it another way, in the neo-monadological approach, reality must be entirely thought [quoting Jacques Rivelaygue] "on the model of the subject," starting from a "subjective substrate," an infinite multitude of forces and subjective and singular points of view, each of which can rightly claim to have access to the totality of that which exists.[4]

In this model, since "the relation...between beings is actually an *internal* relation," we can engage in collective action "without translators or translation," without the mediation of vanguard intellectuals or the direction of central committees.[5] Rather than seeking to transcend differences in the overarching unity of the "universal" or to reduce all struggles to a single category (class, gender, race, ecology, etc.), forces engaged in social struggles can link up with one another, in Félix Guattari's words, along "[a] trans-monadic axis, one of

---

1 Colson, *Trois essais*, 87, trans. my own.

2 Colson, *Trois essais*, 42-43, trans. my own.

3 Leibniz, *The Monadology*, trans. Robert Latta (Oxford: Clarendon Press, 1898), 56.

4 Colson, *Trois essais* 87, translation my own.

5 See the entry for "Secrecy."

transversality."[1] In this way, an infinity of divergent forces might nonetheless find a queer kind of commonality – a "stranger unity," as Deleuze puts it, "that can only characterize the multiple."[2]

As abstract and speculative as this neo-monadology may seem, it suggests a distinctive way of thinking about issues as concrete as the encounter of Palestinian and Israeli activists at a military construction site in Bili'in: how do seemingly disparate and even dissonant movements, groupings, and identities link up in ways that are strong enough to challenge the forces of domination? In forming these links, how can we avoid falling back into another kind of utilitarian means-ends calculation – what Colson calls "the mechanical game of politics in which it is always a matter of defining others…and classifying them as friends or enemies on the chessboard of power so as to conquer or defend them, depending on one's interests and strategy"?[3] How, in fact, do we determine who are our "friends" (and not solely "friends of our friends" or "enemies of our enemies")? What kind of social reality and political value can be ascribed to identities, to what is often derisively called "identity politics"?

In a move similar to Butler's, Colson proposes the Proudhonian concept of "analogy" as an alternative to the kind of reductive strategic analysis in which every form of power must ultimately be tracked back to a single source (so that, for instance, women's oppression is treated as an epiphenomenon, to dissolve spontaneously once "the contradictions of the existing order or system" have been resolved or at best as a subsidiary question to be addressed after the definitive revolution, "deferred to the end of time"): if Church, State, and Capital produce similar effects of power, this is not because they are identical nor because they form a single indissoluble structure. But where Butler emphasizes the non-identity at the core of "analogy" – a primary difference that prohibits "the presumption that one group's suffering is *like* another's" – Colson suggests that not only is the "analogy" between forms of oppression useful, but that we find a world of possible "affinities" among the oppressed, the very logic "[by] which libertarian forces are linked to one another."[4]

All of this can help us to imagine how, in the absence of a single overarching logic of struggle, an infinity of different struggles might nonetheless find a queer kind of commonality, Deleuze's "stranger unity." Analogy and affinity

---

1   Félix Guattari, "Ritornellos and Existential Affects," trans. Juliana Schiesari and Georges Van Den Abbeel, *The Guattari Reader*, ed. Gary Genosko (Oxford: Blackwell, 1996), 167.

2   Deleuze and Guattari, *A Thousand Plateaus*, trans. Brian Massumi (Minneapolis, MN: University of Minnesota Press, 1987), 158 (modifications my own).

3   See the entry for "Friends of our friends."

4   Butler, *Parting Ways: Jewishness and the Critique of Zionism* (New York: Columbia University Press, 2012), 128. See Colson's entries for "Analogy (homology)" and "Affinity (affinity groups, elective affinity)."

can prepare us to understand, for instance, how it is that in the world-historical year of 2011, Egyptian students in Tahrir Square, reaching across the "trans-monadic axis," could greet protesting unionized workers in Madison, Wisconsin with expressions of joyous recognition and how the occupation of Tahrir came to be "mirrored" in Zuccotti Park. Perhaps we could say that this retrieves the subversively universalistic slogan of classical humanism, "nothing that is human is alien to me," but without humanism's normalizing burden: *nothing* is alien to me.

Under these assumptions, Colson's neo-monadology lends to anarchism another way of avoiding the lethal dichotomies in which radical theory so often becomes trapped: not only unity/difference, universal/singular, structure/agency, and theory/practice, but also monism/pluralism, self/other, subject/object, idea/matter, natural/mechanical, human/nonhuman. These are also among the foremost targets of Iwona Janicka's book.

3.

Daniel Colson first published his *Petit lexique philosophique de l'anarchisme de Proudhon à Deleuze* in 2001, the same year Saul Newman published *From Bakunin to Lacan: Anti-Authoritarianism and the Dislocation of Power*. What has since come to be called "postanarchism" is often thought of as a hybrid of poststructuralism and anarchism: anglophone theorists rereading "classical anarchism" through the corrective lenses of "French theory." While often instructive, many of these attempts to read "from Bakunin to Lacan" have been to some degree unsatisfying for a number of reasons.

First, in large part, English-language works of postanarchism have not been deeply informed by the historical experience of anarchism. Relying on a few key thinkers taken as anarchist counterparts to Marx and Engels, as filtered through certain dominant interpretations of those thinkers' texts, the anglophone postanarchists have too often been content to ignore a plethora of other anarchist voices (including the voices of women, non-Europeans, and anybody from the post-World War II generations), as well as the distinction between what theorists write and what militants do.

The first error gives rise to a second. The anglophone postanarchists have almost all read the anarchist tradition as founded on a variety of humanism, a Rousseauian faith in the goodness of "human nature." This interpretation comes largely from the sedimented readings of Proudhon, Bakunin, and Kropotkin (and sometimes Stirner) laid down in past generations by non-anarchist scholars who could scarcely believe that anything else would permit a rational person from expecting something other than a Hobbesian war of all against all to appear in the absence of the State. In fact, those who have attended to the ways in which anarchists actually act together are well aware that they assume human behavior to be a complex product of culture and context as well as nature. Why bother, otherwise, to create practices of federation designed to protect local autonomy from encroachments from above or directly democratic gatherings of delegates bound to their base assemblies by imperative mandate on pain of immediate recall? If anarchists really believe that "nature" is a sufficient source of order, why have they paid so much attention to fine points of organization? Why would believers in innate goodness place such emphasis on education and ethics? But these questions don't arise at all if one's understanding of anarchism is confined to a glance at Kropotkin's *Mutual Aid* or Stirner's *The Ego and Its Own*.

Embarrassed by what they take to be "classical" anarchism's commitment to humanism, the anglophone postanarchists have tended to ignore the actual theoretical resources in the tradition and have chosen instead to reinterpret postmodern theories as already implying an anarchist politics. This allows them to pull postmodernism away from its reformist interpretations, to reinscribe it within the context of May '68. However, they often fail to fully distinguish their interpretation of postmodernism from relativist interpretations. If Foucault insisted that power and knowledge travel together, some postanarchists seem to assume that disrupting claims of knowledge could be tantamount to dispersing the effects of power. Postanarchist practice, then, looks like a game of abstractions, an academic exercise: "The struggle for liberation," Andrew M. Koch announces, "has the character of political resistance to a process of semantic and metaphorical reductionism that serves the interests of control and manipulation."[1] Postmodern anarchism engages in a "symbolic assault upon the semiotic fortresses of modern political economy," aiming at "the overthrow of the Law as an epistemological category," writes Lewis Call.[2] The subject of this "resistance," this "assault" (the term "revolution" has vanished), is defined in terms of thinking and knowing (epistemology) rather than in terms of being and doing (ontology and ethics). The result is sometimes hard to tell apart from what liberal philosopher Richard Rorty approvingly called "textualism": "In the last century there were philosophers who argued that nothing exists but ideas. In our century there are people who write as if there were nothing but texts."[3]

Colson, however, has done more than translate a 19th-century tradition into the terms of a 20th-century discourse. Rather, in his *Little Philosophical Lexicon*, anarchism illuminates poststructuralism, putting postanarchism on an entirely different footing. The difference might be belied by the parallel language of Newman's "from Bakunin to Lacan" and Colson's "from Proudhon to

---

1   Andrew M. Koch, "Poststructuralism and the Epistemological Basis of Anarchism," *Philosophy of the Social Sciences* 23.3 (1993): 348.

2   Lewis Call, *Postmodern Anarchism* (Lanham, MD: Lexington Books, 2002), 5.

3   Richard Rorty, *Consequences of Pragmatism: Essays, 1972-1980* (Minneapolis, MN: University of Minnesota Press, 1982), 139.

Deleuze." Where the former is really organized as a march, chapter by chapter, *from* the anarchism of Bakunin (read as insightful but immature, burdened by humanism, not yet equipped with the radical tools of psychoanalysis and deconstruction) *to* the poststructuralism of Foucault, Deleuze and Guattari, Derrida, and Lacan, Colson's book presents no such narrative. Taking advantage of the generic architecture of "dictionaries and handbooks" (by way of a slight "parody"), it presents us not with an array of definitions that would have the pretension of being complete and authoritative (see the introduction and the definition of "Definition"), but with a rhizome – a centerless network of interrelated nodes between which meaning can be transmitted in multiple directions. This rhizomatic structure allows for a much more open-ended and multilateral relationship between anarchism and poststructuralism (and other instances of subversive and illuminating thought, including, significantly, non-Western voices), so that it is not only a matter of reading Deleuze as the inheritor of Proudhon, but we are also allowed to reread Proudhon through a Deleuzian lens.

In this way, Colson begins to do for Proudhon (and Bakunin, Cœurderoy, Déjacque, Michel, Makhno, Pouget...) what Marxist scholars like Antonio Negri have long since done for Marx. Where Negri gives us, in the title of his book, a *Marx Beyond Marx* (1979), Colson produces a "Proudhon beyond Proudhon," a creative reinterpretation that demonstrates its loyalty to the subversive spirit of the founding texts by turning them against themselves – or, in Colson's Deleuzian terms, by demonstrating their potential to "go beyond their limits," to be "more than themselves."[1] Negri helped reopen a discussion of the relevance of Marxism by rereading Marx's work in a postmodern mode, i.e. "in the margins" and "against the grain." Reading Marx "in the margins" meant taking on an incomplete, transitional work, *The Grundrisse*, that had previously appeared as peripheral to the Marxian corpus and showing that it deserved attention in its own right, that it was not merely a preparation for or an incomplete version of a more canonical works. Reading "against the grain" meant reinterpreting Marx's text in opposition to certain received ideas about what "Marx" meant and did, e.g. that Marx was an "objectivist and determinist" thinker for whom the scientific analysis of economic development ultimately precluded workers' subjectivity, spontaneity, or choice of historical direction. Instead, Negri finds grounds for reading Marx as a thinker of workers' "subjectivity" and self-activity, so that Marx retroactively becomes a prophet of Negri's "autonomy" – a concept that has almost no place in Marx's conceptual armamentarium. Likewise, where Proudhon failed the test of his own radical ideas, lapsing into misogyny and bigotry, Colson allows his best concepts (e.g. "collective force," "collective reason," and "resultant") to serve as

---

1   See the entries for "Limits" and "Limitlessness of the limited."

a kind of immanent critique, making Proudhon go "beyond his own limits."[1]

At the same time, Colson allows us to radically reassess the meaning of post-structuralism, to redescribe it in terms of genuinely anarchist concepts. This translation takes place perhaps most profoundly through the Proudhonian triad of "collective being," "collective force," and "collective reason" (see these entries). If, as Murray Bookchin complained, relativist interpretations of postmodernism tend to produce a privatized experience of the world, a kind of subjectivism without a subject in which emancipation appears as the freedom to imagine that one is free,[2] the *Little Philosophical Lexicon of Anarchism* restores its properly social dimension: emancipation entails dreaming, to be sure, but it is a collective project. I do not know how consciously Colson set out to do this, but his book also does much to rescue Deleuze and Guattari from the "accelerationist" elements of their thought, according to which advanced capitalism is already doing the work of undoing itself – almost a parodic exaggeration of similarly teleological elements in Marxism. We find no celebration here of the privatized fashioning of self-images or the liberatory potentials of consumerism. Nor is there any room for textualism: "All that I attempt to 'say' in this *Lexicon*," as Colson has remarked elsewhere,

> consists precisely in, on the one hand, never separating action and idea, force and signification, and on the other hand, never privileging the one to the detriment of the other… This Deleuzian position is at the heart of militant libertarian discourse itself, at the heart of the concept of direct action, and of course at the heart of the concept of propaganda by the deed, a major concept of the emergent anarchist movement, a concept at once practical and theoretical, demonstrating in itself what it affirms: the indissociable character of action and idea, force and significance.[3]

Here, Deleuze's creative appropriation of Baruch Spinoza's *Ethics* plays an important role. Just as Spinoza proposes a "parallelist" ontology – an account of reality for which "thought" and "extension" (or, more famously, "God or Nature") are just two aspects of the same thing – so both Proudhon and Deleuze sidestep the reductionist question that has bedeviled Western thought from its very beginnings, the question of whether ideas or matter are more real.

---

1   See, for instance, the entries for "Monad" and "Labor."

2   Murray Bookchin, *Social Anarchism or Lifestyle Anarchism: An Unbridgeable Chasm* (Oakland, CA: AK Press, 1995).

3   Colson, "Réponse de Daniel Colson à Eduardo Colombo," *Réfractions* 8 (2002): 144 (trans. my own).

This, in turn, clears the ground for a distinctively non-vanguardist understanding of the relations between theory and practice.[1]

What emerges from this reconstruction of Proudhon via Deleuze and of Deleuze via Proudhon is a kind of anarchism (or postanarchism) that is recognizably true to itself, of a piece with its historical development, while also standing apart from some of our most durable received notions about it. It is not solely or even primarily a critical stance, a "negation of the negation," definable in terms of a list of oppositions, ultimately determined by the very oppressive forces that it would like to overcome; it is profoundly affirmative, "the *affirmation* of the multiple, the unlimited diversity of beings and their capacity to compose a world without hierarchy, domination, or forms of dependence other than the free association of radically free and autonomous forces."[2]

4.

Of course, the definitions in any "brief" lexicon cannot claim to be definitive. For instance, one might ask about the significance of many omissions. Colson's selection and evaluation of anarchist thinkers has proven contentious:[3] entire currents such as primitivism do not even merit mention, and while the book testifies to an enormous respect for the legacy of revolutionary syndicalism and anarcho-syndicalism, class-struggle anarchists will doubtless take issue with the discussions of "Class," "Movement," and "Organization." Furthermore, Foucault, Deleuze, and Guattari are represented here,[4] yet Jacques Lacan – the terminus of Newman's postanarchist narrative and a key referent for contemporary radical philosophers – is conspicuously absent.

Indeed, Colson can be classed among the harshest critics not only of the "Lacanian left" but of an entire genealogy of radical thought indebted to a certain reading of Hegel's *Phenomenology of Spirit*. A number of other anarchists have recently elaborated parallel critiques of what Richard J. F. Day identifies as "the politics of recognition" and what Andrew Robinson calls "the political theory of constitutive lack" at the heart of the works of Ernesto Laclau,

---

1   See the entry for "Theory/practice."

2   See the entries for "Anti-something," "Emancipation (affirmation)," and "Anarchy."

3   See the entries for "Selection" and "Evaluation," as well as Eduardo Colombo's critique, "L'anarchisme et la philosophie: À propos du *Petit lexique philosophique de l'anarchisme* de Daniel Colson," *Réfractions* 8 (2002): 127-41.

4   As well as Michel de Certeau, Giorgio Agamben, and, not without controversy, some of the stranger sources for Deleuze's ontology: not only theists like Leibniz and Spinoza but also the largely apolitical Gilbert Simondon and the virulently *anti*-anarchist Gabriel Tarde, a magistrate and criminologist (see Colombo, "L'anarchisme et la philosophie").

Chantal Mouffe, Alenka Zupančič, Alain Badiou, and Slavoj Žižek.[1] Hegel's concept of desire as marked by a quest for "recognition" in the form of a struggle for domination between warring subjectivities (the famous "master-slave dialectic"), since imported into Lacanian theories of subjectivity as such, implies that the kind of "transversal," egalitarian, horizontal order to which anarchism aspires is, in fact, impossible. "[I]t is one thing," Graeber remarks, "to say that the quest for mutual recognition is necessarily going to be tricky, full of pitfalls, with a constant danger of descending into attempts to dominate or even obliterate the Other. It is another thing to assume from the start that mutual recognition is impossible."[2] Colson is far more blunt: "[I]n the theory of desire as lack, the encounter with the other becomes impossible."[3]

While Janicka notes that Butler's thought, too, is strongly marked by Hegel's master-slave dialectic, Butler is sharply critical of Lacanian theory ("a kind of 'slave morality,'" as she brands it in *Gender Trouble*) for its tendency to hypostasize "lack" into a new quasi-mythic foundation.[4] And although Colson may dispute the need for any privileged "translators" to mediate between monads, he does not deny the "essential role" of signs in permitting the formation of "much vaster collective beings…able to 'translate,' in the field of signs and language, the 'modalities of action' that these collective beings contain." Indeed, both Butler and Colson are wary of the "trap[s]"[5] posed by signs that are permitted to "congeal," to become "sedimented and reified"[6] into rigid constructs, "conferring absoluteness upon what is created by human beings."[7] Butler and Colson share an interest in questioning and undermining "the regulatory practice of identity itself" as a primary form of reification: the identities "woman" and "homosexual" for Butler and "working class" or even "anarchist" for Colson.[8] Moreover, they share an approach to undoing

---

1   David Graeber, "Consumption," *Current Anthropology* 52.4 (August 2011): 494; Richard J. F. Day, *Gramsci Is Dead: Anarchist Currents in the Newest Social Movements* (London: Pluto Press, 2005), 18; Andrew Robinson, "The Political Theory of Constitutive Lack: A Critique," *Theory & Event* 8.1 (2005).

2   Graeber, "Consumption," 494.

3   See Colson, entry for "Lack."

4   Janicka, *Theorizing Contemporary Anarchism*, 26-7; Butler, *Gender Trouble*, 72; Butler, *Bodies That Matter: On the Discursive Limits of "Sex"* (New York: Routledge, 1993), 201-2.

5   Colson, entry for "Symbols (signs)."

6   Butler, *Gender Trouble*, xxi, xxiii.

7   Colson, entry for "Symbols (signs)"

8   Butler, *Gender Trouble*, 32; Colson, entries for "Class (social, sexual, generational, etc.)," "Movement," and "Anarchism." The parallels are really striking: "Any politico-ideological force that claims to found its own existence and the significance of its struggle on the belief in an all-powerful first principle at the origin of that which exists – a foundation that

this appearance of fixity, one that perhaps signals their mutual proximity to Tarde. The corollary to Tarde's declaration that "everything is a society" is that "society is imitation": Tarde's monads, Janicka writes, "have a tendency to associate and 'to associate always and everywhere means to assimilate, that is, to imitate.'"[1] Through what Butler calls "subversive resignification" and what Colson calls "libertarian repetition," they discover not the tragic inevitability of humanism but "an infinite capacity to interpret and reinterpret the signification of events and facts."[2]

Given the many affinities and intersections between the *Little Philosophical Lexicon of Anarchism* and the works of a leading feminist theorist, it is all the more surprising – and disappointing – that references to feminism here are both infrequent and sometimes strikingly misinformed. Francis Dupuis-Déri observes that while Sébastien Faure's *Encyclopédie anarchiste* (1934) includes an entry on "feminism," the *Little Philosophical Lexicon of Anarchism* lacks such an entry.[3] Instead, an empty header for "Pro-feminist" leads to the entry "Pro-something," in which Colson expounds on the familiar dangers of activism driven by white straight male guilt. This phantasmatic feminism finds

---

justifies its struggle (God, State, Capital, Patriarchy, etc.) – merely participates in the power of what it pretends to combat," writes Colson (entry for "Class"). "The mobilization of identity categories for the purposes of politicization always remain threatened by the prospect of identity becoming an instrument of the power one opposes," writes Butler (*Gender Trouble*, xxvi). Both emphasize that identities are effects rather than causative origins – in Colson's terms, *en aval* ("downstream," the product or consequence of something else, *a posteriori*) rather than *en amont* ("upstream," foundational or *a priori*): "[T]he foundational categories of sex, gender, and desire [are] *effects* of a specific formation of power…designating as an origin and cause those identity categories that are in fact the effects of institutions, practices, discourses with multiple and diffuse points of origin" (*Gender Trouble*, xxix). Or, as Colson puts it, "For libertarian thought, the great cleavages that run through and structure our societies (workers/bourgeoisie, men/women, young/old, Whites/Blacks, urban/rural, high/low, in/out, left/right, dominators/dominated, etc.) are not at the origin of the numerous relations of force and domination that comprise our lives. They are, on the contrary, the effects of the ensemble of these relationships" (entry for "Class").

1   Janicka, *Theorizing Contemporary Anarchism*, 96.

2   Butler, *Gender Trouble*, xxxi; Colson, entries for "Repetition" and "Eternal Return."

3   Dupuis-Déri, "L'anarchisme face au féminisme: comparaison France-Québec," *Le sexe du militantisme*, ed. Olivier Fillieule and Patricia Roux (Paris: Presses de la Fondation nationale des sciences politiques, 2009), 198-99n10. In fact, volume two of Faure's anarchist encyclopedia features two entries on "féminisme," one by Jean Marestan and the other by Madeleine Pelletier; see *Encyclopédie anarchiste* (Paris: Librairie internationale, 1934), vol. 2, 804-5. Both the *Encyclopédie* and Colson's lexicon can be faulted for inadequate attention to questions of racism, ableism, and other important modes of oppression.

an echo in the entry for "Rendering of accounts," a ritual supposedly practiced by unnamed "currents emerging from North America" in which "each rebellious force" is required to "immediately subordinate itself to one that is more dominated than itself, to 'render account' to this other, to act and think 'under its supervision.'"[1] If this seems, at best, like a caricature of the "political correctness" denounced by conservatives, it may reflect the relatively slow and difficult uptake of feminist and anti-racist discourses in a French anarchist milieu that, according to Dupuis-Déri, is still strongly influenced by the "universalism" of French "republican discourse."[2] Perhaps it also reflects the gendered biases of Colson's source material: what can be expected if one tries to write an article about "Sexuality" that only cites Spinoza (whose *Political Treatise* declares that "women have not by nature equal right with men") and Proudhon (who speculated that it might be wise to "put woman in seclusion," since she could be only "courtesan or housewife")?[3] Even if he denies any "anatomical or discursive" foundation to masculine power, when Colson insists that "virility, in the libertarian sense of the term, is unrelated to the categories of gender and sex," a symbolic expression for "affirmation" and "force," it is hard to take this at face value, nor can we avoid hearing an echo of the Proudhon who wrote that "genius is...the virility of the mind, its power of abstraction, of generalization, of invention, of conception, of which the child, the eunuch, and woman are equally deprived."[4]

To be fair, North American anarchists often complain – in good as well as bad faith – about the readiness with which discussions can devolve into an "Oppression Olympics," a rhetorical contest in which relative lack of privilege can be converted into a kind of "subcultural capital."[5] Even if they never amount to the authoritarian "rendering of accounts" Colson depicts, anarchist social practices of "holding people accountable" for oppressive behaviors, as Laura Portwood-Stacer notes, "can easily be mistaken for (or actually devolve into) self-righteous moralism and arbitrary boundary policing."[6] All

---

1   Colson, entry for "Rendering of accounts."

2   Dupuis-Déri, "L'anarchisme face au féminisme," 193, 196.

3   Benedict de Spinoza, *A Theologico-Political Treatise and a Political Treatise*, trans. R.H.M. Elwes (New York: Dover, 1951), 387; Proudhon qtd. in Jenny d'Héricourt, *A Woman's Philosophy of Woman; Or, Woman Affranchised: An Answer to Michelet, Proudhon, Girardin, Legouvé, Comte, and Other Modern Innovators* (New York: Carleton, 1865), 84.

4   Proudhon, *De la Justice*, 4.197.

5   Abbey Volcano, "Police at the Borders," *Queering Anarchism: Addressing and Undressing Power and Desire*, ed. C. B. Daring, J. Rogue, Deric Shannon, and Abbey Volcano (Oakland, CA: AK Press, 2012), 34; Laura Portwood-Stacer, *Lifestyle Politics and Radical Activism* (New York: Bloomsbury, 2013), 60.

6   Portwood-Stacer, *Lifestyle Politics and Radical Activism*, 90.

of this, however, coexists alongside the survival of a wide array of oppressive behaviors in the anarchist milieu, from microaggressions and manipulation to racism and rape. Indeed, Colson is right to observe that "[t]raditional divisions…and practices of submission to extrinsic authorities" – including all the vicious hierarchies of gender, race, sexuality, ability, and more – "continue to operate within the actions that seem to be the most peaceful and free."[1] All the more need, then, for "continually discussing and modifying the most minute relationships," for a continuous evaluation of and experimentation with "the most tenuous realities and relations, the thousands of ways of living and working, of eating and getting dressed, of loving and learning, of giving birth and aging."[2]

Would it be perverse to read Colson's text as calling for precisely the kind of internal scrutiny in which anarchist collectives are currently engaged? According to Colson, a certain "prickliness," "sensitivity," or even "hypersensitivity," "a vigilant attention to the diversity and the nuances of…relationships," "an obsession with details," and "a kind of exaggerated democracy" is in fact proper to any anarchist movement worthy of the name, as a continuous practice of evaluation aimed at ensuring "autonomy and respect to the forces that it associates." "[L]ibertarian self-management," he writes, "is always placed under the sign of *tension…*, of *conflict*, and of an unstable balance that must be constantly sought."[3] And Colson identifies a crucial guarantee of this "balance," of internally egalitarian relations, as the right and capacity of individuals and groups to break away from associations and federations, to form parallel or autonomous collectivities: "The demand of the women's movement for separate associations," he writes, is entirely in keeping with the "foundational demand of the anarchist project…[and with] the need to constitute an infinity of radically autonomous collective forces charged with proving concretely, through experimentation with the various methods of association and disassociation, their effectively emancipatory character."[4]

Ultimately, the *Little Philosophical Lexicon of Anarchism* prefigures the kind of feminist rereading and appropriation that might be made of the *Little Philosophical Lexicon of Anarchism* itself. Perhaps an astute reader of Judith Butler would be well positioned to "open [it] up to the infinity of the possibilities and significations that [it] contains" so that it can "[go] beyond its own limits," as Colson's text seems to prophesy:

---

1   Colson, entry for "Hierarchy."

2   Colson, entry for "Common notions."

3   See the entries for "Sensitivity," "Class (social, sexual, generational, etc.)," and "Self-management."

4   Colson, entry for "Separatism."

It is in this sense that the misogynist Proudhon can nonetheless enable us, a century and half later, to think and perceive the nature and the value of women's emancipatory movements, as well as the affirmation and meaning of their most radical feminist currents."[1]

Here, then, is the promise of this book: it is open to resignification, to translation.

You are the translator now.

5.

"FIND EACH OTHER," urged the Invisible Committee in *The Coming Insurrection* (2009), finding an echo in a call for action against the inauguration of Donald Trump: "Find your friends and accomplices."[2] If, as anarchists, we are aware that "the 'state of emergency' in which we live is not the exception but the rule,"[3] that does not prevent us from being seized with horror at the present world crisis, at the ways in which it mirrors the dark years of a globally ascendant fascism in the last century, but also at the ways in which it is unprecedented, as the fundamental processes of life on Earth are rapidly coming undone even while technological advances open up new possibilities for domination. In this situation, the need we have to find our friends is great. So is the need for the arts of association and assembly, experimentation with and evaluation of relationships, described by the *Little Philosophical Lexicon of Anarchism*.

May it be a useful tool in your hands. May it modify you – and may you modify it.

---

1   Colson, entry for "Multiple."

2   Invisible Committee, *The Coming Insurrection* (New York: Semiotext(e), 2009), 97; "Seattle Call for Autonomous Action on #J20," *It's Going Down* (24 Dec. 2016).

3   Walter Benjamin, *Illuminations*, trans. Harry Zohn, ed. Hannah Arendt (New York: Schocken Books, 2007), 257. For a poignant Colsonian reading of Benjamin's essay, see Daniel Colson, "L'ange de l'histoire," *Monde libertaire* 1377 (18-25 Nov. 2004).

PREFACE

ANARCHISM, OWING TO ITS COLORFUL AND SOMETIMES CRUEL HISTORY, THE extremity of its demands, and the marginality or folkloric character of its protagonists – but also owing to the nature of its most theoretical texts – has never truly been recognized within Western philosophical and political thought. It was not until the second half of the 20th century that the radicality, coherence, and immediacy of its social and theoretical implications finally had a hope of becoming visible. By this time, the reference to anarchism had been transformed bit by bit into a half-remembered curiosity, a negligible, more or less sympathetic reference to which the youth must sometimes pay tribute. It is not to itself that anarchism owes this possibility of a new and perhaps first legibility, of a redoubling of an immediate and implicit experience and perception. As its principal theorists so often affirm, it owes this primarily to the outside: the outside of the events that, for a short time, from Shanghai to Paris, from Washington to Berlin or Tokyo, swept over and shook up so much of the world during the '60s and '70s, but also the outside of a contemporary thought seemingly unrelated to historical anarchism, referring to Nietzsche more often than to Proudhon, to Spinoza more often than to Bakunin or Stirner, while at the same time helping, in a subterranean but undeniable manner, to restore meaning to a political and philosophical project that had been forgotten before it was even able to express what it contained. This, at least, is what this lexicon intends to establish: to show how the Nietzscheanism of Foucault or Deleuze, the rereading of Spinoza or Leibniz that these thinkers permit, and the current rediscovery of Gabriel Tarde, Gilbert Simondon, or Alfred North Whitehead not only give new meaning to libertarian thought (for example, the texts of Proudhon or Bakunin) but also take on new meaning from within libertarian thought. In this way, perhaps, this encounter helps make possible the anarchism of the 21st century.

19

Viewed from the perspective of the richness of the experiences of the libertarian movements in all their implications, this lexicon is limited in its objectives. It contains no history and it does not provide any information on individuals, currents, or organizations. It does not address the events that, for nearly a century (from the European insurrections of 1848 to the Spanish Revolution of the summer and autumn of 1936),[1] constituted the living reality of anarchism. It does not do away with the necessity of reading those accounts and testimonies that best allow us to perceive the meaning of this reality: James Guillaume's *L'Internationale*, for example, or Voline's *The Unknown Revolution*, Abel Paz's *Durruti in the Spanish Revolution* or Alexandre Skirda's *Nestor Makhno*.[2] Even within the limits it sets for itself, this lexicon remains provisional and susceptible to a great number of additions and corrections. In its brevity, it has but one aim, which can be summed up in four points: 1) to demonstrate the possible (and paradoxical) theoretical coherence of a movement that resolutely calls for *anarchy*; 2) to show how, after its long eclipse, the theoretical revival of this movement during the second half of the 20th century returns to its origins; 3) to make visible the secret *affinities* that, from the perspective of this movement, link philosophers and theorists as seemingly disparate as Spinoza, Leibniz, Stirner, Proudhon, Bakunin, Tarde, Nietzsche, Bergson, Foucault, Simondon, and Deleuze, among others; 4) to bring to light a perception of the world and of reality analogous to libertarian practices and experiences, a perception necessary to the development of these practices and experiences, yet which they sometimes rather badly lack.

Some practical counsel for the reader: any genuine lexicon, however limited, is a labyrinth with many possible entrances. In libertarian thought, none of these entrances can claim to occupy a privileged place, play a foundational role, or serve as a first principle. It is, therefore, not essential to rely on the arbitrary order of the alphabet and to begin – out of indifference or habit – with the letter "A." On the contrary, all are invited to choose the entries that best suit them, perhaps because they feel a particular and intuitive *affinity* with such-and-such a word or such-and-such an idea, or because certain ideas already constitute a particularly important crystallization of their way of

---

1 What Hans Magnus Enzensberger quite aptly terms "anarchy's brief summer" (*Anarchy's Brief Summer: The Life and Death of Buenaventura Durruti*, trans. Mike Mitchell [Chicago: University of Chicago Press, 2018]).

2 Voline (V.M. Eichenbaum), *The Unknown Revolution, 1917-1921*, trans. Holley Cantine and Fredy Perlman (Detroit: Black and Red, 1974); James Guillaume, *L'Internationale, documents et souvenirs (1864-1878)* (Paris: Éditions Gérard Lebovici, 1985); Abel Paz, *Durruti in the Spanish Revolution*, trans. Chuck Morse (Oakland, CA: AK Press, 2006); Alexandre Skirda, *Nestor Makhno – Anarchy's Cossack: The Struggle for Free Soviets in the Ukraine, 1917-1921*, trans. Paul Sharkey (Oakland, CA: AK Press, 2004).

thinking, feeling, and perceiving. The index at the end permits this choice. You may want to begin – and to return – there. However, by way of your relation to these suggested concepts, they will also have affinities and correspondences that bind them to one another. This allows for a gradual reading, an approach in which proximity is no more to be respected than the alphabetical order or the demands imposed by the logical imperatives of deduction. From this, two consequences follow. Both are closely related to the nature of the project underlying this lexicon as well as to the methods of its construction:

1. Each definition is self-contained and may be read alone, meaning that the commentary on any word may reiterate certain references and quotations that illuminate and explain it without fear of redundancy.
2. Generally, each entry will also refer to several other entries (indicated in italics in the text) that you might want to or should consult next. These are connections made by the author of this lexicon and that aided in the development of this text, concerning which a few more pointers are needed.

First note: these references to other entries (often placed between parentheses) are sometimes included in the very text of the definitions, at the moment when they meet with or brush up against other possible expositions. These references may also be at the beginning of each entry. Placed between parentheses, they are arranged in rough order of increasing difficulty, opening onto a possible sequence and course. The paths that constitute this lexicon are thus manifold. Some of them are steeper, rockier, and more difficult (as well as more abstract) than others, but generally, they all attempt to communicate with one another (if you find otherwise, please notify the author), either directly or by *analogy* and *internal affinity* (see these terms). If the air becomes too thin for those who take these paths, they can beat an immediate retreat and take an easier one.

Second note: many of the terms that mark these paths (approximately a quarter) are not accompanied by definitions. In anticipation of potential expositions that are present in a more or less latent fashion within other definitions and expositions or linked to them, these usually just point the way. This leaves it to the reader to flesh these terms out, to make a different choice about the importance to be granted to them, to privilege those that best suit them, to develop for themselves the possibilities that they contain, and to give them definitions that would then justify new bifurcations, new sequences.

A third note, therefore: each reader can thus imagine many other passages that are not yet opened. One may also become irritated with the insistent character of these signposts and refuse to follow the directions they propose or be astonished by the absence of a great number of entries that seem possible or essential. One is free to clear one's own path through this selection of libertarian discourse. One can also build oneself another lexicon – a parallel lexicon – or one that explores other territories, that is capable of composing other possible worlds.

One last important note that follows from the previous: the peremptory or didactic tone adopted here – that of dictionaries and handbooks – is obviously a parody, one that is dictated by the grammar of the genre, as Nietzsche and Léo Ferré[1] would say, and intentionally so. Anarchism, because it has no Academy, qualifying exams, pope, high priests, or central committee, authorizes anyone to speak on its behalf. But the absolute *subjectivism* proposed within this lexicon is in no way the justification a kind of *relativism* that refutes, for its part, the importance here attached to the concept of *affirmation* (see these terms). It is merely, so to speak, the *internal* and *subjective* condition of the definition of anarchy suggested by Gilles Deleuze and Felix Guattari, this "stranger unity that can only characterize the multiple."[2]

---

1   Translator's note: Léo Ferré (1916-1993) was one of the most well-loved poets and singers of the French *chanson* tradition, as well as a lifelong anarchist militant.

2   Gilles Deleuze and Félix Guattari, *A Thousand Plateaus*, trans. Brian Massumi (Minneapolis, MN: University of Minnesota Press, 1987), 158 (trans.: modifications my own).

A ***priori*/*a posteriori*** [***amont*/*aval***] (see *eternal return, tradition, chaos, entelechy, past*).

Action (practice) (see *tools/weapons, movement,* and *symbols/signs*). "What can we expect from man? – Only one thing: acts." "Reflection, and consequently the idea, arises in man from action, not action from reflection."[1] "The condition *par excellence* of *life*, health, and *force* in organized beings is action. It is through action that they develop their faculties, that they increase their *energy*, and that they attain the fullness of their destiny."[2] These remarks by Proudhon go to the heart of the libertarian project.[3] Anarchism refuses idealism and its primacy of theory ("think before you act!"), which entrusts to scientists, experts, words, and reasoning the prerogative of dictating what must be done, thought, and desired, so as to continually rein in our acts and desires, all the better to subject them to the order of signs, ranks, and hierarchies. The libertarian conception of action thus refers to two principal standpoints:

- A standpoint that could be described as epistemological or critical, consisting in a refusal to separate things and signs, forces and significations, acts and reasons to act, laws or precepts and their applications. This standpoint diagnoses this separation as one of the principal sources of domination: the capacity of certain forces to separate others from what

---

1   Pierre-Joseph Proudhon, *De la Justice dans la Révolution et dans l'Église*, vol. 3 (Paris: Rivière, 1930), 71-72.

2   Pierre-Joseph Proudhon, *La Guerre et la paix* (Paris: Rivière, 1927), 53.

3   "In nature, all is movement and action: to be means nothing more than to do" (Mikhail Bakunin, "Considérations philosophiques sur le fantôme divin, sur le monde réel et sur l'homme," in *Œuvres*, vol. 3 [Paris: Stock, 1908], 384).

they are capable of by binding them in the snares of language, law, and principles or in the trap of lying words that pretend to stand in for the things of which they speak (see *representation* and *State*).

- A standpoint that pertains to the very nature of the libertarian project. As the most common philosophical definition of this word indicates, "action is the operation of a being regarded as the product of this being itself and not of a cause external to it."[1] In this sense, action is the expression of a project based on the autonomy of beings, on the refusal of any being's submission to or dependence on another. It is also in this first sense that libertarian thought can be compared to Nietzsche's.[2] Because it is an *affirmation* of beings in what constitutes them as free beings solely subject to their own self-*determination*, action is not only opposed to discourse and signs, it is also opposed to *reaction* (see this term), to that passive form of action in which one is content to react to the action of others (see *ressentiment* and *guilt*). And it is in this sense – as the decisive criterion of all that makes us act (actions and reactions, affirmations and negations, activity and passivity) – that libertarian action poses the question of emancipation and posits its necessary conditions.

Active minorities (see *core*, *midst of things*, *direct action*, and *intimate*). A concept from revolutionary syndicalism and anarcho-syndicalism. Not to be confused with the authoritarian concept of the "vanguard" specific to the Marxist parties (in their Leninist or Trotskyite versions), which claim to be able to see farther, higher, deeper, and more from the outside than the great majority of the exploited – thanks to their possession of theory – and therefore to have the right to steer the exploited on their path to emancipation (see *alienation*). The active minorities of revolutionary syndicalism and anarcho-syndicalism think and perceive themselves as the particular expression of a *possibility* (see this term) within a favorable and potentially revolutionary milieu, but one that is varied in its forms of expression, organization, and struggle and that may always be

---

1   André Lalande, *Vocabulaire technique et critique de la philosophie*, 15th ed., vol. 1 (Paris: PUF, 1985), 19-20.

2   The entirety of this brief lexicon hopes to show in a sufficiently convincing way, in spite of the many and radical differences, a profound affinity between Nietzsche and the principal theorists of anarchism. If one must justify this link by a reference that is at once extrinsic and *intimate* (see this term), see the memoir published in 1906 in which Franz Overbeck, one of Nietzsche's few close friends, not only lengthily demonstrates, in the most explicit manner, the connections that may exist between Nietzsche and Stirner (whom the former read), but also "the greatest possible affinity" between Nietzsche and Proudhon. Cf. Franz Overbeck, *Souvenirs sur Nietzsche*, trans. Jeanne Champeaux (Paris: Éditions Allia, 1999), 59-65.

composed differently, according to other *possibilities* (corporatist, reformist, nationalist, reactionary, etc.). While initially appearing on the terrain of *action* (see this term), active minorities present themselves neither as an external model nor as agents of a theoretical knowledge that would authorize them to direct or to lecture to others. While selecting from within their lived experience the forms of and reasons for struggle perceived by them as the most radical or revolutionary, active minorities attempt to act by contagion or imitation, to involve others by expressing within their own practices a relation to the world and others that is potentially present in an infinity of other situations and may be repeated with greater power. In this sense, according to the model of crystallization proposed by Simondon, active minorities, in the libertarian sense of this concept, can only appear in a "pre-revolutionary" context, in "a state of supersaturation…in which an event is really ready to occur," an event able "to traverse, animate, and structure a varied domain, increasingly varied and heterogeneous domains," "to propagate" throughout them.[1]

Affinity (affinity groups, elective affinity) (see *trust, commons, association, repugnance, repulsion,* and *analogy*). A concept from ancient chemistry recovered in modern times by Goethe and Max Weber to theorize human relations, which plays an essential role in the representations and practices of the libertarian movement. "We group ourselves only by affinity!" exclaims Charles d'Avray in his song "Le Triomphe d'anarchie." Contrary to what one might believe, libertarian affinity is not of an ideological nature – except insofar as such-and-such a shared program or platform implies more profound "affinities" between those who subscribe to it. In love as in politics (such as libertarians conceive of it), affinities between militants on this or that position or *plane of reality* (community life, association for a technical task, or, historically, the small activist groups of the FAI[2] in the working-class districts of Barcelona, etc.), involve temperaments, various forms of *sensibility*, various qualities of character, and the various ways in which these can be composed with others. We always change according to the beings, the situations, and the things that we associate ourselves with for some length of time (a car, a companion, an automatic rifle, or a suburban house, for example). Each *association* selects in us and in others particular qualities and predispositions, which are sometimes unsuspected and often surprising. This is why nobody is capable of knowing or envisaging what he or she can do, for good as well as for bad. Association is the art of bringing about good encounters and avoiding bad ones, thereby mobilizing in oneself and from oneself new, untapped resources that are affirmative rather than negative, charged with life rather than death. This presupposes a great deal of

---

1   Gilbert Simondon, *L'Individuation psychique et collective* (Paris: Aubier, 1989), 53, 54, 63.

2   The Iberian Anarchist Federation.

finesse, flair, and *practical sense*, which circumstances and the crudity of the schemas and roles imposed by the current order generally make very difficult. An example of affinities which were fruitful in their contents and their effects: the "intimate circles" in which Bakunin never ceased to participate. A much more questionable example of affinities (both on the theoretical and practical level): the Nechayev-Bakunin association or the militarization of the militias in Spain in 1937.

Affirmation (see *emancipation*).

Alienation (see *lack, desire,* and *appetite*). Separated from that which they are capable of by an oppressive and damaging external order, unable to discover in themselves the infinite resources that they contain, *collective forces* are led to try in vain to to fill the *lack* (see these terms) caused by this distortion, to desperately seek a remedy for their powerlessness in the exteriority of other beings (see *exterior/interior*). Whether this identification with the other takes the form of love or hate, whether it takes place through the abject submission of the *masses* (see this term) to bosses and powerful persons or through the envious and hateful struggle that these figures inspire, or through the illusions of distance provided by negation and the dialectic, the collective being, separated from its own capacities, is dispossessed of itself. And it is in this sense that it can be said that one is alienated: one is entirely dependent on the other – friend or enemy – and exists only through the other. This is the case not only in one's acts (see *master/slave*) or the image that one has of oneself, but in the very heart of one's *subjectivity* (see this term). Alienation thus justifies two types of oppression, which are symmetrical even as they pretend to be opposed to one another: 1) the oppression of existing dominations, which can feed on the forces that they have captured and that identify with them; 2) the oppression of future dominatory orders fed by the impotence of those same forces that they claim to liberate, to which they deny any autonomy since, as alienated forces, they are said to depend entirely on a domination and a liberation external to their being, external to what they are capable of doing by themselves. Marxists or Christians, revolutionaries or humanitarians, the *servants of the people* (see this term) – the spokespersons and defenders of the "poor" and the "oppressed" – are indeed (in the words of Proudhon concerning Marx) the "tapeworms" of *emancipation* (see *classification*).[1]

---

1   Translator's note: in Proudhon's diary entry for Sept. 23, 1847, he responds angrily to Marx's publication of *The Poverty of Philosophy*, a book attacking Proudhon's own *Philosophy of Poverty*: "Marx is the *tapeworm* of socialism" (*Carnets*, vol. 2, ed. Pierre Haubtmann [Paris: Rivière, 1974], 200).

Alliance (see *friends of our friends* and *association*). The concept of alliance plays a great part in the history of the libertarian movement, from Bakunin's International Alliance of Socialist Democracy to the *active minorities* of anarcho-syndicalism. It is, then, synonymous with the *intimate circles* (which are very often secret) founded on *affinity* (see this term). In this very particular sense, this concept radically escapes the meaning generally given to the word "alliance" when it is used to indicate political, economic, or matrimonial agreements between States, parties, families, or enterprises (see *friends of our friends*). In this common sense of the word, for libertarian thought, "alliance" is opposed to *association*. If association allows the associated beings – through *composition* and *affinity* (see these terms) – to liberate the internal *forces* and *possibilities* that each of them contains, thus displaying and affirming the power of that which exists, an "alliance" – whether political, military, or economic – is always a mere external addition of forces (families, parties, clans, nations, businesses), a utilitarian grouping according to the (equally external) exigencies or necessities of fear, domination, or profit.

Altruism (see *implication*).

Analogy (homology) (see also *affinity* and *in the midst of things*). A concept that Proudhon uses to theorize the common character of Capital, State, and Church: "Capital, the analogue of which, in the political order, is Government, has as a synonym, in the order of religion, Catholicism…What Capital does to labor and the State to freedom, the Church inflicts, in its turn, on intelligence."[1] Analogy is an important concept for understanding the logic and the nature of libertarian emancipation. In anarchism, the revolution is not primarily the product of the contradictions of the existing order or system, the dialectical product of this system, or its negation (see *power of the outside*). It is born from the outside of the currently dominant system, from what this system does not manage to enclose, from the infinity of possibilities that this system ignores, plunders, suppresses, and denies, the potential forces that always haunt this system with the fact that it is merely one possibility among an infinity of other possibilities (see *anarchy*).[2] The libertarian movement is not born from the

---

1   Pierre-Joseph Proudhon, *Confession d'un révolutionnaire* (Paris: Rivière, 1929), 282.

2   On this relation between the inside and outside of systems, cf. the distinction suggested by Michel de Certeau in *The Practice of Everyday Life* (trans. Steven F. Rendall [Berkeley, CA: University of California Press, 2011], 35-36), but also the way in which, as Alain Caillé explains, Claude Lefort refuses to consider "society as a flat and homogeneous space totally covered by the various systems without any remainder" (Alain Caillé, "Claude Lefort, les sciences sociales et la philosophie politique," in *La démocratie à l'œuvre. Autour de Claude Lefort*, eds. Claude Habib et Claude Mouchard (Paris: Éditions Ésprit, 1993], 63-64). (On

order that it refuses, even if this order is contradictory, but from the anarchic profusion of forces and possibilities that are alien to this order or from those that this system dominates and damages. To compose another arrangement from this profusion of forces, to select from among all the possible forces those that permit the free development of the others, to order or seriate these forces in such a way that none of them prevents the others from *doing all that they are capable of:* such is the nature and the ambition of the libertarian project. If *affinity* defines the experimental and subjective way in which libertarian forces are linked to one another, analogy helps us to think the logic that would be at once common to all of these forces and proper to each of them and that makes it possible to verify – by *intuition* and theoretical clarification – the validity of the reasons for uniting and the relevance of the affinity that guides this association. Affinity can always be established on false pretenses, and it often is, stemming from bad judgments or bad reasons (see *common notions*): for example, uniting against a common adversary, according to the principle (absurd from the libertarian point of view) that the enemies of our enemies are inevitably our friends. Analogy makes it possible to think the *selection* of the forces capable of embodying the libertarian movement. Because it is always internal to these forces, however, it presupposes a great deal of finesse and practical sense. From a libertarian point of view, the forces closest to one another within the current order – those most alike in outward form or identity – are not always the ones best joined together. On the contrary, in certain situations, it is sometimes most desirable and pregnant with emancipation for this libertarian association – based on a desire for and a logic of freedom and autonomy – to be with the most dissimilar and distant forces from the point of view of identity and appearances. This is expressed, in certain circumstances, by the slogan "The police are with us!" and historically demonstrated by the union of the anarcho-syndicalists of Barcelona with the assault guards during the insurrectionary days of July 1936. It is in this sense that Proudhonian analogy makes it possible to understand, with Spinoza, how a plow horse and a racehorse, on a certain *plane of reality* (see this term), have less in common than a plow horse and a cow.[1]

Anarchism. The designation – in the classificational and identitarian register of the categories of the dominant order (Christianity, Marxism, liberalism, syndicalism, feminism, etc.) – of the practices, ideas, movements, and organizations that identify themselves with anarchy. Anarchism thus has two faces:

---

this point, see Jacques Dewitte, "La mise en abyme du social: Sur la pensée politique de Claude Lefort," *Critique* 635 [Apr. 2000]: 346-66.)

1   See Gilles Deleuze, *Spinoza: Practical Philosophy,* trans. Robert Hurley (San Francisco: City Lights Books, 1988), 124.

- As a freely available title, commensurate with that which it seeks to express, it is at the service of all those who recognize in it the best means of designating what they feel, what they experience, and what they desire. In this sense, because it applies to everything, anarchism has the precious possibility of speaking of a project that is common to a multitude of situations, to an infinity of manners of understanding, perceiving, and acting. It is the best means of expressing that "stranger unity" of which Deleuze speaks "that can only characterize the multiple" (see *multiplicity* and *localism*).[1]

- As a classificational category in the register of the dominant order, comparable to many others and in competition with them, anarchism always risks negating the anarchy of which it is the theoretical and organizational expression. Like its religious and political rivals, anarchism thus tends to give birth to institutions locked up inside their own identities – each possessing an *interior* and an *exterior* – with their rituals of induction, their dogmas, their police and priests, their exclusions, their schisms, their anathemas and excommunications. Anarchism transforms itself from the *direct* and *immediate* expression of *multiple* and *different* forces into an overarching entity, a symbolic power (Proudhon) analogous, in its own way, to all the great dominations (Church, Capital, State) that it claims to combat. In this manner, its original multiplicity tends to be transformed into a juxtaposition of sects or individuals struggling with one another because all of them aspire to command the totality of an overall project, which is reduced to a logo, a flag, or a business enterprise (see *ideomania*).

Anarchism of the right (see also *neoliberals*). An ill-tempered and acrimonious mode of being that, in being drawn to select *reactive* (see this term), often macho and paranoid forces, continually risks giving rise to beings with bad digestion, incapable of *revolt*, pervaded by *ressentiment*, the *nihilism* of which refuses any *affirmation*. Contrary to what it is often thought to be (and regardless of disputes over whether it deserves the name of "anarchism"), *right wing* anarchism (see this term) is not altogether foreign to certain currents and aspects of what is called the anarchism "of the left," as shown by the most immediate militant behaviors, as well as, for example, the long and blind tolerance that certain currents of the libertarian movement expressed toward the anti-semite and man of *ressentiment* who was Paul Rassinier.[2] Examples of famous anarchists of the right: the writers Céline and (at the end of his life) Léo Malet.

---

1   Deleuze and Guattari, *A Thousand Plateaus*, 158 (trans.: modifications my own).

2   On this point, cf. Nadine Fresco, *Fabrication d'un antisémite* (Paris: Seuil, 1999).

Anarchist chemistry (see *propaganda by the deed, passage to the act, focal point*). The *attentats* and bombings of the years 1880-1890 gave anarchist action a lasting reputation as the violence of a desperate minority. Moreover, it is not certain that these *attentats* were not partly the product of two tendencies that are unacceptable from a libertarian point of view: 1) the utilitarian and mechanical illusion that one can change the world order by attacking those who believe themselves to be its foundations or keystones, i.e., kings and heads of State; 2) *ressentiment* (see this term), in this case the *ressentiment* of the poor and weak against the rich and powerful, a *ressentiment* that, as a substitute for *revolt* (see this term), would blossom into the disgusting crimes of the so-called "Bonnot Gang" (see *cynicism*). This negative image of the *attentats* of the end of the 19th century must not, however, obscure their importance in relation to libertarian thought, particularly with regard to the manner in which the anarchist movement appropriates science and its technical applications. It is significant that it was a large international assembly of delegates issuing from the First International (the Congress of London, July 1881) – who had adopted the modes of action previously theorized by the principal leaders of the anarchist movement (Kropotkin, Reclus, Malatesta, etc.) and who believed "that the era of a general *revolution* is not far off" – were the ones who decided to study the technology and chemistry of bomb-making. Largely negative in their effects (causing the death of their authors and of their victims), the "explosive" character of the anarchist bombs would nevertheless symbolically convey the meaning of libertarian action and a libertarian manner of conceiving the world for half a century onwards. Indeed, instantaneous in its effect, charged with expressing all the aspirations of an irrevocable and final act, all the fears and hopes of an individual *will* (see this term) confronted with life and death, the anarchist bomb is directly charged (in its very materiality) with the idea of the "explosion" of the world order, of the radical recomposition of the elements that compose it. Foreign to modern conceptions of science and politics, anarchist chemistry thus takes on meaning within the double register of metaphor and practical action. As both symbolic and real, it is charged with an infinite signification in which the local (see *localism*), the individual, and the directly experienced furnish the visible referent for the revolutionary idea and desire, in which Science and Society, Technology and Social Transformation, Explosion and Revolution come to live together for a little while in the test tube of the dynamiter, in the manner of the *liujia* Daoists.[1] Like the "tradecraft" of the

---

1   The "dynamiters of the old world" (or "demolishers") manufacture their own explosive products, and the majority of the anarchist journals of the time have a technical and scientific section devoted to this activity. On this point, see Jean Grave, *Quarante ans de propagande anarchiste* (Paris: Flammarion, 1973), 166 et passim, and Daniel Colson, "La science anarchiste," *Réfractions* 1 (Winter 1997): 89-118.

First International and the future syndicalism of direct action, anarchist chemistry disregards the boundary between culture and nature, between ideal *liberty* and material *necessity* (see these terms). In alchemical fashion, it attempts to unite that which has been separated: humanity and nature, idea and matter, the purely utilitarian technical operation and the mystical concern with a radical transformation of the world. Like alchemy, it attempts to compress space and time into a single, immediate act: space, in the minuscule operation of a mixture of nitroglycerin and fulminate of mercury capable, through their "propagation," of transforming the order of the world and society from bottom to top; time, in the messianic certainty that the moment of the gesture corresponds to that of history, that the Revolution is near, that the hour of the *Great Evening* (see this term) has arrived.

Anarcho-syndicalism (see *direct action, active minorities, movement, Great Evening*, and *general strike*).

Anarchy (see *power of the outside*). The founding notion of the libertarian movement, which has lost its provocative, subversive, and theoretical sense with the passage of time, being little by little transformed into "anarchism," a body of ideas and organizations often contrary to what the term "anarchy" originally meant in the writings of its first inventors: Déjacque, Cœurderoy, Proudhon, Bakunin, etc. Contrary to what is often believed, anarchy is not reducible to a utopian political model, deferred to the end of time: the absence of government. As is prefigured by its most pejorative common meaning and as is manifest in its erudite origin (the Greek meaning of the word *an-arche*), anarchy is first of all the refusal of any first principle, of any first cause, of any primary idea, any dependence of beings with respect to a single origin (which always ends up being identified with God).[1] Anarchy, as origin, goal, and means (see *entelechy*), is the *affirmation* of the multiple, the unlimited diversity of beings and their capacity to compose a world without hierarchy, domination, or forms of dependence other than the free association of radically free and autonomous forces (see *multiplicity*). In this sense, the concept of anarchy refers to two states of being, one prior and one posterior to what a being is capable of. First of all, the word anarchy refers to an *a priori* condition of things, to the blind chaos of forces and powers randomly encountering one another (see *common notions* and *collective reason*). Secondly, it refers to an *a posteriori* condition (if this distinction is still meaningful), in which anarchy is to be thought as the voluntary construction of new subjectivities, as the capacity of beings to

---

1 "The first cause has never existed, could never have existed. The first cause is a cause that itself has no cause or that is the cause of itself. It is the Absolute creating the Universe, pure spirit creating matter, a nonsense" (Bakunin, "Considérations philosophiques," *Œuvres*, 3:349).

express the power that they contain. This latter condition is what Proudhon will attempt to think, some time after the events of 1848, through the term *positive anarchy*, in the form of autonomous and contradictory or antithetical forces that struggle only to be recognized by one another and to associate with one another, rather than to resolve the difference that opposes them. These are an anarchic excess of forces and affirmations that – in seeking to establish association between mutually contradictory terms, to polarize one another in the manner of the two poles of an electric battery[1] – settle, so to speak, for "seriating" their profusion, trying to discover and to construct what Bakunin called the order of life.

Anguish (see *power of the outside*).

Anti-authoritarian/anti-power. Anarchism is not first and foremost a political movement whose (very relative) originality would consist of opposing the State (along with the ultra-liberals; see *neoliberals*) or in denouncing "Power" as a mysterious essence incarnated in the State, the Law, or the domination of one *class* over another. Libertarian struggle operates from the *interior* (see this term) of the totality of relationships constitutive of that which exists, as disparate and minuscule as they may be. The qualifier "anti-authoritarian" serves to indicate the breadth of the anarchist struggle and project. This is why the libertarian movement, through its constant practice, can (in part) endorse the manner in which Michel Foucault renders an account of *power*, which we reiterate here nearly word for word:

- Power is not primarily identified with the sovereignty of the State, with Law, with the principle or total unity of a domination.
- "Power is not something that is acquired, seized, or shared, something that one holds on to or allows to slip away; power is exercised from innumerable points, in the interplay of non-egalitarian and mobile relations…
- "Relations of power are not in a position of exteriority with respect to other types of relationships (economic processes, knowledge relationships, sexual relations), but are immanent in the latter; they are the immediate effects of the divisions, inequalities, and disequilibriums which occur in the latter, and conversely they are the internal conditions of these differentiations."
- "Power comes from below." It does not depend on an all-encompassing binary opposition between dominators and dominated, a duality that is

---

1   Pierre-Joseph Proudhon, *Selected Writings of P.J. Proudhon*, ed. Stewart Edwards, trans. Elizabeth Fraser, (Garden City, NY: Anchor Books, 1969), 229.

echoed from top to bottom, down to the depths of the social body (see *system* and *determinism*). On the contrary, it is the multiple relations of force in working life, in family life, in *immediate* relations (see this term) that are the foundation of and condition for the large-scale relationships of domination and that, through their intensity, make possible the effects of conformity, homogenization, serialization, and convergence of relations.

- "Power relations are both intentional and non-subjective...[T]hey are imbued through and through with calculation...But this does not mean that it results from the choice or decision of an individual subject...[nor of] the caste which governs, nor the groups which control the state apparatus, nor those who make the most important economic decisions."[1] "The rationality of power is characterized by tactics that are often quite explicit at the restricted level where they are inscribed..., tactics which, becoming connected to one another, attracting and propagating one another, but finding their base of support and their condition elsewhere, end by forming comprehensive systems: the logic is perfectly clear, the aims decipherable, and yet it is often the case that no one is there to have invented them, and few who can be said to have formulated them: an implicit characteristic of the great anonymous, almost unspoken strategies which coordinate the loquacious tactics whose 'inventors' or decisionmakers are often without hypocrisy."[2]

Anti-something (see *pro-something*). Anti-capitalism, anti-clericalism, anti-statism, anti-militarism, anti-colonialism, anti-nuclear, anti-fascism, anti-racism, anti-imperialism, anti-anti-semitism, anti-productivism, anti-authoritarianism, anti-sexism, anti-speciesism, anti-sizeism, anti-anti-dwarfism, anti-meatism, etc. Despite what this long (and not exhaustive) list might lead one to believe, anarchism is neither an ideological program nor a catalog of demands, generally negative, that would become elaborated over time into new rubrics and new moral and behavioral prohibitions. Anarchism is an *affirmative* force that breaks the chains of *domination* through revolt only in order to better affirm, in the very movement of rupture, another *possibility*, another *composition* of the world (see these terms).

---

1 In this sense, libertarian thought radically dissociates itself from the analyses of certain currents of the far left or those close to Situationism, analyses very often founded on the theme of conspiracies and hidden forces manipulating reality from the shadows.

2 Michel Foucault, *History of Sexuality, Vol. 1: The Will to Knowledge*, trans. Robert Hurley (Harmondsworth, UK: Penguin, 1990), 94 et passim.

Anti-speciesism (anti-speciesists) (see *anti-something, suffering, utilitarianism,* and *rendering of accounts*). In its history as a *milieu* (see this term), anarchism has always been linked to movements of particular ideas (naturism, vegetarianism, pacifism, etc.) that sometimes develop into *ideomanias* (see this term and *integral pacifism*). This is the case with anti-speciesism, to give a more recent example. The anti-speciesist position, analogous to anti-racism or anti-sexism, can be formulated as follows: "Species is not an ethically relevant category, no more than gender or race. Anti-speciesists thus fight against speciesism, i.e., discrimination based on species."[1] In its recognition of animal life, its refusal of the radical distinction between mankind and other species, its denunciation of a standardized and technologized violence and cruelty behind the scenes of our world, anti-speciesism echoes many aspects of libertarian thought. However, it also differs from libertarian thought in three important ways:

1. Anti-speciesism speaks of animal "liberation," of "struggles" and a movement for animal liberation, a vocabulary and a conception of the action of beings common to a great number of other emancipatory movements. It is here that anti-speciesism is apparently, on the plane of words, nearest to the libertarian movement's modes of expression while, at the same time, moving further away from them for a reason that could be formulated as follows: anarchism calls for emancipation, supports struggles for emancipation – all the struggles for emancipation, as different as they may be – but on one condition: that this emancipation is the work of the interested parties themselves, of the forces that have need of liberation, through *direct action*, apart from any representative, any *representation* (see this term) claiming to speak in the name of others, to act for others, in the interest of others. How can animals emancipate themselves, liberate themselves? Such is the first problem that leads the anti-speciesists to differentiate themselves from the libertarian project. Like it or not, the anti-speciesists cannot help situating themselves as the animals' "spokespersons" or "representatives," "representing" the animal cause and, at the same time, benefiting from this *representation* (see this term). Animals are neither slaves, nor women, nor proletarians, nor undocumented immigrants [*sans-papiers*], nor oppressed minorities. What distinguishes them is not a transcendent difference in nature. From the anarchist point of view, it is a practical, immediate, concrete, and singular difference. Minorities, women, the unemployed, workers, and *sans-papiers* can fight and

---

1   Yves Bonnardel and David Olivier, "Antispécisme: pour une solidarité sans frontière," *La Griffe* no. 10 (1998).

organize themselves directly, constituting collective beings and acting without intermediaries and representatives (see *direct action*). They can develop their own points of view by themselves, confronting the points of view of other forces. Animals cannot. They can do other things, an infinity that opens up a great number of possibilities in the relations that we maintain with them, as well as with all that exists. But they cannot struggle in the manner of women, the young, workers, or any other minority. This permits the anti-speciesists to reduce the existence of animals to human realities, to speak on their behalf, to translate what the animals are supposed to want, to subject them to interests and considerations that they cannot themselves affirm, and thus to profit from their silence, while forbidding themselves to acknowledge what this silence makes possible for human beings as well as for other animals.[1]

2. The second divergence follows partially from the first. Since the animals do not speak and anti-speciesism is a movement of human beings alone, the anti-speciesists could be content to speak for themselves, to say why the animal cause is so important for them, to unfold the becoming-animal that they themselves contain. They could say what they experience in their relationships with animals, how they experience it, and what this experience implies.[2] But anti-speciesism, as an ideological current, is not satisfied with this subjective standpoint, the only one that could, from a libertarian point of view, aspire to the emancipatory recomposition of that which exists, opening human beings up to the totality of that which exists and thus to the other animal species. Faithful to the "human, all too human" interest that they take in defending animals, the anti-speciesists do not renounce the possibility of working out a general point of view that would give animals a human voice, in which the animals would have rights, a status recognized – under the same title as that of humans – as one of *equality* (see this term). But because this general point of view cannot be produced from the practical, immediate, and direct confrontation of all the interested parties – and, more precisely still, those most interested among the interested parties, the animals themselves (see *common notions* and *collective reason*) – the anti-speciesists are obliged to appeal to a third party, a third point of view, a *universal* (see this term), objective, and transcendent point of view: a sort of Judge of the Peace, ethics committee, or divinity, as external

---

1   On this point, see Elisabeth de Fontenay, *Le Silence des bêtes: La philosophie à l'épreuve de l'animalité* (Paris: Fayard, 1998).

2   In this regard, however, see David Olivier, "Le goût et le meurtre," *La Griffe* no. 13 (1999).

to human subjectivities as it is to animal subjectivities but capable of saying or measuring what these subjectivities feel in an objective way and, according to this external measurement, pronouncing the equality of their *rights* (see *law/rights*). This third party, this Justice of the Peace or divinity, is *utilitarianism* (see this term), which assumes this role under the threefold aspect of a traditional morality (I must take account of the suffering of others, a suffering that I do not experience), an objective science (I must be able to determine objectively who suffers and with what intensity), and a casuistry or political economy of morals (I must always be able to calculate with precision the best allocation of my acts and my resources within the framework of a general market of happiness and suffering).

3. The third and final great divergence between anarchism and anti-speciesism, which makes it possible to understand the first two: in its practical dimension, in its concern for animals, for their lives and points of view on the world, anti-speciesism may seem to call into question and destabilize what is commonly called "humanism," this mixture of values and rights inherited from Christianity which – from property to the soul or spirit, to the State and morality – serves as a mask and a foundation for all sorts of relations of domination and exploitation. But anti-speciesism goes at once too far and not far enough in its critique of humanism – too far on the surface, not far enough in depth. By highlighting the innocent, indifferent, and supposedly natural cruelty of the relations that bind human beings to animals, anti-speciesism indeed opens up the possibility of thinking differently about our world and thus of inventing radically new relations. But in order to do that, anti-speciesism would have to renounce the magical boundaries of humanism, its hegemonic and facile representations. It would have to renounce the traditional representations that make human beings separate, self-contained subjects equipped with powers, interests, and rights, concerned only to determine what they do or do not have the right to appropriate from the world that surrounds them, to determine who deserves the status of "subject," who is worthy of "interest" (in both senses of this expression). Anti-speciesism does not renounce humanism but is content to extend it to some nonhumans, hence the outrage it inevitably provokes and hence the nonsense of the discussions provoked by this outrage. The divine and sacred prerogatives of the Western white male having been extended to men of color, then to women and children, the anti-speciesists now propose to extend them to certain animals, under the threefold patronage of law, morality, and science. Anti-speciesism does not destroy the limits and schemas of

thought that, for anarchism, are at the foundation of relations of domination and exploitation. It is content to renew them by applying them to a certain number of other living species. How do we put an end to the oppressive and absurd prerogatives of humanism? Such is the question that anarchism aspires to answer on the very terrain of the relations that we maintain with other living species. Such is the question that anti-speciesism does not answer.

Apeiron (see *power of the outside*). A Greek concept, simultaneously meaning ignorance and infinity. Used by Anaximander to think the indefinite and unspecified foundation from which the infinity of beings is perpetually born, the concept of *apeiron* – imported into modern thought by Gilbert Simondon in particular – is very close to the concept of anarchy and contributes to the thought of anarchy, as well.[1]

Appetites (see *desire, force, repugnance, repulsion*, and *affinity*). A concept used by Gabriel Tarde. It is synonymous with desire, but also indicates how other *collective forces* can be included in the *will* of each being (see *monad* and *lack*). If the encounters or the avoidances among beings are never subject to the mere chance of the coldly mechanical and *extrinsic* conceptions of quantum physicists (see *common notions*), it is precisely because each collective force existing at a *given moment* is marked, via its particular *arrangement*, not by the *lack* of the other (see this term), but on the contrary, by the desire to encounter these beings – a desire corresponding to the *possibilities* that each one, from a certain *point of view*, contains with *superabundance*. This is why anarchism can endorse the formula of René Thom: "The famished predator is its own prey."[2]

Application (see *utilitarianism*). Because, in its eyes, the meaning, value, and *determination* of things are always internal to the *beings*, the *situations*, and the *events* themselves, anarchism refuses any notion of "application," this particular subjection of acts and practices to a first principle, an extrinsic judge or measure, in a relation in which it is always precisely a question of "applying oneself" to a task, answering to a taskmaster, doing what *he* asks you to do as *he* requires (see *rendering of accounts*).

---

1   Simondon, *L'Individuation psychique et collective*.
2   René Thom, "Morphologie et individuation," in *Gilbert Simondon: Une Pensée de l'individuation et de la technique*, ed. Gilles Châtelet (Paris: Albin Michel, 1994), 101.

Arrangement (collective arrangement) (see *collective beings*).[1] A Deleuzian term. This word allows us to avoid the biologizing presuppositions of the concept of *organization*. Arrangement is the mode of *composition* of a *collective being* that determines the quality of its desire and its degree of *power* and *autonomy*. From this point of view, any collective being or collective force is an arrangement.

Association/disassociation (see *collective*). As the analyses of Simondon and Proudhon allow us to demonstrate, associations and the collective force that corresponds to them are never merely the sum of the individuals who associate such as they exist at the time of this association. They always function on the basis of what is not yet individuated within these individuals (see *individuation*), on the basis of the *more-than-themselves* or the *indeterminate* that they contain and that justifies their *will* to join others, to create a new being, and thus to exceed their own limits as individuals such as they exist at a *given moment*. In this sense, because it mobilizes forces that are not yet individuated, one never knows what a new being is capable of – for good or for bad. Any association requires many experiments and many past experiences of association, but also a certain intuitive finesse, an attentiveness to those new forces and potentialities that each association mobilizes within ourselves.

From a libertarian or emancipatory point of view, three kinds of forms or methods of association and disassociation between *collective forces* (see this term) can be considered, all of which are marked by positivity, by occupying the register of *affirmation*.

1. A force can avoid other forces, avoid bad encounters, encounters that cause *sadness* and thus a diminution of its *power*. Because it has

---

1   Translator's note: the French word *agencement*, as used (very frequently) in the works of Gilles Deleuze and Félix Guattari, is generally translated as "assemblage." However, as Jasbir Puar notes, this is an "awkward" rendering, bordering on mistranslation, because it suggests something more solid or static than *agencement* requires (Puar, "'I Would Rather Be a Cyborg Than a Goddess': Intersectionality, Assemblage, and Affective Politics," *EIPCP: European Institute for Progressive Cultural Policies*, Jan. 2011, http://eipcp.net/transversal/0811/puar/en; see also John Phillips, "Agencement/Assemblage," *Theory, Culture & Society*, 23, nos. 2-3 [2006]: 108-109). In common usage, *agencement* may refer to nothing more permanent than the configuration of furniture in one's living room or the placement of notes in a song (J. Macgregor Wise, "Assemblage," in *Gilles Deleuze: Key Concepts*, ed. Charles J. Stivale [Montréal: McGill-Queen's University Press, 2005], 77, 79). It seems to me that as used by Deleuze and Guattari and particularly as used by Colson, the term might be better rendered as "arrangement" in order to connote the open-endedness of a process (see also Graham Livesey, "Assemblage," in *The Deleuze Dictionary*, rev. ed., ed. Adrian Parr [Edinburgh: Edinburgh University Press, 2005], 18-19).

everything in itself (see *monad, autonomy,* and *potential*), a force can always choose – briefly or for a long time – the greatest solitude, relying only on itself, on the possibilities that it contains, while waiting for better times, other encounters, other *situations,* other *events* (the only things that can actualize these possibilities), in a kind of hibernation or, more colorfully, like a "spy" in deep cover or a "virus" that has gone "dormant." The real thus contains an infinity of forces that have withdrawn into themselves, into their own capacities, limiting external relationships to a minimum or to specific *planes of reality* (see this term) – whether voluntarily or out of necessity – but that are pregnant with an infinity of possibilities, both for *good* and for *bad* (see these terms). And this is what permits Spinoza to say that nobody knows what a body is capable of, what each force is capable of, what each of us is capable of within a given situation or *arrangement* (see *body*).[1]

2. A force can also be entangled in relations of domination and dependence and choose to liberate itself through *revolt* (see this term) from the bonds that link it to other forces, bonds it perceives as relations of *oppression* (see *direct action*). Any revolt (a strike, an insurrection, a teenager running away, or the falsely negative formula of Melville's Bartleby: "I would prefer not to") is, as Michelle Perrot puts it, a "beautiful escape,"[2] a rent in time and in the fabric of things (see *stoppage*), a moment when indeed everything becomes possible.

3. Always fleeting, this emancipatory rift or fissure can thus create the conditions for an emergence of new forces and a recomposition of the relationship between forces, a third method of association and disassociation. Liberated from the bonds of subjection, from the limits imposed on them by an order that is extrinsic to what they contain, the forces in revolt can freely join other forces and, thanks to this association, go to the limits of their capacity – beyond the limits heretofore imposed on them – by giving rise to more powerful forces through this association, by composing through this association another world entirely devoted to *affirmation,* to *power,* and thus to *freedom* (see these words, but also *balancing of forces*).

Autonomy (see *nomos, nomad, scientific laws,* and *monad*). A term recurring within libertarian and anti-authoritarian movements (from "the autonomy of syndicalism" to the "Autonomists" of the '70s). Contrary to its pseudo-erudite

---

1 Spinoza, *Ethics,* Part III, Scholium to Proposition 2, in *Spinoza: Complete Works,* trans. Samuel Shirley, ed. Michael L. Morgan (Indianapolis: Hackett Publishing Inc., 2002), 280-82.

2 Michelle Perrot, *Workers on Strike: France 1871-1890* (New Haven, CT: Yale University Press, 1987).

definition, autonomy does not indicate the capacity of a being to give itself its own laws, to subject what constitutes it as a being to legal forms of which it can imagine itself to be the master. In the common sense of the word (see *law/rights*), all law is *external* and forms part of the relations of domination, including those "laws" that are called "natural" – as Gabriel Tarde demonstrates – in Leibniz's vocabulary, when he offers "to explain natural laws…by the triumph of certain *monads* [see this term] who desired these laws,…imposed these forms, subjected to their yoke and levelled with their scythe a people of monads thus subjugated and made uniform, although born free and original, all as eager as their conquerors to dominate and assimilate the universe."[1] In libertarian thought, all law is singular, specific to the nature of each being – a conception that Bakunin formulates as follows: "Each thing contains its *own* law, i.e., its particular mode of development, existence, and action, within itself [emphasis in original]" (see *entelechy*).[2] It is in this sense that anarchist autonomy refers to the forces constitutive of beings, to their capacity to develop in themselves the totality of the resources that they need in order to 1) affirm their existence and 2) associate with others and thus to constitute an ever more *powerful* force of *life*.

Avant-garde (see *active minorities*).

---

1   Gabriel Tarde, *Monadology and Sociology*, ed. and trans. Theo Lorenc (Melbourne: re.press, 2012), 27.

2   Bakunin, "Considérations philosophiques," *Œuvres*, 3:352-354.

B

Balance. A Proudhonian term borrowed from the accountancy of his time. See *balancing of forces.*

Balancing of forces (see *struggle, autonomy, limits, dialectic, hierarchy,* and *tension*). A Proudhonian concept according to which "society must be thought of not as a hierarchical system of functions and faculties, but as a system of free forces balancing each other."[1] In libertarian thought, every force seeks to *go to the limits of its capacity,* i.e., beyond the limits imposed on it by an *external* and *dominatory* order (see these terms). But each force also has its own limits, limits intrinsic to that which constitutes it. This is due, on the one hand, to the fact that it is always a *singular* force, *different* from all the other forces (see these terms), and on the other hand, paradoxically, due to the fact that each force, by virtue of what constitutes it, is always capable of more than what its *singularity* or its *individuation* (see these terms) initially allows it to do. Following Proudhon, who here appropriates Leibniz's vocabulary, one could say that each force is a monad or a composite of monads, inwardly possessing all that exists. This possession is the basis of a force's autonomy, its possibility of affirmation as a free force, sufficient unto itself, but only from a certain *point of view* and through a certain quality of *power* (see these terms) that constrains it and that it must exceed. In the vocabulary of Gilbert Simondon, one could say that, as a singular being, as an individual, the drama and uncertainty of any existing force are due to the fact that it is always capable of more than what it is: "The individual is nothing but itself, but it exists as superior to itself because it contains within itself a more complete reality not exhausted by the process of *individuation,* which remains new and potential, animated by potentials…

---

1 Proudhon, *Selected Writings of P.J. Proudhon,* 59.

the individual does not feel alone in itself, does not feel limited as individual to a reality that would be merely its own."[1] From this double modality of the existence of forces – as absolute singularities, as inwardly possessing all the potentialities of that which exists – arise the three questions that form the foundation of the libertarian project: 1) the importance of the modalities of encounter between forces, the methods of *association* or *disassociation* (see these terms) that, at a *given moment*, bind or separate beings; 2) the autonomy of each force and thus the possibility for each to break from any association, in the name of the totality of that which exists; 3) the perpetual possibility for *collective beings* to attempt to create another mode of the composition of forces, the better to express all the power of the real.

It is within this conception of beings that it is possible to approach the Proudhonian concept of the *balancing of forces*.[2] Any force immediately gives rise to its contrary (see also *fractiousness*) as a resistance to the imperialism of its singularity, as an affirmation of the limits inherent to its point of view, as the other of that which it affirms. Many examples could be provided here. The affirmation of the necessary solidarity of forces within a larger power directly corresponds to the affirmation of the autonomy of these forces and the possibility of their seceding from or revolting against the bonds that link them at a given moment and for the purposes of a given action (see *hierarchy*). The assertion (all too "assertive") in a given situation of the exigencies of a particular *plane of reality* (see this term) – whether economic, physical, military, romantic, administrative, etc. – directly corresponds to the different and thus immediately contrary (or opposed) affirmation of the more or less circumstantial or immediate exigencies of one or several other planes of reality.[3] Contrary to the Hegelianism that some attribute to Proudhon (in order to reproach him

---

1   Simondon, *L'Individuation psychique et collective*, 194.

2   Perhaps it is here that Proudhon radically distinguishes himself from another possible Nietzsche, a Nietzsche who, according to Deleuze's inverted and broadened formula, would no longer encounter Spinoza and Leibniz, would have no further possibilities of association with them. On a (debatable) interpretation of Nietzsche's conception of force in terms of simple relations, thought apart from all subjectivity, apart from the constant imbalances, and especially apart from the constant struggles for domination, cf. Wolfgang Müller-Lauter, *Nietzsche, physiologie de la volonté de puissance*, trans. Jeanne Champeaux (Paris: Éditions Allia, 1998), and Pierre Montebello, *Nietzsche, la volonté de puissance* (Paris: PUF, 2001).

3   If one has once participated in a collective enterprise, even a short-lived one, one knows from experience this ceaseless struggle between the contradictory needs that arise in any collective work, that it is always a question of evaluating, seriating, and prioritizing them, and that the attempts of sociology to relate them to a limited number of regimes of justification or determination are in vain.

for not having understood it), in no way do these contradictions arise from a dialectic: first of all because of the anarchy of their manifestation, but also because they are completely foreign to the negation and synthesis that form the basis of Hegelian and Marxist dialectics.

Let's begin with negation: in the libertarian conception of contradictions, the contrary or opposing force has nothing to do with the negation of the force that elicits or polarizes its existence. Rather, it is the singular affirmation of what this force excludes or damages through its singularity, at a given moment and in a given situation. Contradiction, for Proudhon (both in his thought and in his writings), is always an anarchic overflowing of forces and affirmations that – in seeking to oppose one another at every point, to polarize one another – are content to "seriate" their profusion, to try to discover and construct an order within the anarchy of the real (see *serial dialectic*, *positive anarchy*, and *tension*). The submission of one collective being to another – as a limitation of its power – as well as the destruction of one being by another – as a loss of power or sometimes, more positively, as a condition for the emancipation and recomposition of forces and of the relations that link them (see *rebel*) – is always the immediate horizon of the relations between contrary forces, the most probable effect of their meeting. But this loss of power, which generally follows the confrontation between opposed forces – even in moments of struggle and revolt and even when, in the libertarian conception of revolution, these confrontations are imagined as being as brief as possible (see *Great Evening*, *general strike*) – is exactly what Proudhonian anarchism attempts to abolish through its conception of the seriated balancing of contrary forces, in which "forces do not struggle for even a moment except to recognize themselves, to control themselves, to confirm and classify themselves."[1]

From this comes a second fundamental difference between the libertarian conception of contradictions and that of the Hegelian and Marxist dialectic. Within emancipatory movements, the opposition between two forces does not have to be resolved either by the victory of one over the other or by the synthesis of both (a "synthesis" of which the State, the Capital, the Church, and all the other absolute, dominatory, and overarching powers are the inevitable manifestation). They must be "balanced," Proudhon tells us, not in order to contradict one another, but so that they may be extended as far as possible: "I had shared Hegel's belief[2] that the two terms of the antinomy, thesis and antithesis, were to become resolved in a superior term, *synthesis*. But I have since come to realize that just as the two poles of an electric cell do not destroy each other, so the two terms of the antinomy do not become resolved. Not only are

---

1   Proudhon, *La Guerre et la paix*, 134.

2   That is, up to the *System of Economical Contradictions* (*Système des contradictions économiques*, 1846).

they indestructible, but they are the very motive force of all action, life, and progress. The problem is not to bring about their fusion, for this would be death, but to establish an equilibrium between them – an unstable equilibrium, that changes as society develops."[1] Paradoxically, in achieving a momentary balance, two forces or two series of contrary forces are not neutralized. On the contrary, through the *tension* (see this term) and thus the instability of this balance, they can liberate the infinite power that they contain and that their contradictory encounter contains. They can make it possible to surpass the limits of their points of view and the determinate characters of their singular powers, enabling the emergence of other forces, other associations of forces, the relations of which they must then also learn how to combine and balance so that yet other forces can be born, ad infinitum. The composition of a world that would make it possible for each force to do all that it is capable of, to deploy all the power that reality contains, thus requires an entire practice of *selection* and *experimentation* (see *experiment*) with good and bad contradictions, good and bad associations. At which moments and for how long, in a given arrangement, must collective beings agree to subject themselves to the balancing, to the *tension* or ranking (see *hierarchy*) of the relations that connect them in a given context, in order to obtain certain effects of power? At which moments must they imperatively break off their association, creating others, in order to prevent one of them from imposing its domination in a lasting way, to prevent circumstantial hierarchies from becoming "petrified" (as Bakunin puts it)?[2] How can we balance the multiple components so that each quality, each possibility of a force and its associations with other forces, can be fully expressed, can do all that it is capable of? What are the little oscillations, the *imperceptible* reminders of autonomy within the tiniest interactions, that make possible a range of complementarities, on a given plane of reality and at a given moment, without which these interactions might turn into tyranny? What overall relations must the various collective arrangements maintain so that none of them can impose itself on the others, so that none of the forces within these arrangements can subject the others to its point of view and its desire, for example in the name of external relations? How can we evaluate, at every moment, the quality of the relations between forces, the affinities or enmities that draw them together and pull them apart? Which *collective reasons* or *common notions* are necessary to this evaluation, to the establishment of *trust* between different or contrary forces, making it possible to perceive and think "the other," to perceive and think the discrepancy and plurality of beings? So numerous are the problems that libertarian practice attempts to solve. Furthermore, for

---

1   Proudhon, *Selected Writings of P.J. Proudhon*, 229.

2   Mikhail Bakunin, *The Political Philosophy of Bakunin: Scientific Anarchism*, trans. G.P. Maximoff (Glencoe, IL: The Free Press, 1953), 259.

solving these problems, the balancing of forces constitutes the touchstone, since, beyond its own effects (on the planes of equality, autonomy, power, and thus freedom), it constitutes the concrete sign of the capacity of libertarian and emancipatory forces to escape their own limits, to select good contradictions, and thus to express all the possibilities that these forces contain – possibilities that only an agreement with other forces, contrary to them, can liberate.

Base (horizontality). In the functioning of organizations and associations – both those formed around the working class and others – the concept of the "base" plays an important part, in particular in the event of conflict ("let the base decide!" "return the leadership to the base," "give voice to the base," etc.).[1] This call to the "base" has always had a libertarian connotation, provided that one sees clearly that it constitutes only the first steps of a movement (often quickly stifled) and a *rupture* (see this term) in which the word "base" would no longer need to be used. A base always presupposes a "summit," a higher authority for which it would form the base or that would be supposed to express the wishes of the base, to execute its will. In anarchism, there exists neither base nor summit, but the absolute horizontality of a multiplicity of autonomous and sovereign collective beings entering into relations directly, without overarching authorities to coordinate them. In this sense, base and horizontality are the spatial expression of the idea of *equality* (see this term).

Becoming (see *movement, eternal return*). For libertarian thought, as Bakunin writes, being is identified with becoming: "To be real…is to become…: i.e., movement always and eternally resulting from the infinite sum of all the particular movements down to the infinitely small, the totality of the mutual actions and reactions and the ceaseless transformations of all the things that appear and disappear in turn."[2] This is a conception that one finds at the heart of Gilbert Simondon's thought when he explains that "becoming is a dimension of the being, not something that happens to it following a succession of events that affect a being already and originally given and substantial."[3]

---

1   Translator's note: the term "base" is not widely used in English-language anarchist discourse, but a similar problematic arises around expressions such as "from below" (e.g., Bakunin's "spontaneous movement from below" (Mikhail Bakunin, *Bakunin on Anarchism,* ed. and trans. Sam Dolgoff [Montreal: Black Rose Books, 2002], 200). See Todd May, *The Political Philosophy of Poststructuralist Anarchism* (University Park, PA: Pennsylvania State University Press, 1994), 48-9, for parallel reflections on "'top' and 'bottom' imagery" in anarchist discourse and Marina Sitrin, *Horizontalism: Voices of Popular Power in Argentina* (Oakland, CA: AK Press, 2006) for the many resonances of "horizontality" (vi, 3).

2   Bakunin, "Considérations philosophiques," *Œuvres,* 3:345.

3   Gilbert Simondon, "The Genesis of the Individual," trans. Mark Cohen and Sanford

Being (see *intimate being* and *one*).

Beyond its limits (beyond what one can do) (see *limitlessness of the limited*).

Body (human body) (see *person*, *subject*, *brain*, *sexuality*, and *power of the outside*). "[N]obody as yet has determined the limits of the body's capabilities: that is, nobody as yet has learned from experience what the body can and cannot do, without being determined by mind, solely from the laws of its nature insofar as it is considered as corporeal...[We] do not know what the body can do, or what can be deduced solely from a consideration of its nature."[1] In libertarian thought and its manner of conceptualizing *collective forces* (see this term), the concept of "body" applies to all beings, whatever they may be, whatever their degree of *spontaneity* (see this term) and their power to affect or be affected. But it is precisely because human beings have a great capacity to be affected and to affect other beings – and consequently, through their activity, to give birth to ever more vast, complex, and powerful collective forces[2] – that the human body takes on particular importance within a process of emancipation that calls on the power of *nature* as a whole, which the body carries with it (see this term and *power of the outside*).

As a "composite of powers,"[3] a "composite of *spontaneities*"[4] (see this term) like any other collective force, the human body is multiple. Once again, as Proudhon explains with regard to the *person* (see this term), "What is it, indeed, that we call *a person*? And what does this person mean when he says, 'me'? Is it his arm, his head, his body, or his passion, his intelligence, his talent, his memory, his virtue, his conscience? Is it any of his faculties? [emphasis in original]."[5] Or, as Nietzsche puts it: "We are richer than we think, we have in the body wherewith to make many persons, we take for 'character' what

---

Kwinter, in *Zone Vol. 6: Incorporations*, ed. Jonathan Crary and Sanford Kwinter (New York: Zone, 1992), 311.

1   Spinoza, *Ethics*, 280-81.

2   "[I]n any organized or simply collective being, the force that is its resultant is the freedom of that being, so that the more this being, whether crystal, plant, or animal, approximates the human type, the greater will be its freedom, the greater the range that free will shall have. In man himself, free will manifests itself all the more energetically as the elements that generate him by their community are themselves developed in power: philosophy, science, industry, economy, law" (Proudhon, *De la Justice*, 3:433).

3   Proudhon, *La Guerre et la paix*, 128.

4   "Man can be regarded as a composite of spontaneities that are linked to one another, but each of which, by the effect of circumstances, solicits him from its own side" (Pierre-Joseph Proudhon, *Économie*, bibliothèque municipale de Besançon, 2863 [74]).

5   Proudhon, *De la Justice*, 3:172.

belongs only to the 'person,' to *one* of our masks…We deceive ourselves when we judge a man according to isolated acts: such acts warrant no generalizations [emphasis in original]."[1] A plurality of "minds," of "forces," "souls," and "wills to power,"[2] the human body – particularly in its brain, the supposed seat of its consciousness – is a "node of forces" (using, this time, the vocabulary of Tarde) that transmits "impulses that come from afar and are intended to travel afar."[3] This is why the human being must detach itself from its self in order to liberate the power that it contains. It must liberate itself from the convenient illusions of its *conscience* and of the *ego*, wherein the dominant order finds the best means to reproduce itself (see *self-discipline, responsibility, ego*). By opening up to the other that it contains – to the *apeiron*, the *power of the outside* that its body carries in itself – the human being breaks up its *ego*, only to gain a "lucidity that was more vast" and a "new cohesion":[4] "From this point on, Nietzsche would no longer be concerned with the body as a property of the self but with the body as the locus of impulses, the locus of their confrontation."[5] By expropriating the "ego," in becoming other, the human being restores "thought to these 'corporealizing' forces (impulses)," to the *self* of which Nietzsche speaks, from which alone "every creative force, every evaluation" can spring, the "*Self*" that "exists in the body only as a *prolonged* extremity of *Chaos*."[6]

How is a new body created? How can the human body give itself a new cohesion, an emancipatory unity, and thus liberate, by means of its points of view and its acts, the power of the world that surrounds and traverses it? Such is the question posed by libertarian emancipation. In the world we inhabit, this unification of the body was for a long time ensured by the bonds of religion, by God or his substitutes, by submission and obedience to God and the very particular order guaranteed by the figure of God. And it is undoubtedly Christianity as conceived and practiced by Saint Paul, through the concept of the "resurrection of the body," that most thoroughly unified and confined what the human body is capable of by subjecting it to "faith," by subjecting

---

1 Nietzsche, *Nachgelassene Fragmente* (1884), 26 [370], qtd. in Didier Franck, *Nietzsche and the Shadow of God*, trans. Bettina Bergo and Philippe Farah (Evanston, IL: Northwestern University Press, 2012), 128.

2 On this point, see Franck, *Nietzsche and the Shadow of God*, especially 135.

3 See Jean Milet, *Gabriel Tarde et la philosophie de l'histoire* (Paris: Vrin, 1970), 172: "The case of the human being is particularly significant. Its body, and particularly its brain, are mechanisms for the transmission of psychic impulses that come from afar and are intended to travel afar."

4 On all of this, cf. Pierre Klossowski, *Nietzsche and the Vicious Circle*, trans. Daniel W. Smith (Chicago: University of Chicago Press, 1998), 30 et passim.

5 Ibid. 30-31.

6 Ibid. 33.

the multiple wills of the human body to a single will, that of God, who gives it a new body. In opposition to the *anarchy* of the forces that constitute us, for which each force, each will, "wants something different and is inevitably opposed to all the others," for which "the body is no longer…exclusively what I am but also what I have, and that to which I am connected" (see *possession*), theology thus put forward the governing principle of God, the unification of the various human wills in "their common submission" to God and to an external power that the various figures of authority both embody and transmit.[1] How do we "get rid of God" (as Bakunin puts it) and of the narrow and coercive order that he founds and guarantees? How do we give human beings a new body, a body that would liberate all the powers it contains? How do we invent methods of association and a *balancing of forces* and of wills that allows them to do all that they are capable of? Such are the questions that anarchism attempts to answer.

Bombs (see *anarchist chemistry*).

Boss (see *leader* and *hierarchy*). The external domination of one collective being over others, guaranteed by an oppressive order or based on simple violence. Anarchism hates bosses.

Brain (see *body* and *monad*). Gabriel Tarde asserts that "living bodies are machines," albeit composed of elements – "carbon, nitrogen, oxygen, hydrogen, etc." – that "contain hidden psychic elements."[2] And this is why, especially in the human being, the "body," and "particularly its brain, are mechanisms for the transmission of psychic impulses that come from afar and are intended to travel afar."[3] A seemingly strange conception, an intuition that is perhaps poorly explained, but one for which certain developments in cognitive science open wide vistas.[4]

---

1   Franck, *Nietzsche and the Shadow of God*, 58. For a slightly different analysis, cf. Klossowski, *Nietzsche and the Vicious Circle*, 23 and et passim.

2   Qtd. in Milet, *Gabriel Tarde et la philosophie de l'histoire*, 172.

3   Ibid.

4   For a first approach, cf. Georges Vignaux, *Les Sciences cognitives: Une introduction* (Paris: Éditions La Découverte, 1992).

C

Capital (see *God, State, neoliberals, class,* and *utilitarianism*).

Capture (see *domination, planes of reality, symbols*).

Care for the self (see *implication*).

Causes (see *scientific laws*).

Chaos (see *possibilities, anarchy, apeiron, power of the outside, body*). A Greek concept, used by Hesiod to describe the original state of the world – a world subsequently endowed with an order, with completely differentiated beings (the "cosmos"). In the modern and libertarian use of the word, chaos ceases to refer to a temporal origin, transcended by a linear and temporally oriented process of becoming. On the contrary, it constitutes the ever-present substrate of all the possibilities that reality contains. In this sense, chaos is synonymous with Anaximander's *apeiron* and, as the common usage aptly perceives, with the *anarchy* that justifies the existence of the libertarian movements, not *a posteriori* [*en aval*] as a remote objective to come, but *a priori* [*en amont*] (if this distinction is still meaningful) – an *a priori* without temporal depth, an *a priori* which is always present (see these terms). As many libertarian texts demonstrate, from Cœurderoy and Proudhon to Bakunin (see *power of the outside*), the anarchy or chaos to which anarchism bears witness is not at all synonymous with the arbitrary – this arbitrariness which serves as the illusory foundation of all utopias – but, on the contrary, with *necessity* (see this term) – a necessity that comprises the sole foundation of anarchist *freedom* precisely because it expresses all the power of that which exists. Once again, it is from this point of view that anarchism can be compared to Nietzsche, in spite of the many and fundamental differences that separate them, especially when he explains how "the total character of the world, by contrast, is for all eternity chaos, not in the sense of a lack of necessity but of a lack of order."[1]

Chaplain (see *direction of conscience, rendering of accounts*). Representative of a church or a religion (all the great religions have their chaplains) charged with seeing to it that collective beings are correctly subjected to the standards and values of an external or transcendent collective authority. Under the name of "political commissar," authoritarian communism was happy to recover from religious institutions a practice and apparatus of inspection that had long ago proven its effectiveness. The force of contemporary capitalism undoubtedly lies in its capacity – after the already promising experiments of the guardian angel and especially of the "conscience" (see *responsibility, discipline*) – to base the economy on an organization of external control (and a rather cumbersome one at that) and to transform the chaplains and political commissars of other times into an internalized superego. In this way, through an intimate identification with the law of the market, each individual is his or her own chaplain, his or her own commissar, his or her own representative in the order of the market, his or her own judge of what it is best to do or not to do, to hope for, or to be satisfied with.

Charge of nature (see *indeterminacy*). Concept used by Gilbert Simondon to indicate the *power of the outside* (see this term) that every collective being contains. The charge of nature is another word for anarchy. For this reason, anarchism, in the myopic view of its detractors, may look like an absolute and especially dangerous *naturalism* (see this term). Indeed, libertarian thought refuses to divide reality into two radically distinct substances (see *dualism*): matter and mind, body and soul, nature and culture. This is why it rejects all the presuppositions and frameworks of so-called anthropology – as if human realities could be distinguished from radically different "nonhuman" realities! As Proudhon affirms, the human composite does not differ in any respect from any other composition, from all that constitutes nature, except in degree of power: "The living human being is a group, like the plant or the crystal, but to a higher degree than those others; it is all the more alive, sensitive, and sentient to the degree that its organs, secondary groups...form a more extensive combination."[2] Like Gilbert Simondon, anarchism does not consider the

---

1   Friedrich Nietzsche, *The Gay Science,* trans. Josefine Nauckhoff and Adrian Del Caro (Cambridge, UK: Cambridge University Press, 2001), 109. On the importance of "left Nietzscheanism" for libertarian thought, cf. Michel Onfray, *Politique du rebelle: Traité de résistance et d'insoumission* (Paris: Grasset, 1997).

2   Pierre-Joseph Proudhon, *Philosophy of Progress,* trans. Shawn Wilbur and Jesse Cohn (n.p.:

expression of human specificity and its full flourishing to consist in our being distinguished from nature. On the contrary, it consists in the capacity of humans to find within themselves and outside of themselves – since their "inside" is only a fold of the *outside* (see this term) – the nature from which they issue, even if their provisional and reductive *individuation* prompts them to regard it as an external environment to be exploited and dominated (see *subject*).

Christian anarchism (religious anarchism) (see *Great Evening*). As curious as it might seem, there exists or has existed a Christian anarchism (formed mainly around the work of Tolstoy). However, this bizarreness is only apparent. Indeed, the anarchist theory of the *composite* character and *nature* of collective forces (see these terms) makes it possible to understand that a given being or reality contains much more than what has been assigned to it by a crude and extrinsic spatial classification of political and ideological confrontations and hatreds. Therefore, anarchism can at once be violently distant from Christianity – as from any religion – and intimately close to certain dimensions of religious practices and perceptions. As global and universal experiences, inscribed from their very beginnings in relation to a non-alienated world,[1] religions have not only given rise to churches, dogmas, sacred texts, and obligations (alimentary, ritual, moral) that tend to separate collective forces from what they can do and to subjugate them to external powers that damage them. They retain in themselves and in a certain number of their practices (even in the most authoritarian monotheisms) a relation to the world (generally indicated by the term "mystic"[2]) that is immanent to reality and the possibilities that reality

---

LeftLiberty, 2009), 23 (trans.: modifications my own). This position can also be found in the work of Gabriel Tarde (*Monadology and Sociology,* 28 et passim) and in that of Gilles Deleuze and Felix Guattari when they explain: "even when they are nonliving, or rather inorganic, things have a lived experience because they are perceptions and affections" (*What Is Philosophy?*, trans. Hugh Tomlinson and Graham Burchell [New York: Columbia University Press, 1994], 154).

1   What Gilbert Simondon calls "the primitive magical unity," this "vital connection between man and the world, defining a universe that is at once subjective and objective prior to any distinction between the object and the subject, and consequently prior to any appearance of the separate object" (*On the Mode of Existence of Technical Objects* trans. Cecile Malaspina and John Rogove [Minneapolis, MN: University of Minnesota Press, 2016], 177).

2   For a reevaluation of the connections between anarchism and mysticism, cf. Onfray, *Politique du rebelle*. This is why anarchism can endorse the "Dreyfusard mysticism" of which Charles Péguy speaks, "a step toward the culmination of three mysticisms: Jewish, Christian, French" (Charles Péguy, *Notre jeunesse* [Paris: Gallimard, 1933], 63). On Christian mysticism cf., in particular, Michel de Certeau, *The Mystic Fable: The Sixteenth and Seventeenth Centuries*, trans. Michael B. Smith (Chicago: U. of Chicago Press, 1995).

contains and that attempts – by circumventing priests, dogmas, rites, and all the authorities claiming to speak in the name of the divine – to express directly, without intermediaries, the forces and *possibilities* that the existing order denies (see *direct action*).

Circumstances (see *event, arrangement*).

Class (social, sexual, generational, etc.) (see *anti-authoritarian, power, possibilities*). Anarchism distinguishes itself in two ways from the very numerous Marxist or Marxian analyses that, for many decades, have been commonplace in the discourses of workerism, third-worldism, feminism, etc. on the left or far left.

For libertarian thought, the great cleavages that run through and structure our societies (workers/bourgeoisie, men/women, young/old, Whites/Blacks, urban/rural, high/low, in/out, left/right, dominators/dominated, etc.) are not at the origin of the numerous relations of force and domination that comprise our lives. They are, on the contrary, the effects of the ensemble of these relationships, effects that then come to bear on local confrontations, traverse them, bind them, place them in a *series* (see this term), and give them meaning. As Foucault and Proudhon have shown, large-scale dominations are the hegemonic effects of a multitude of immediate and minuscule interactions, which continually sustain these dominations and furnish them with the force and intensity that they need in order to reproduce themselves and to pretend to be the origin of their own power (for Foucault's analyses, see *anti-authoritarian*). In libertarian thought, neither State, Capital, God, Patriarchy, nor any other metaphysical divinity is either a cause or an origin; they are *resultants* (see this term). Any politico-ideological force that claims to found its own existence and the significance of its struggle on the belief in an all-powerful first principle at the origin of that which exists – a foundation that justifies its struggle (God, State, Capital, Patriarchy, etc.) – merely participates in the power of what it pretends to combat. Whatever its size, it can only constitute a body of priests, police officers, professors, and scientists, an authoritarian apparatus aspiring, in its turn, to profit from the illusions of despotism, to rob the dominated of their right to struggle and of the possibility of struggling everywhere they find themselves, to prohibit them from becoming the masters of their own struggle (see *alienation*). The *spontaneism*, the *localism* (see these terms), and the sometimes small size of libertarian struggles are often badly misinterpreted, reduced to a kind of exaggerated democracy, an obsession with details, a hypersensitivity, a dispersal of demands: in short, indulgences or distractions from the clash of the Titans undertaken by serious militants and organizations (conscious of their duty and, above all, of their knowledge) against Capital, the State, the Church, Patriarchy, or any other overarching or structural power. On the contrary, the spontaneism, localism, smallness, immediacy, and heterogeneity of libertarian struggles, far from being wasteful indulgences, are the expression of another perception of reality, other methods of action, the only ones able to oppose and, perhaps, even put an end to relations of domination.

To this first difference between anarchism and Marxism with respect to classes (social, sexual, generational, racial, or other), it is necessary to add a second, which arises in part from the first. Because they depend on a multitude of power relations and not on a first principle or a determining totality, because they are in a continual state of flux that never corresponds to a phony and illusory historical determinism, because they combine with a great number of other constantly changing relations of exchange and domination, no class relations of any kind can ever claim to found the existence of a revolutionary class, a class subject of emancipation ("workers," "youth," "women," "Blacks," etc.), no matter how oppressed this class may be. Since they are the resultants of changing relations, but also because they are closely dependent on the domination that is essential to them and that defines their being at a *given moment* (see *emancipation*), dominated classes contain only an emancipatory *possibility*, depending on a great number of conditions. These include their power to *revolt* and especially their capacity to *compose* a greater *power* (see this term) in combination with other forces and with all that escapes the relations of domination that define them (see *stoppage* and *analogy*). In short, the position of the dominated is in no way the sufficient guarantee or source of the emancipatory possibility of a world without *domination* (see this term).

Class struggle (see *master/slave*, *dialectic*, and *class*).

Classification (see *analogy* and *series*). Because it calls for *becoming* and *movement* and because, with Bakunin, it defines nature as "the sum of actual transformations of things that are and will ceaselessly be produced within its womb,"[1] libertarian thought is opposed to any classification, which is inevitably external, reductive, and oppressive. For this reason, Proudhon (like Gilles Deleuze and others) can, within the framework of the natural sciences, take the side of Geoffroy Saint-Hilaire against Cuvier: "Yes, as Geoffroy Saint-Hilaire says, all the animals of creation are evolved from one another; otherwise they would not form genuses and species. And what the error made by Cuvier, the king of classification, demonstrates, is that in claiming to refute the theory of Geoffroy Saint-Hilaire, he contradicts himself; outside of the unity of generation, the orders, classes, genera, species, varieties, no longer have a *raison d'être*; like the constitutional regime, it is a fiction of the mind, a chimera."[2]

---

1   Bakunin, *The Political Philosophy of Bakunin*, 53.

2   Proudhon, *Économie*, 2863 [104]. For Deleuze's references to Geoffroy Saint-Hilaire, cf. Deleuze and Guattari, *A Thousand Plateaus*, 45, 254. Translator's note: historian of science

Collective (social). For Proudhon, every collective is an individual and each individual is a collective, a "composite of powers."[1] But it is undoubtedly Gilbert Simondon who best enables us, from a libertarian point of view, to think this reality of the social or the collective via three great propositions.

First proposition: "the individual," in the psychological or traditional sense of the word, like any other form of *individuation*, is always more than itself (see *more than oneself, balancing of forces, genealogy, limitlessness of the limited*). A paradox that Simondon formulates as follows: "The individual is nothing but itself, but it exists as superior to itself because it contains within itself a more complete reality, one that the process of individuation did not exhaust, that remains new and potential, animated by potentials...[T]he individual does not feel alone in itself, does not feel limited as an individual to a reality that would be merely itself."[2]

Second proposition: this more-than-itself of individuals is at the foundation of the collective. In other words, the collective is not the sum of individuals, the consequence of individual strategies, or a contract that individuals make with one another. It is not an association of individuals (what Simondon calls the "interindividual"). It arises, on the contrary, from the more-than-itself of individuals, from what, strictly speaking, is not them (as individuals; see *subject*): "Collective consciousness is not constituted by the union of individual consciousnesses any more than the social body is derived from individual bodies. Individuals contain something that can become collective, but that is not already individuated in the individual."[3] "The collective is an individuation that unites the natures contained by several individuals but that is not contained in the already-constituted individuations of these individuals; this is why the discovery of the signification of the collective is at once transcendent and immanent with respect to the anterior individual."[4]

Third and final proposition: this *preindividual* reality of individuals from which the collective individual arises is being thought as becoming, the *apeiron*, *Nature*, the *indeterminate*, the *limitlessness of the limited*. In this sense,

---

John Tresch offers some useful historical context for Proudhon's engagement with the Cuvier-Geoffroy debate. As alluded to in the passage Colson quotes here, Proudhon sided with Geoffroy Saint-Hilaire's proto-Darwinian vision of life as continually evolving in response to "the circumstances in which it developed" as opposed to "Cuvier's view of four fixed 'embranchements,'" an unchanging taxonomical schema (326). See Tresch, "The Order of the Prophets: Series in Early French Social Science and Socialism," *History of Science* 48.3-4 (2010): 315-342.

1 Proudhon, *La Guerre et la paix*, 128.

2 Simondon, *Individuation psychique et collective*, 194.

3 Ibid. 195.

4 Ibid. 197.

the collective individual, like any individual, is also more than itself. It, too, contains the indeterminate and the preindividual charged with potentials, with new problems to be resolved in new forms of individuation and through a movement of *eternal return* to being (see this term) in which historical time, novelty, and the future always proceed in reverse, in advance [*en amont*] of what, in traditional anthropology, constitutes the basis of beings and individuals: the adventures, the wills, and the histories from which they seem to emerge.

Collective beings (see *collective force, arrangement,* and *planes of reality*).

Collective reason (public reason) (see especially *common notions* and *theory/ practice,* but also *representation, expression, symbols/signs,* and *entelechy*). A Proudhonian concept. For anarchism, reason does not exist in itself, in the heaven of ideas or logical imperatives. Dependent on language and on signs, reason is always the expression of the relationship between beings or collective forces. To be strictly accurate, there is only one reason: the reason of things or beings and of the relations that bind them. It is in this sense that Proudhon writes, following his readings of Leibniz – even if only to draw back before a thought too "bold" (and undoubtedly too gradualist [évolutionniste] in his eyes) – that "intelligence is everywhere, latent or conscious...: intellect sleeps in the stone, dreams in the animal, reasons in the man. Why would it not also reason in humanity?"[1] It is also in this sense that Gilbert Simondon carries out his critique of language, of the human-all-too-human, when he explains that "it is not language that creates signification"; rather, "signification" is anterior to language: "if there were no signification to support language, there would be no language."[2]

With Deleuze and Guattari (and following Spinoza), one could say that all reality has two distinct and yet indissociable aspects: a discursive aspect, the world of expression, language and signs; and a "machinic" aspect, the world of contents, the body, reality, and forces.[3] Because of this, collective reason is the other side of collective force, both distinct and indissociable from it.[4] "The act and the idea are really inseparable," Proudhon writes (see *action*).[5] Even

---

1 Proudhon, *De la Justice*, 3:267.
2 Simondon, *Individuation psychique et collective*, 200.
3 Deleuze and Guattari, *A Thousand Plateaus*, 88.
4 "The organ of the collective reason is the same as that of the collective force: it is the group assembled for labor, for study; the company, whether industrial, scholarly, or artistic; academies, schools, municipalities; it is the national assembly, the club, the jury; any meeting of men, in a word, formed for the discussion of ideas and inquiry into questions of right" (Proudhon, *De la Justice*, 3:270).
5 Ibid. 2:298.

when it claims to be "pure," reason is always the expression of an arrangement of forces, an arrangement that this very pretension to purity always marks as an apparatus of domination and oppression. In such a case, reason is always a "State reason [*raison d'État*]," which points back to the State itself, to the Church, to Capital, or to the illusions of that little State called the "ego": the illusions of individual reason and *free will*, the foundations and transmitters of domination, everywhere the "absolute," on whatever scale, aspires to substitute itself for the relations constitutive of reality. As Proudhon explains, anarchism proposes to "purge" ideas of all that is absolute, "to reveal the reason of things," "to determine, by means of historical observation and the study of social trans-actions, the relations or the reason of human acts without mixing in any-thing of the human absolute, much less anything of the superhuman absolute, whatever names these might take: angel, archangel, domination, principality, throne, community, Church, council, Parliament, cathedral, personality, prop-erty, etc., up to and including the head of this incommensurable hierarchy, the Absolute of absolutes, who is God."[1] Reason is always "collective" because it is the expression and point of view of an *arrangement* of forces. But because any *arrangement* seeks to go to the limits of its capacities, as seen from the limits of its own point of view, of its particular composition of forces, its *raison d'être* tends to transform itself into an absolute and an illusion, to want to subject other forces, external to and constitutive of its being, to its own desire and point of view (see *totality/totalitarianism*). Only encounters and clashes with other forces, a recognition of their otherness, and the discovery of the power that this encounter induces when it is transformed into association can make a collective force aware of the collective and relative character of its *raison d'être*, as well as the collective character of any reason. That is when reason, like *law* (see *law/rights*), can be transformed into the expression of an increasingly pow-erful and free arrangement of forces, revealing to itself its character as *resultant* (see this term), becoming a true "public reason," when, founding itself on the "greatest contradiction" (see *balancing of forces*), it gives itself "for organ, the greatest possible multiplicity."[2]

Common notions (see *collective reason* and *practical theory*). A term employed by Spinoza. The importance of this term for a libertarian reading of this philoso-pher has been demonstrated by Gilles Deleuze. What has always, historically, separated anarchism from Marxism is well-known. In place of a revolution-ary project that tasks politics with accomplishing human emancipation and assigning meaning to the numerous concrete interactions and events of the reality it proposes to transform by translating them into the register of political

---

1   Ibid. 3:248.
2   Ibid. 3:270.

classifications, *identities*, and injunctions (right/left, proletariat/bourgeoisie, appearance/reality, friends/enemies, etc.), anarchism has instead affirmed two stances:

1. A refusal of politics' claim to *represent* (thus to enclose, define, and denature) all other realities within its partisan, symbolic, and official forms.

2. A binding (and thus an infinite extension) of the forces of emancipation to the totality of those lived realities, things, and situations that are the most immediate, the most everyday. These are those realities called social and professional, individual and inter-individual, romantic, economic, artistic, etc., which enlist the totality of the relations that human beings can establish among themselves and with things: their ways of eating, working, loving, treating animals – the most minute of the relations and practices of living that constitute that which exists.

Deleuze's reading of Spinoza helps us to think this project and these emancipatory practices, to redouble and intensify them through thought, in a manner that can justly be called libertarian. The originality of this reading could be summed up as follows: to show how knowledge obtained through the senses, through affects and signs – this confused and erroneous knowledge, dominated by prejudices and imagination, which so often plunge us into anger, love, hatred, ressentiment, and finally enslavement – can also constitute the starting point of an adequate knowledge of the world and a means (in fact, the only means) of our emancipation. In place of an idealistic or political interpretation of Spinoza, which entrusts the liberation of human beings to the mere faculties of reasoning or to a "political" imagination purged of its "natural" origins, the libertarian reading of Spinoza posits a contrary movement toward emancipation, a movement rooted in the power of the Nature from which humanity emerges and that never ceases to act within us, to our benefit as well as to our misfortune, for our oppression and our emancipation.[1]

For Deleuze's Spinoza, it always a matter of acting on the level of existence itself, in the obscure constitution of the real, "at the deepest level of the obscure mixture of bodies," as Deleuze tells us, where the "combat between servitudes and liberations" unfolds.[2] For Deleuze, it is true that the signs and affects of

---

1 For a more detailed treatment of these questions, cf. Daniel Colson, "L'imagination spinoziste et l'idée d'émancipation," in *Les Incendiaires de l'imaginaire*, ed. Alain Pessin and Mimmo Pucciarelli (Lyon: ACL, 2000) and "Anarchist Readings of Spinoza," trans. Jesse Cohn and Nathan Jun, *Journal of French Philosophy: Bulletin de la Société Américaine de Philosophie de Langue Française* 17 no. 2 (Summer 2007): 86-129.

2 Gilles Deleuze, *Essays Critical and Clinical*, trans. Daniel W. Smith and Michael A. Greco

existence are inadequate ideas and passions that bind human beings to the domination and illusions of the first kind of knowledge, which are particularly opposed to the notions of the second kind, those "adequate ideas from which true actions ensue."[1] However, as "dark precursors," these signs and affects are nonetheless the condition of human emancipation in two senses: 1) they are what assures the production of concepts, by "*selection* of the passional affects, and of the ideas on which they depend," through the experiences of joy and sadness, augmentation and reduction of the power to act;[2] 2) the concepts, once produced, are what ensure the lasting emancipatory power of the signs and affects of existence by embodying them, by preventing them – at the price of "an inexpiable affective combat in which one risks death" – from falling into the hands of the Despot and the Priest, those "terrible 'judges' of life."[3] A "passional struggle" in which "signs confront signs and affects clash with affects," this selection and construction within the most intimate moments of lived experience of the world in which we want to live is always "the very condition" for human liberation.[4]

How do we pass from the confusion and tension of lived situations and relations to what Proudhon calls a *collective reason* (see this term)? This would be a reason that never loses its connection to the forces that produce it, that does not autonomize itself into an external and dominatory authority, a reason that would be the expression and point of view of an emancipatory arrangement of collective forces. By means of common notions, answers the Deleuzean Spinoza: notions shared by at least two bodies (*collective beings*, in Proudhon's vocabulary) that have the capacity to select "ideas" compatible with the forces and beings that encounter and associate with one another. Gradually and through increasing involvement [*implication*], these notions move from being merely "common to" two beings to increasingly general and universal notions, to a recomposition of the totality of that which exists, constituting "a world that is increasingly wide and intense."[5]

It is undoubtedly here – from this perspective of common notions – that the Deleuzean Spinoza is closest to the libertarian movement. He is close to its

---

(New York: Verso, 1997), 146.

1   Ibid. 143. The traditional interpretation of Spinoza distinguishes between three kinds of knowledge: knowledge of the first kind, sensory knowledge, confused and erroneous; knowledge of the second kind, rational knowledge, which makes it possible to reconstruct the logic of things and events; and finally, knowledge of the third kind, an intuitive knowledge that gives access to the essence of things and their relations.

2   Ibid. 144.

3   Ibid. 145.

4   Ibid. 145, 144.

5   Deleuze, *Spinoza: Practical Philosophy*, 126.

critique of science, when, as Bakunin remarks with regard to *matter* (see this term), it considers that "a common nature, a common character does not exist in itself, by itself, apart from the distinct and real things or bodies to which it is attached."[1] He is close to the way in which the libertarian movement conceives of association, federalism, and what it calls relations of *affinity* (see this term). He is close to its taste for experimentation, even of the strangest and riskiest kinds. He is close to its will to base its existence on the free *association* and *dissociation* of the forces that compose existence at a *given moment*, starting with the most tenuous realities and relations, the thousands of ways of living and working, of eating and getting dressed, of loving and learning, of giving birth and aging, of continually discussing and modifying the most minute relationships, and thus refusing to identify them with any fixed and final representation. Instead, they are continually evaluated according to the sole criterion of how each being feels at a given moment, according to its internal composition and its constitution in conjunction with other beings, therefore as a common "idea" and project.[2]

Where do common notions come from and how do they function? To put it another way: how, for the Deleuzean Spinoza, can existence and experience allow human beings to free themselves from error and sadness, from the dominations that, internally and externally, chain them to their own misfortune, prevent them from thinking for themselves and from deploying their power to act in a very different world? Through association and experimentation, Deleuze tells us: "The common notions are an Art, the art of the *Ethics* itself: organizing good encounters, composing actual relations, forming powers, experimenting."[3] This art of the *Ethics* never ceases to operate within the most immediate experience, every day, from the place where fate has thrown us, from the (fortunate and unfortunate) chance encounters that life imposes on us from the beginning (those of family, sex, social background, skin color, culture, country, and nationality), in which "signs refer to signs as effects refer to effects, following an *associative chain* that depends on the order of the simple chance encounter between physical bodies [emphasis in original]".[4] As the *Ethics* attempts to demonstrate, we can cease to subject ourselves to these chance relations and encounters – the outcome of mere circumstance – and instead seek relations and encounters on the basis of happy affects and passions.

---

1   Bakunin, "Considérations philosophiques," *Œuvres*, 3:351.

2   "The interior is only a selected exterior, and the exterior, a projected interior" (Deleuze, *Spinoza: Practical Philosophy*, 125). For an approach to libertarian conceptions of association, federalism, and affinity groups, cf. Claude Parisse, *Les Anarchistes et l'organisation* (Lyon: ACL, 1989).

3   Deleuze, *Spinoza: Practical Philosophy*, 119.

4   Deleuze, *Essays Clinical and Critical*, 143.

To do this, we have only to experimentally "select" the beings and associations that suit us, that increase our joy and our power to act: "[f]rom a random encounter of bodies, we can select the idea of those bodies that agree with our own and give us joy, that is, that increase our power…There is thus a *selection* of the passional affects, and of the ideas on which they depend, which must liberate joys, vectorial signs of the augmentation of power, and ward off sadnesses, signs of diminution. This selection of the affects is the very condition for leaving the first kind of knowledge, and for attaining the concept through the acquisition of a sufficient power [emphasis in original]."[1]

Association and *selection*. Through this twofold process, the associated forces can then form "common notions," composing ever newer relations, increasingly broader and more intense, involving more and more possible beings, in pursuit of a total recomposition of that which exists. The world in which human emancipation takes place then ceases to be a plane of organization or development – even if such a plane were infinite.[2] It ceases to be a plane of appropriations or captures.[3] As a plane of composition and association on which there is no end to experimentation with the effects of encounters between ever different and ever new forces, between possible associations, it is transformed into a *plane of immanence* (see this term), "always variable," "constantly being altered, composed and recomposed, by individuals and collectivities."[4]

Common sense/good sense (see *experience*). Libertarian thought rejects the pretensions of the *science* that claims to break with common sense and ordinary *experience* – like the thought of Durkheim and Bourdieu, as well as that of Lenin, Althusser, and other pretenders to epistemological rupture – in order to dictate the meaning of one's life, the destiny and the determinisms that shape it, from an *external* position. Anarchism affirms, on the contrary, the capacity of collective beings to possess in themselves, from a certain point of view, the totality of meanings of that which exists, that is to say, its *possibilities* (see *common notions* and *collective reason*). For anarchism, the point of view of science is only one point of view among others, whose self-satisfaction, fatalism, and pretensions to exteriority and superiority are the surest sign of its oppressive, damaging, and damaged character (see *power*). However, with Whitehead, libertarian thought is not therefore to be confused with *good sense*, that mixture of clichés and received ideas that is always charged with persuading collective forces to surrender to the cynicism of the existing order (like Professor Ramsay

---

1   Ibid. 144.
2   Deleuze, *Spinoza: Practical Philosophy*, 128.
3   Ibid. 126.
4   Ibid. 128.

in Virginia Woolf's *To the Lighthouse*).[1] Present in the most ordinary judgments as well as "in the most ambitious theoretical statements" (and thus in science itself), good sense aspires to put each thing in its place within a world order that has been fixed once and for all. By contrast, common sense, the "insistent murmur" under "the authority of theories" and clichés, in the "interstices of the authorized discourses,"[2] affirms the infinite power of invention, creation, and innovation of that which exists.

Commons (common project, common arrangement). The commons is the *plane of reality* (see this term) and of the existence – enduring or provisional, yet always revocable at any moment and in any way – that autonomous forces bring about by their association (economic, political, ludic, romantic, etc.). A union, a bookshop, a cooperative, a football team, or a romantic relationship are a common *arrangement*, creating a collective project and a collective being that is shared in common by all who freely join together to make it work. Any association or collective being resulting from this association is a different and more powerful being or force than those forces that, in joining, contribute to its existence. It relies entirely on *trust*, since each is free to unmake it whenever he or she desires, in order to found another association that seems more appropriate or useful. The commons is never a terrain of struggle, an external framework that external forces would seize and fight over like a bone, a chair, or the wheel of a car. The commons is neither a setting (like a "common" waiting room or a gymnasium) nor a tool. While it is greater than the sum of the forces that constitute it, it is never external to them, since it comes from their association and does not exist otherwise. To associate (in love as in politics or in any other activity) is to agree to transform oneself within this association, it is to run the risk of becoming a different being (for better or for worse!). In this sense, all true association presupposes trust. Only the experience of the effects of such a transformation, tested and found to be *good* or *bad*, can lead one to withdraw from association. (Conversely, as one example among others of the subjugation and instrumentalization of collective beings emptied of all their own content and deprived of any autonomy, cf. the infiltration of the unions by the Communist Party shortly after the First World War.)

Communication (see *mediation*).

Commutation (see *justice*). A Proudhonian concept. Libertarian thought distinguishes between two types of justice:

---

1   On this point, see also *L'Effet Whitehead*, ed. Isabelle Stengers (Paris: Vrin, 1994), 12.
2   Ibid.

- A distributive justice that it rejects and fights against, which is exercised in an authoritarian fashion and originates from an overarching authority – the State, the court, the school principal or factory manager, God – who, through a judgment, distributes rewards and punishments according to merit measured from the outside by reference to some law, on a graduated scale from evil to good.
- A commutative and libertarian justice founded on direct exchange, on the equality of the things exchanged, on the equivalence of obligations and burdens, and on contracts or pacts of *association* or *alliance* (see these words and *law/rights*). This is a commutation internal to the beings' association, excluding any third person or intermediary and any external authority.

Components. Collective beings or forces in their relations of association within a larger collective being or force.

Composed unity. Concept employed by Bakunin (at the same time as *universal causality*, *nature*, etc.) to think the totality of being (see *multiplicity*).

Composition (see *association*, *balancing of forces*, and *serial dialectic*). A Proudhonian concept borrowed from chemistry (along with the physical concept of equilibrium – see *balancing* – and the physiochemical concept of *tension*) to account for the manner in which libertarian forces associate and join with one another. This association may well take the legal form of a contract or internal regulation (see *law/rights*). Because it is a *resultant* and because it calls forth unsuspected resources from the *collective beings* that it associates, it deeply modifies the nature of these beings and is itself an entirely new being. Indeed, contrary to what a juridical vision of the world would have us believe, the relations and associations between beings (as well as the conflicts among them) are not external to that which constitutes these beings. Said associations implicate these beings entirely. It is within what is deepest inside themselves, within what is *more-than-themselves*, that the possibility is determined of truly revolutionary associations capable of modifying the existing order from bottom to top, of containing another world (see *intimate*, *affinity*, *analogy*, *intuition*).

Concept. Opposed to *definition* (see this term).

Conformism (see *herds*, *mass*, *multitude*). A form of equality in which it is a matter of resembling others so as to lose oneself in the uniform mass. Anarchism violently denounces this form of equalization in the name of an equality that is radically different because it is founded on the absolute *difference* and *singularity* of beings (see these terms).[1]

Consciousness (see *person*, *ego*, and *body*).

Constraint (see *necessity*).

Contract (see *law/rights*).

Contradictions, contradictory (see *violence*, *balancing of forces*, *dialectic*, and *serial dialectic*). The *anarchy* and plurality of collective beings or forces necessarily imply that they are bound to collide and clash with one another by the very fact of their differences and their will to increase their power rather than to remain as they are. Only *practical sense*, experimentation, revolt, and the art of avoiding bad encounters and seeking good ones, can teach us how to avoid the domination of one force over another and the suicidal struggle of forces among themselves, and above all how to favor the development of *collective beings* that draw a greater power from the free association of the forces that compose them. Even in this case, contradictions are not just inevitable but desirable. They are both the sign of the freedom of the associated forces and the guarantee of the power and vitality of the beings resulting from this association – of their capacity to encompass and reorder all of the determinations of the real. Anarchist contradiction has nothing to do with Marxist (or Hegelian) contradiction. The concept of a "dialectical" development of nature and humanity is foreign to libertarian thought. For anarchism, there are bad and good contradictions: some contradictions kill and decrease the power to live, while others nourish and increase this power. It is necessary to avoid the first kind – to prevent them from occurring – and to carefully maintain the second kind without ever presuming to resolve them (see *balancing of forces*).

Contrariety (see *affinity*).

Convention (see *law/rights*).

---

1   On the other hand, on the characteristics and effects of conformism among libertarians where it takes the guise of a mass movement (see this term), cf. Eduardo Colombo, "Quelques réflexions sur les relations entre l'idéologie et la composition sociale du mouvement anarchiste," in *Composition sociale du mouvement anarchiste* (Lausanne, Switzerland: CIRA, 1972).

Core. Concept used by Monatte and the editors of the journal *La Vie ouvrière*[1] to define the small militant groups capable of galvanizing the trade unions from within, thanks to their "ardor" and taste for books. The revolutionary syndicalist "core" is aligned with (in a more moderate register and in a period of low ebb) the *active minorities* of revolutionary syndicalism at their height and, in a more primordial way, with the Bakuninian *intimate* circles (see these terms).

Culture (see *manual/intellectual*).

Cynicism. The lasting effect of an aborted revolt that is transformed into negation. It takes the form of a twofold *ressentiment* that is not content to disparage and devalue others, but which turns against the very being that experiences it. The cynic is thus a man of *ressentiment* raised to the second power who, fortunately, for this very reason, generally eschews libertarian milieus.

---

1   Translator's note: Pierre Monatte (1881-1960) was a French revolutionary syndicalist who founded *La Vie ouvrière* (*Workers' Life*), the official journal of the CGT, in 1909. The anarchist sympathies of his earlier life, which led him to participate in an international anarchist congress in Amsterdam in 1907, later gave way to Marxism. Jeremy Jennings notes that "*La Vie ouvrière* was built around a group or '*noyau*' of regular contributors." See Jennings, *Syndicalism in France: A Study of Ideas* (New York: St. Martin's Press, 1990) 146-48, 167, 75.

D

Daoism (see *neo-Confucianism*). The proximity between anarchism and Chinese Daoism is a commonplace in the historiography of China.[1] It can be justified by a great number of historical and sociological observations in connection with peasant revolts, the individualism and nonconformity of the erudite Daoists, the sexual practices of this movement, its assertion of equality between men and women, its radical critique of language and hierarchy, its rejection of Confucian humanism as well as the official totalitarianism of "the Legalist school." But it is on the terrain of philosophy (with which we are concerned in this little lexicon) that the homology between anarchism and Daoism is at the same time strongest and most implicit. Among the many possible translations of the *Dao De Jing*, the enigmatic text of Laozi, that of Bernard Botturi undoubtedly best expresses the proximity between anarchism and Daoism. See, for example, at the beginning of chapter 42: "The Dao gave birth to the Primordial Unity, the Primordial Unity gave birth to Heaven and Earth, Heaven and Earth gave birth to the Interval, the Interval gave birth to the ten thousand living things."[2] Like Daoism, in its action as in its thought,

---

1   See, in particular, Wolfram Eberhard, *A History of China*, trans. E.W. Dickes (Berkeley, CA: University of California Press, 2004), 42 and 45; Isabelle Robinet, *Taoism: Growth of a Religion*, trans. Phyllis Brooks (Stanford, CA: Stanford University Press, 1997); Étienne Balazs, *Chinese Civilization and Bureaucracy: Variations on a Theme*, trans. H.M. Wright (New Haven, CT: Yale University Press, 1964), 158, 243 et passim; Jacques Gernet, *Ancient China from the Beginnings to the Empire*, trans. Raymond Rudorff (Berkeley: University of California Press, 1968), 118-19.

2   Lao-tseu [Laozi], *Tao-tö king: la Tradition du Tao et de sa sagesse*, trans. Bernard Botturi (Paris: Cerf, 1983) (Translator's note: while translations of the *Dao De Jing* are plentiful, none available in English seem to echo Botturi's adequately. Hence, this is a rendering of

anarchism never begins from existing *identities* (see this term), from what defines or distinguishes them within a given space and according to a given order, and thus from what inevitably opposes them to one another (alliance then being itself an effect of this opposition; see *friends of our friends*). It always arises from within the *midst of things* (see this term), in the interval, the only place in which an infinity of possibilities can emerge (the "ten thousand living things" of the *Dao De Jing*). Anarchism always tries to avoid the deadly trap of direct confrontations between entities distinct from and thus external to one another (see *class, class struggle, power*, and *subversion*).[1] It identifies itself with vast affirmative and emancipatory movements that subsist solely on their own power and their own development. It recurs continually within all that exists as the welling-up of forces of *subversion* (sometimes infinitesimal), as another possibility, and as the polymorphous condition of an emancipatory affirmation of the whole.

Death (see *war/warlike, putting to death*, and *intimate being*).

Definition (see *classification*). In libertarian thought, the definition is opposed to the concept. Whereas the concept emerges from the midst of things in order to bring to light and express *focal points* of meaning – the *nodes of forces* (see these terms) that can recompose the totality of that which exists – the definition, as this word indicates, always attempts to fix things within preestablished limits, within a given framework, in order to try to articulate them in an external fashion within a reductive and oppressive order. In place of the definition, libertarian thought affirms the indefinite, the unspecified, the *apeiron* of Anaximander and Simondon, this reserve of being from which the concepts and conditions of a new world can emerge.

Dependency (see *government* and *domination*). The submission of a *collective being* to an external force that separates it from its own capacities and damages its power of *subjectivity*.

Desire (see *will, collective force, power, appetite, lack*, and *alienation*). The subjective and internal definition of force, of that which wants in it, equivalent to the Nietzschean *will to power*.[2]

Botturi's French into English).

1   Precisely in the autumn of 1936, when the summer's insurrection opposing the military coup was finally transformed into a civil war – a confrontation between two camps – the Spanish libertarian revolution definitively sealed its defeat, in reality as well as in idea.

2   For a neo-Leibnizian approach to the link between force and desire, cf. Tarde, *Monadology and Sociology*, 19. On the distinction between force and will to power, cf. Gilles Deleuze,

Determination (see *will*). Concept employed by the libertarian movement in a sense close to that of *will* (as when one says that somebody is "determined," that one shows "determination"). Despite what one might believe, libertarian determination is not opposed to the *indeterminate* (see this term). It is opposed to the concept of *determinism* insofar as, contrary to the latter, libertarian determination is entirely *internal* to the being that expresses it. It is the expression of the *power* and the *will* (see these terms) that constitute this being at a given moment and in a given situation. It is in this sense that Proudhon can speak of the "power of determination."[1]

Determinism. A concept linked to domination, which posits beings as entirely dependent on causes and conditions *external* to that which defines their *subjectivity* (see these terms). Libertarian thought opposes *determination* to determinism.

Devil (diabolic, demonic) (see *power of the outside, symbols/signs*). At the risk of worsening the image of a movement that is already identified with *anarchy* in the most commonplace sense of the term, most of the principal libertarian theorists refer frequently and positively to the figure of the devil and of demons – whether it is Bakunin's "*diable au corps*," the witch's cauldron of the *affinity* groups and secret societies,[2] or Proudhon's glorification of Satan, the chief of the rebellious angels, the adversary of God: "Come, Satan, come, you who are calumniated by priests and kings, that I may kiss you, that I may clasp you to my breast! Long have I known you, and you have known me too. Your works, blessed of my heart, are not always

---

Nietzsche and Philosophy, trans. Hugh Tomlinson (New York: Columbia University Press, 1983), 49 et passim. On the (contestable) contestation of this interpretation and the issues in this debate, see Paolo D'Iorio, "Les volontés de puissance" in Mazzino Montinari, *"La volonté de puissance" n'existe pas*, trans. Patricia Farazzi and Michel Valensi (Paris: Éditions de l'Éclat, 1996), 119-191; Müller-Lauter, *Nietzsche, physiologie de la volonté de puissance*; and Montebello, *Nietzsche, la volonté de puissance*.

1   Proudhon, *De la Justice*, 3:375.

2   Cf., among many possible examples, Bakunin's letter to Jean-Louis Pindy of January 11, 1873 in connection with Elisée Reclus: "He does not have all the *diable au corps* that one could wish. But it is a matter of temperament, and a man can do no more than he can" (*Œuvres complètes*, vol. 7 [Paris: Champ libre, 1979], xxxi).

Translator's note: *Diable au corps* ("devil in one's flesh") is "Bakunin's favourite expression to describe unbounded revolutionary energy and initiative," Max Nettlau explains ("The Sight of Nature and the Works of Man, and Practical Life, These Form the College in Which the True Education of Contemporary Society Is Obtained," in *Élisée and Élie Reclus: In Memoriam*, ed. Joseph Ishill [Berkeley Heights, NJ: Oriole Press, 1927], 200).

beautiful and good, but they alone give meaning to the universe and prevent it from being absurd."[1]

While the anarchist opposition between the devil and God offers a model that will sound familiar to everyone (in a manner that is undoubtedly too explicit or violent), it obviously has nothing to do with religion. As Didier Franck demonstrates elsewhere in connection with Nietzsche,[2] it has to do with a radical and general ontological position in which the expression "the devil in one's flesh" employed by Bakunin ceases to be a lighthearted pedagogical remark (as in the Countess of Ségur's "good little devils";[3] see *body*). In opposition to the person of God as guarantor of the unity of the human body – and thereby the unity of a totally "humanized," universally ordered world without any "remainder" – anarchism affirms a world freed from the "bonds" of *logos*, as well as those of religion. In this world, what Nietzsche calls "the time of anarchy"[4] would correspond to what Proudhon calls the "anarchy" of the "powers" constitutive of the human being, in which "all of nature's spontaneities, all the fatal instigations of Being, all the gods and demons of the universe converge."[5] Varuna and Mitra, the magician-king and the priest-judge, the despot and the legislator, the gods of the bond and the pact, are opposed by Indra, the warlike god, the god of "pure and immeasurable multiplicity," the god of "the ephemeral" and "metamorphosis," the god who "unties the bond just as he betrays the pact"[6] (see *war/warlike*). The *sym-bolic* of order and domination that binds and attaches is opposed to the anarchist *dia-bolic* that breaks and separates[7] (see *direct action*), affirming the *autonomy* of beings, making possible associations of an altogether different nature.

Dialectic (see *emancipation, master/slave, contradiction*, and *balancing of forces*). Confronted with the ordering of *representations* (see this term), their will to fix the *future* and to waste the power of that which exists by enslaving it to the pettiness of their interests, the dialectic pretends to introduce *movement* (see this term), both in thought and in reality. But as Deleuze has shown, the dialectic

---

1   Proudhon, *De la Justice*, 3:433-434. For a clarification of the enigmatic character of the essential role that Proudhon confers on Satan in the significance of the universe, see *power of the outside*.

2   Franck, *Nietzsche and the Shadow of God*.

3   Translator's note: Sophie Rostopchine, the Comtesse de Ségur (1799-1874), was famous for her moralistic children's books, including *Un Bon Petit Diable* (*A Good Little Devil*, 1865).

4   Friedrich Nietzsche qtd. in Franck, *Nietzsche and the Shadow of God*, 174.

5   Pierre-Joseph Proudhon, *Contradictions économiques*, vol. 2 (Paris: Rivière, 1923), 253.

6   Deleuze and Guattari, *A Thousand Plateaus*, 352.

7   On this distinction and this etymology of the word "devil," cf. Gilbert Hottois, *Simondon et la philosophie de la "culture technique"* (Brussels: De Boeck Université, 1993), 125.

– whether it calls itself idealist or materialist, Hegelian or Marxist – is always a "false movement," an "abstract logical movement," that is to say a "*mediation*" (see this term and *direct action*).[1] Unlike dialectical thought, libertarian thought rejects all mediation in favor of struggling *directly* and *immediately*, both in reality and in thought. In this way, from the perspective of thought, the libertarian project can recognize itself in the philosophical tendency of Nietzsche or Kierkegaard: "to put metaphysics in motion, in action…to make it act, and make it carry out immediate acts" (see *passage to the act*). Indeed, as Deleuze writes, thinking – like art, revolt, and all emancipatory struggle – does not mean "propos[ing] a new representation of movement; representation is already mediation. Rather, it is a question of producing within the work a movement capable of affecting the mind outside of all representation; it is a question of making movement itself a work, without interposition; of substituting direct signs for mediate representations" (see *direct action*).[2] It is in this sense, following Déjacque this time, that thought and writing, too, can be replaced by *propaganda by the deed* (see this term): "This book is not written in ink at all; these pages are not leaves of paper at all. This book is made of steel folded in octavo and loaded with fulminate of ideas. It is an authoricidal projectile that I hurl in a thousand copies upon the pavement of the civilized. May its shards fly far and mortally pierce the ranks of the prejudiced. Let the old society crack down to its very foundations! *This book is in no way a piece of writing; it is an action*…[I]t is forged of heart and logic, of blood and fever. It is a cry of insurrection, a ringing of the alarm bell with the hammer of the idea, which resounds in the ear of the popular passions…This book is hatred, it is love [emphasis my own]."[3]

Differences (see *contradictions*, *point of view*, *multiplicity*, *equality*, and *indiscernibles*). Following Leibniz (and his theory of *indiscernibles*), anarchism (from Stirner to Bakunin) affirms the absolute singularity of beings.[4] In the libertarian conception, the identity of a being is not defined in an external and objective way by its limits and the place that it occupies in space and time. This is a police perspective in which it is always a question of pinning things down, knowing where they are (address, nationality, age, profession), being able to "locate" them (see *localism*) and thus to control them. Identity is inherent in each being, in its *raison d'être* (its reason for being itself rather than something

---

1   Gilles Deleuze, *Difference and Repetition*, trans. Paul Patton (New York: Columbia University Press, 1994), 8.

2   Ibid. (trans.: modifications my own).

3   Joseph Déjacque, À bas les chefs! (Paris: Champ libre, 1971), 86-87.

4   "Ownness…is my whole being and existence, it is I myself" (Max Stirner, *The Ego and His Own*, trans. Steven T. Byington [New York: Benjamin R. Tucker, Publisher, 1907], 206).

else) and in the singular *force* that gives it existence at a *given moment* (see these terms).

Dignity (see *equality, autonomy*). The subjective perception of one's own autonomy, of the *equality* of all beings, and of their right to *do all that they are capable of.*

Direct (see *monad*). Directness is opposed to *mediation* (see also *direct action*) and to *representation* (see this term). Libertarian thought is opposed to any notion of instrumentality, of neutral and objective tools and buffers entrusted with maintaining the bond between *collective forces* (see this term). For anarchism, everything is a collective force, good or bad, transmitting *oppression* or *emancipation*. It is from the direct and *immediate* encounter (see this term) between these forces and from the *interior* of what constitutes them that a world without *domination* can be born (see these terms).

Direct action (see *propaganda by the deed, passage to the act, plastic force*, and *transduction*). In a book on the work of the painter Francis Bacon, Gilles Deleuze explains how "painting directly attempts to release the presences beneath *representation*, beyond *representation* [see this term]. The color system itself is a system of *direct action* upon the nervous system."[1] This is a practical and theoretical notion invented by revolutionary syndicalism and anarcho-syndicalism and a continuation of the earlier precedent of anarchist *propaganda by the deed*.[2] In its libertarian sense, direct action embraces the totality of human activity in and relations with the world, from the social struggle to painting, from philosophy to manners. In a circumstantial way (but for anarchism, there are only *circumstances*), the concept of direct action provides an essential key to understanding the nature of the libertarian project in the economic and social context of the early 20th century. Émile Pouget, one of the leaders of the French CGT[3] before 1914, gives it the following definition: "Direct Action, the manifestation of the workers' strength and determination, shows itself in accordance with circumstance and setting, through acts that may well be very gentle, just as they might as easily be very violent. It is simply a matter of what is required. *Thus, Direct Action has no specific form* [emphasis my own]."[4]

---

1   Gilles Deleuze, *Francis Bacon: The Logic of Sensation*, trans. Daniel W. Smith (Minneapolis, MN: University of Minnesota Press, 2003), 45 (trans.: emphasis my own).

2   On the connection between direct action and propaganda by the deed, as well as their significance in the history of the anarchist movement, cf. Colson, "La science anarchiste."

3   Translator's note: the CGT (*Confédération Générale du Travail*, or General Labor Confederation) was founded as a revolutionary syndicalist union confederation in 1895.

4   Émile Pouget, *Direct Action*, trans. Kate Sharpley Library (London: Kate Sharpley Library,

As a *plastic force* (see this term) that opens to an infinity of possibilities – and therefore quite close to the concept of *species activity* in Nietzsche or Deleuze's *univocal being*[1] – the experience that embodied the idea of direct action is closely related to the practice of syndicalism as conceived by anarcho-syndicalism. This is achieved through two broad operations, which take place successively or simultaneously:

1. First of all, a foundational operation. It is imperative that the revolutionary union free itself from the symbolic traps of law, representation, and negotiation through conflict and *rupture* (see this term). It must refuse to be the "intermediary," the "*chargé d'affaires* of the workers' interests."[2] On the twofold *plane of reality* of the labor movement and of its relations to other social forces, it must refuse to be the "middle-man" who, by virtue of its status as "representative," separates what it claims to connect, transforming the bond that it proposes into chains and hindrances, prohibiting any direct association or effective combination of the "physical, intellectual, and natural forces" of the working class.[3] Refusing to unfold itself within the falsely rational, transparent, and orderly theater of law and representation, the union must not only withdraw into the "irregularity," the "diversity," and the apparent "incoherence" of "working-class life," but, adding fold upon fold, it must also include and implicate itself in its solitary *intimacy* as an "autonomous grouping."[4] Because of this condition – the *autonomy* of its preserved intimacy and the concentration that it supposes – the union is capable, for its part, of perceiving and *focalizing* (see this term), from

---

2003), 23 (trans.: modifications my own).

1 Deleuze, *Difference and Repetition*, 36 et passim.

2 Fernand Pelloutier, "Du rôle des Bourses du travail," in Jacques Julliard, *Fernand Pelloutier et les origines du syndicalisme d'action directe* (Paris: Seuil, 1971), 41; and Pouget, *Direct Action*, 23.

3 Fernand Pelloutier, "L'organisation corporative et l'anarchie," in Julliard, *Fernand Pelloutier*, 407. A "bond-separation" that, following Guy Debord, Giorgio Agamben clarifies as follows: "What hampers communication is communicability itself; humans are separated by what unites them" (Giorgio Agamben, *The Coming Community*, trans. Michael Hardt [Minneapolis, MN: University of Minnesota Press, 1993], 81). An affirmation that corresponds, almost word for word, to the declaration of the delegate from Sète to the international anarchist congress held in Geneva on August 13-14, 1882: "We are united because we are divided" (qtd. in George Woodcock, *Anarchism: A History of Libertarian Ideas and Movements* [Harmondsworth, UK: Penguin, 1986], 214).

4 Victor Griffuelhes, *Le Syndicalisme révolutionnaire* [1909] (Toulouse, France: CNT-AIT, 1977), 14.

a certain point of view, a "working-class life that is too complex in its manifestations and details to be entrusted to the hands of inept leaders"[1] and also of "expressing" this "working-class life," becoming the "tribune" and "echo" of the "worker's intimate concerns."[2]

2. As a "laboratory of economic struggles," in Pelloutier's words,[3] a "living and vibrant agglomeration," having "vitality" and "influence" corresponding to its "organism" for Pouget,[4] a new alchemical crucible of the social revolution for Griffuelhes,[5] the union can then, on this condition, connect with and confront others, extend its singular intimacy to the totality of organized labor (other unions, cooperatives, various groupings, labor exchanges, trade or industrial federations, confederations, internationals). By means of this association and confrontation, each union increases its own force, increases the intensity of its perception of working-class life and expands the acuity and richness of its point of view in order to finally "bring to light" the power of life thus created and accumulated, to "develop" it further, until the "supreme struggle that will comprise the revolutionary general strike."[6]

Direct democracy. Direct democracy is opposed to representative democracy (see *representation*). It is generally identified with three principal procedures: 1) the sovereign general assembly gathering all the members of a given collectivity in order to decide on whatever concerns the life of this collectivity. This is done most often through *common* accord, the vote (with hand raised or by seeking the views of all present) serving to make known the points of view of those present and to enable a consensus; 2) revocable delegation, with any delegate subject to being replaced at any moment; 3) the imperative mandate, the delegate being unable to take decisions other than those that he has been mandated to take by the collectivity that delegated him, with any new problem needing to be submitted for the discussion of that collective. Paradoxically, because it is direct, libertarian democracy takes time. To function well, it requires of its participants a great number of other conditions (*equality, affinity, trust, practical sense*, etc.). The new means of communication (internet, mobile phones, possibilities for small groups to coordinate themselves in an immediate way and

---

1   Victor Griffuelhes, *L'Action syndicaliste* [1908] (Paris: Éditions syndicalistes, 1982), 15-16.

2   Griffuelhes, *Le Syndicalisme révolutionnaire*, 29-30.

3   Ibid. 404.

4   Ibid. 8 and 4.

5   Ibid. 10.

6   Ibid. 30; Georges Yvetot, *A.B.C. syndicaliste* [1908] (Toulouse, France: CNT-AIT, s.d.), 39-40.

at a distance, etc.) in part permit the resolution of those problems of slowness that pertained merely to the physical difficulties of meeting and coordinating. Thanks to the subversive appropriation [*détournement*] and judicious use of the new means of communication, the coordination of general assemblies, as well as the revocability and imperative mandates of delegates, can function in an almost immediate fashion, but one must not forget that the slowness of taking decisions also very frequently constitutes a requirement essential to libertarian practice.

Direction of the conscience (see *chaplain* and *political commissar*). An old Christian practice in which each being is supposed to subject its acts, thoughts, intentions, and most intimate perceptions and internal movements to the judgment of an external authority that, in the name of transcendent norms, is tasked with knowing, evaluating, and correcting this being, subjecting its power to an external order. This Christian model for the subjection of collective forces found wide use in the practices and conceptions of Marxist revolutionary movements. It is deeply inscribed in the cultures that are called Western, even in certain currents that claim to belong to the libertarian movement (see *rendering of accounts*).

Disassociation (see *association*).

Discipline (self-discipline). A *constraint* (see this term) that aims to subject collective beings to an order external to that which constitutes them. Discipline can be internalized by these beings (we then call it "self-discipline"), but only by disabling them, rendering them incapable of the movements that their nature makes possible – as when one says that someone has a stick up his ass [*il a avalé un parapluie*].

Domination. The composition of collective forces in which certain forces impose their own will on others, separating them from what they are capable of, subjecting them to a general order in which they are *separated from themselves* (see this term). Anarchism opposes all domination to the extent that it proposes a composition of free and *autonomous* forces (see *autonomy*) enabled to do all that they are capable of, a composition of forces that are all the more powerful because they refuse any negativity, any distortion of possibilities, any capture or cooptation of potential forces. This is why anarchism is close to the Deleuzean Spinoza: "But now it is a question of knowing whether relations (and which ones?) can compound directly [see *direct*] to form a new, more 'extensive' relation, or whether capacities can compound directly to constitute a more 'intense' capacity or power. It is no longer a matter of utilizations or captures, but of sociabilities and communities."[1] How can collective forces compose themselves so as to form a superior collective force without damaging or oppressing some of them, respecting and preserving the totality of the power that each contains? Such is the question that anarchism poses and attempts to answer.

Dualism (see *monism*).

Duty of memory (see *eternal return*).

---

1   Deleuze, *Spinoza: Practical Philosophy*, 126.

E

Economy (see *statistics* and *neoliberals*). References to the economy play a large part in libertarian discourse and thought, even, at times, decked out in its most mathematicized trappings: in the writings of Proudhon, for example, but also more generally in the polemical manner in which libertarian workers' movements have always striven to resist the traps of politics, the State, morality, and religion. The adversaries of the libertarian movement have not missed the opportunity to point out (not without reason) that this importance given to economics was not necessarily accompanied by a great competence on their part within this academic discipline, as can be seen in the coarse mockery to which Marx subjects Proudhon's work, *The System of Economical Contradictions.*[1] Indeed, in its will to recompose the totality of that which exists – as in the radicality of its critique – anarchism refuses to treat economics as a separate domain and science, detached from other aspects of life, through which emancipatory critique is obliged to pass in order to make its proposals credible. As the totality of this brief lexicon should make clear, anarchism is foreign to any notion of a program or proposals (see *anarchy, exterior/interior, entelechy,* etc.), as well as to any demand for it to justify itself before the courts of the existing order. The separation and hypervalorization of the economy – particularly in its mathematical representations, with their ambitions far exceeding their ability to account for reality – constitute for libertarian thought the clearest sign of an oppressive and reductive order, founded on domination, the distortion and repression of our capacities, paid for by an infinity of *suffering,* waste, and loss of power. This can be seen, if we are willing to see it, in our own experiences and through our relations with others.

---

1   Karl Marx, *The Poverty of Philosophy,* 1847.

Effectiveness/efficiency [*efficacité*] (see *ends/means, exterior, given moment,* and *utilitarianism*). A utilitarian and party-political concept that defines the value of a being or an action with respect to an objective or an interest external to this being or this action. Anarchism is often accused of being ineffectual, but this is done in ignorance of the reasons for this apparent weakness, from the myopic and self-serving point of view of the codes and ledgers of the very order that anarchism aspires to transform from bottom to top. In opposition to the effectiveness of beings or their mechanical and external instrumentalization, anarchism proposes the consideration of that which constitutes beings by themselves and for themselves at a *given moment* and in a given *situation* (see these terms). In libertarian thought, the encounter and association between two beings can never be defined in an external way. It may be that one of them integrates a dimension of the other into its own plans and interests (slave and master, employee and company, people and leaders, etc.). Or it may be that the association of both takes its meaning from the beneficial effects that they bring to a third party (for example, the alliance of the petite bourgeoisie and the working class as the conjunctural condition of the Communist Party's rise to power during the Spanish Civil War).

In opposition to tactical and strategic association defined by separate or external interests (the enemies of my enemies are my friends), anarchism proposes the *affinitary* encounter founded on an *intimate* and *internal* agreement (see these terms) – an agreement able to modify the nature of the associated beings and to increase their power.

Ego (see *body* and *person*). A subjective illusion, which masks the great diversity of the forces and possibilities that constitute us, thereby preventing us from giving birth to other *subjectivities* endowed with more *power* and thus more *freedom* (see these terms).

Élan vital (see *vital/vitalism*).

Emancipation (affirmation) (see *anti-speciesism*). In the libertarian project, emancipation is always considered in the form of an *affirmation*: an affirmation of radically different relations, of other modes of being that enable a more intense and freer life. The desire and will for emancipation often spring from a past or present situation or condition of oppression and domination. This can be a situation experienced negatively as unbearable or unacceptable, a condition (as a "slave," "employee," "housewife," "soldier," "child" subjected to the authority of his/her parents, etc.) in which the forces and identities capable of aspiring to another life are forged. These potentially emancipatory forces are thus thrice characterized by negativity and dependency with respect to domination: 1) through the oppression they endure, of which they are products; 2) through their own struggles, which are always in danger of being confined to a mere refusal of oppression; 3) through the *means* (see this term) by which they undertake this struggle, generally molded and dictated by the demands of the struggle and, ultimately, by the enemy that is to be fought and destroyed. Thus this easily verifiable historical consequence: the eternally repeated victory of an oppression that, even in the event of an apparent victory by the oppressed, immediately returns via the *means* and identities that the oppressed have adopted in order to win. Thus the central question of the libertarian project, a question that is at once theoretical and practical: how do we transform this situation of a threefold dependence on the dominant into one of affirmative, autonomous forces, masters of that which constitutes them? How can the collective beings produced by domination transform themselves into subjects of emancipation? How can the means of struggle be made simultaneously into the ends of this struggle? (See *entelechy* and the fiercely debated question of whether "revolutionary unions" are merely a means of struggle or the administrative organs of the society that they aspire to give birth to; the question of the militarization of the militias in Spain; the frequently misunderstood anarchist refusal of revolutionary "discipline," hierarchical effectiveness, and, finally, the State, which always ends up being presented as the surest and most effective means of emancipating those whom it oppresses.) The libertarian movement believes in neither the mysteries and magic tricks of the dialectic nor divine providence (even dressed in the scientist rags of "historical materialism"). From this point of view, liberation struggles are not automatically endowed with an emancipatory quality. Each must be evaluated individually, practically, in every last detail of that which constitutes them: in terms of the means that they employ, in terms of the will that animates them, and in terms of their capacity to affirm, from this moment forward, another world, opposed to all oppression and domination, present and future. It is, among other things, because it federates different and contradictory forces, each acting on their own plane of reality, that the libertarian movement can escape the traps of the relations belonging to each form of domination, relations produced by this very domination.

Encounters (see *association*, *event*, and *situation*).

Ends/means (see *entelechy*). Anarchism refuses the utilitarian and Machiavellian distinction between ends and means (the "ideal" end justifying the most repugnant or coercive means). In particular, it refuses the kind of mastery over time that this distinction presupposes (a long-term strategy operating through a series of manipulations and maneuvers in the short and middle terms). For libertarian thought and practice, the end is necessarily contained in the means. The final objective is entirely contained in the present moment. Not only does this standpoint imply, historically, the anarchist refusal of the so-called "dicta-torship of the proletariat" through which the Party-State claimed to pave the way to the future happiness of the people at the price of the worst kinds of sub-jection. This standpoint also informs the most immediate militant practices (e.g., revocable delegation and the imperative mandate given to delegates [see *direct democracy*]). It implies, through these immediate practices, the refusal of what has long been the strategy of Marxism.

Energy (see tension). A term borrowed from physics that serves, in the revolu-tionary syndicalist and anarcho-syndicalist vocabulary, to define the quantity of force at the disposal of a *collective being* (see this term). This energy, the quantity of which varies according to the being in question, is not given once and for all. It depends on the nature of the *composition* of the being under consideration and its relations with other beings. The revolutionary syndicalist and anarcho-syndi-calist appeal to "energy" is a call to continually recompose the forces constitutive of collective beings ("individuals," tradecrafts, unions, union federations) in a different way, to implicate them in a new *arrangement* (see this term) that is more powerful and less dependent on others (see *autonomy*), capable, as Deleuze explains, of "transcend[ing] its limits in going to the limit of its capacities."[1]

Entelechy (see *project, collective reason*). An old philosophical concept, recu-perated by Leibniz and then by Proudhon (see *collective reason*), which makes it possible in particular to think the relationship between *collective force, free-dom*, and *reason* (see these terms).[2] As employed by Aristotle and then by the Scholastics, "entelechy" traditionally indicated a being's state of completion (and thus of perfection). In this conception, it is the "goal" of the *movement*, like a "final cause," that permits a passage from the "power" to do something to the "act" of doing it. In place of this static succession of "states," in which the entelechy would designate the final state, Leibniz posits a dynamic model of movement. In his work, the term "entelechy" indicates a "tendency," present from the beginning, that leads each being – through a process of "dilation" or "unfolding" – to discover *what it can do,* that which it has contained from the beginning of its constitution. This excludes all "finalism." The "goal" (or "end") is not what one tends toward, in an *external* fashion, as an external purpose, *posterior* to our *action*, and as a function of the illusions of conscious-ness, logic, or reason. Rather it is that which makes us act, *prior* to it, as *will* and *desire*, in the deepest and most obscure part of ourselves, according to the *arrangement* that constitutes us at a *given moment.*[3]

---

1   Deleuze, *Difference and Repetition*, 37 (trans.: modifications my own).

2   Proudhon, *De la Justice*, 3:267.

3   On the concept of entelechy in Leibniz, cf. "De philosophiae emendatione et notione

Entity. Concept used by Alfred North Whitehead, synonymous with *thing* and with *being* (see these terms).

Equality (see also *autonomy, differences, base, hierarchy, limits,* and *balancing of forces*). Libertarian equality is synonymous with *autonomy, freedom,* and *balancing*. It has nothing in common with the abstract legal equality of *democracy* and human rights, which, under the guise of an abstract ideal, justifies all kinds of real hierarchy, domination, and inequality (as demonstrated by the machinations of its promoters). Nor does it have anything to do with the barracks equality (quite historically real) of authoritarian socialism, in which the vast majority of people, dominated by party leaders and State bureaucrats, are subjected to *conformism* and obedience. Against these false equalities, either illusory or imposed from the outside, anarchism affirms *differences* (see this term), all differences, the absolute singularity of each being in terms of that which constitutes it at a given moment (see *indiscernibles*). Anarchist equality is not an equality of measurement, an equality imposed from the outside. On the contrary, it is an equality based on the *anarchy* of beings, on their absolute autonomy, on the possibility for each of them to *go to the limits of* the aspirations, desires, and qualities of which it is capable at a *given moment,* according to the principle that "the smallest becomes equivalent to the largest once it is not separated from its own capacities" (see *balancing of forces*).[1] In this sense, libertarian equality is synonymous with *autonomy* and *freedom.* This requires libertarian forces to be capable of composing a world based on this *autonomy* and this *freedom,* on the refusal of any one being's submission to another, on the unquestioned value of every revolt, whatever it may be, and on the *immediate* solidarity that this revolt evokes among those who are truly inspired, through that which constitutes them at a given moment, by this kind of *freedom* (see these terms).

Eternal Return (see *chaos, past, given moment,* and *power of the outside*). An obscure and controversial concept within Nietzsche, but one that is important to understanding the nature of the libertarian project and, more particularly, its relation to time and history. The anarchist movement has often been reproached for its untimely character, its refusal of historical laws and determinations, of necessary stages. "We want everything, right now!" Such could

---

substantiae," *Opuscula philosophica selecta,* qtd. in Gilles Châtelet, *Figuring Space: Philosophy, Mathematics, and Physics,* trans. Robert Shore and Muriel Zagha (Dordrecht, Netherlands: Kluwer Academic Publishers, 2000), 23; and Émile Boutroux, "La Philosophie de Leibniz," in Gottfried Wilhelm Leibniz, *La Monadologie* (Paris: Le Livre de Poche, 1991), 133n1 and 254-255.

1   Deleuze, *Difference and Repetition,* 37 (trans.: modifications my own).

be the motto of the libertarian movement in the eyes of its blinder detractors with regard to its most intense moments of affirmation: from the *general strike* of the end of the 19th century to May '68, including, in a more tragic way, the events of Munich in 1919, the Russian and Spanish revolutions, or the proclamation of libertarian communism in a certain number of Andalusian villages during the winter of 1932. At times, it might appear that anarchism endorses the idea of progress, that illusion born in the 19th century, a casualty of the disasters of the following century. But in its practices as well as in the imaginary that accompanies them, anarchism's relation to time has always been radically different from that of all "progressivisms," whether revolutionary or bourgeois, material or moral. As the libertarian interpretation of Spinoza demonstrates, anarchism is foreign to a linear conception of time. The time to which it refers and that defines it is a multiple and qualitative time that has to do with the duration of beings, with that "reality of enduring things" of which Bernard Rousset speaks, and with the relations of composition, recomposition, and decomposition that increase, decrease, or destroy these existing things' power to act.[1] Here, the libertarian interpretation of Nietzsche's eternal return helps to clarify the originality of the anarchist relation to duration and the order of things.

In their blindness regarding Nietzsche, Karl Löwith and, before him, Otto Weininger undoubtedly best illuminate the libertarian significance of the eternal return, albeit negatively and in spite of themselves.[2] What does Nietzsche add to the ancient and mythical conception of cyclical time?, wonders Löwith. Nothing, he concludes, if not an affirmation that is terrible within the context of modernity, since it amounts to a refusal of the irreversible and inescapable time bequeathed by Christianity. Thus, it is a refusal of the past and the future, the beginning and the end, a refusal of waiting and hoping, of the "sense" of history (in the double "sense" of the word "sense" [i.e., "meaning" and "direction"]). For this reason, it is a refusal of all change, all progress, all possibility of anything new. "The teaching of the eternal return" as the repetition of the identical and as "the *most extreme* form of nihilism":[3] such is the interpretation suggested by Löwith and Weininger, an interpretation whose sole and distant libertarian echo would be the punk "no future" of the '70s and '80s. Everything

---

1   Cf. Bernard Rousset, "Le réalisme spinoziste de la durée," in *L'Espace et le temps* (Paris: Vrin, 1991), 176 et passim, and Colson, "Anarchist Readings of Spinoza."

2   Karl Löwith, *Nietzsche's Philosophy of the Eternal Recurrence of the Same*, trans. J. Harvey Lomax (Berkeley, CA: University of California Press, 1997). Otto Weininger (1880-1908). Löwith refers mainly to two of Weininger's works: *Sex and Character*, trans. Ladislaus Löb (London: W. Heinemann, 1906) (German edition 1903) and *On Last Things*, trans. Steven Burns (Lewiston, NY: Edwin Mellen Press, 2001) (German edition 1904).

3   Löwith, *Nietzsche's Philosophy of the Eternal Recurrence of the Same*, 115.

returns, in the manner of stars and universes that die and are reborn, without goal or completion. For Löwith's Nietzsche, in the face of an absurd, alien world that utterly penetrates it (see *power of the outside*), the human being, crushed by the blind power of a nature indifferent to its own existence, would have to content itself with accepting its destiny. This would mean saying yes to this indifference and absurdity and thereby breaking with the lie of rationality and meaning with which human beings had so long aspired to invest their life, breaking definitively with the frustrations and illusions of humanism: the illusions of a properly human history capable of dominating the cosmos by means of religion, morals, science, and technology, of becoming its center, of humanizing it and giving it a meaning.

Quite incorrectly, Löwith and Weininger thus reproach Nietzsche and his conception of the eternal return with three things: 1) his *naturalism* and refusal to distinguish between humanity and nature, to recognize the transcendent and symbolic dimension of a human being created and interpellated by a God to whom humanity appeals that he may enter the world and pledge it to the story of its salvation; 2) his fatalism and refusal of *free will*, this freedom that obliges the human being to be responsible for his acts (see this term and *guilty party*) and to render an account of himself before his creator, before the courts, or before the "moral law" within; 3) finally, his obstinate refusal of memory, this "memory, by means of which man can recall his entire existence," as Löwith explains, "gives man the inner continuity that makes responsibility possible [see *guilty party*] and is itself already a moral responsibility."[1] Without this memory, it is impossible, Löwith insists, to be free, it is impossible to build a history with a past that one remembers, a present in which one remembers, and a future that one prepares through this recollection.[2] At the same time, however, from a libertarian point of view, these reproaches are all to Nietzsche's credit. They constitute an affirmation of exactly the opposite of what they intend to establish: the affirmation of another freedom; the affirmation of another conception of time; the affirmation of a culture, a meaning [*sens*], and a new humanity freed from the traps of modern humanism, in which freedom is synonymous with slavery, culture with oppression, and memory with guilt, a burden, and a prison.

Precisely by grounding themselves solely in the affirmation of the power of beings, in the positivity of the forces and the desires present at a *given moment* and in a given *arrangement* (see these terms), Nietzsche and anarchism reject what is generally understood by memory. In the name of the "untimeliness of the present" of which Paul Ricœur speaks, "the interruption the lived-through present brings about in regard to, if not the influence of the past, at least its

---

1   Ibid. 160.
2   On all of this, cf. ibid. chapter 7, 156 et passim.

influence over us," Nietzsche and anarchism indeed radically reject a dominant form of humanism that has, for such a long time, "transformed our ability to remember...into a burden"[1] and the education that accompanies it into a "preparation for death."[2] For Nietzsche and libertarian thought, memory, the "duty to remember," and the type of duration that they install within the old skeptical paradox of time are at the foundation of a fool's bargain in which – in the name of its capacity to remember and to base its present and its future on this memory – the human being is immediately called upon to recognize the radical "ontological deficiency" of the time from which it takes its life and to entrust itself entirely to the transcendence that feeds on this infirmity.[3] The past is no longer, the future is not yet, and the present passes without any reality but this passage that is incessant, *fleeting, imperceptible* (see these terms), and without content, in which, in order to exist, the human being can only remember what is no more, answering for what it so briefly was before a transcendent (divine or moral) court that is the sole judge of its future.

For Nietzsche and libertarian thought, the memory of the past, this perpetual monument and tomb in which humanism would like to imprison the human being – this mourning, this absence, and this infinite debt to which it would subject us – is merely invented by the oppressive, ferocious powers to devalue the life and force of the beings that they dominate, to deprive them of any possible initiative, to reduce them to the powerlessness of regret and guilt. With the eternal return, conversely, only the present moment counts, the moment as a "synthesis of time," at once present and past, present and future.[4] And it is on this point specifically that the humanist critique of eternal return cannot sustain its anger or mask its true face and the ugly machinery of its interests. Indeed, despite what one might believe, that with which Löwith, Weininger, and humanism reproach Nietzsche is not really wanting to forget the past – to ignore it, to refuse to remember it – but, on the contrary, with wanting its return. For humanism, one must always remember the past since it is through this memory, this attachment to that which is no longer, that which one can no longer change and for which one is eternally responsible, that humanity definitively ensures its servitude, its infinite debt, its perpetual

---

1   Paul Ricœur, *Time and Narrative*, vol. 3, *Narrated Time*, trans. Kathleen Blamey and David Pellauer (Chicago: University of Chicago Press, 1988), 312n42 and 235-236. It is remarkable that a philosopher opposed to Nietzsche and libertarian thought best grasped in what respect these present a true alternative to the "duty" of memory.

2   Cf. Bernard Edelman, *Nietzsche, un continent perdu* (Paris: PUF, 1999).

3   On this point and on the aporias of time in the Western tradition, cf., regarding Saint Augustine's *Confessions*, Paul Ricœur, *Time and Narrative*, vol. 1, trans. Kathleen McLaughlin and David Pellauer (Chicago: University of Chicago Press, 1984), 5 et passim.

4   Cf. Gilles Deleuze, *Nietzsche and Philosophy*, 48 et passim.

remorse.[1] But this past must never return, because then it becomes real again: it ceases to be past, it can be lived for a second time, a third, an infinite number of times. Therefore, it can be remade, modified, thus releasing the human being from any debt, sin, or guilt, while making us the contemporaries of and participants in a reality that never ceases to be present, in a relation to the world in which everything is always given, without any remainder other than that which emancipatory relations have yet to recompose.

Now the most serious charges that humanism levels at the eternal return – fatalism and the refusal of freedom, naturalism and the refusal of the human, as well as the refusal of meaning and the symbolic – fall, so to speak, on the heads of those leveling them. Now they show themselves for what they are: the indignant denials of an order founded precisely on the absence of freedom, on *determinism* (see this term), on the submission of beings to a univocal and simplistic meaning [*sens*] that is given once and for all. This order perceives very well in what respect Nietzsche and the eternal return radically threaten its hypocrisies and slaveries: by rendering its proclaimed ideals effective, while it works to render them impossible.

One must always listen attentively to humanist discourse so as to hear what it is really saying behind its principles and expressions of indignation. According to this discourse, Nietzsche, with his concept of the eternal return, would reduce humanity to nature, to its blind forces and imperious instincts, with no regard for human specificity, for culture and meaning. According to this discourse, Nietzsche and the eternal return would subject humanity to the eternal repetition of the same, depriving the human being of any freedom. But behind these words, we can hear others that say exactly the reverse.

First, let us consider culture and the symbolic. Humanism calls for and prides itself on meaning and signification. This meaning transcends the order of the world by conferring on humanity its "proud loneliness…in the whole of the extra-human world."[2] But it also transcends that very human being within whom it operates, in Kantian fashion, in the imperative form of a Law: a categorical imperative that radically distinguishes it from the rest of the world, but of which it is not the master.[3] This is why, as opposed to what they affirm else-

---

1   A past founded, in the monotheistic religions, on the myth of Adam and Eve and an original sin, an insolvent debt that only God can redeem.

2   Löwith, *Nietzsche's Philosophy of the Eternal Recurrence of the Same*, 162.

3   "And therefore he [man] also has a law within himself, therefore he is himself all law and no gushing arbitrariness…That is the gruesome greatness: it makes *no further sense* for him to obey the call of duty…But he must comply with the relentless, nonnegotiable *categorical* demand *in himself*." And if he would still like to act, to lament, laugh, dance, or rebel, let him learn once and for all that "*Kant's* loneliest man does not laugh and does not dance, he does not howl and does not rejoice" since the sole "yes" that he has to give is a yes to his solitude

where, what Weininger and Löwith reproach Nietzsche with so vehemently is not just wanting the past to return but especially wanting to indefinitely redefine the "meaning" of this past through this return, to declare that its signification is never fixed once and for all. What humanism reproaches Nietzsche and the eternal return for is not depriving humanity of the power of interpretation – subjecting it to the blind destiny of the world's forces and instincts – but, on the contrary, for equipping it with an infinite capacity to interpret and reinterpret the meaning of events and facts. Humanism does not accuse Nietzsche of depriving humanity of its *raison d'être* but, on the contrary, of providing it with an infinity of these and especially of refusing to subject them to a meaning that comes from elsewhere, a definitive, univocal and imperative meaning imposed by God. Worse still, he invites humanity to seize this power of interpretation (hitherto so poorly employed) and to multiply it ad infinitum in a becoming in which everything is always to be resumed, repeated, and revalued anew.

A lack of signification on one side – in which Nietzsche is shown to reduce the human to absurdity and to the blind forces of an indifferent nature – and an excess of it on the other side – in which Nietzsche is shown to equip the human being with an infinite power of meanings and confabulations. One should not be easily deceived by the multi-level contradictions, hidden agendas, and bad faith of humanist discourse. It is, indeed, with much hypocrisy that Weininger and Löwith accuse the Nietzschean will to eternal return of a "lie" and of "false history," of interpreting the past ad infinitum, of continually inventing new versions, of saying everything and its opposite.[1] They know very well that, for Nietzsche, one can never separate reality and its interpretation. But for Löwith, Weininger, and humanism, it is precisely a matter of continually separating reality from interpretation, violently refusing (without any explanation) to imagine that they may be merely two sides of the same reality (see *collective reason* and *common notions*). The past returns with all its power of life and determination, and it is because it returns that it can change both in its meaning and in its reality: such is the libertarian interpretation of the eternal return. This is why the crime and scandal of the eternal return (in the eyes of the humanists) lie neither in a supposed abandonment of signification nor in an excess of meaning, synonymous with lies and confabulation. On the contrary, they lie in the fact of being able to render these multiple interpretations true by affirming the infinite power of things and words, of the forces and points of view they contain, being able to render them effective and thus

---

and the Law which founds it: "only that is morality" (Otto Weininger, *Sex and Character*, qtd. in Löwith, *Nietzsche's Philosophy of the Eternal Recurrence of the Same*, 162).

1   "Every lie is a falsification of history…The lie is unethical, is the *reversal* of time: since the will to alter, here, concerns the past instead of the future" Weininger, *On Last Things*, qtd. in Löwith, *Nietzsche's Philosophy of the Eternal Recurrence of the Same*, 164-165.

making an attack on the immutable order of time and the things willed by God, Science, and Morality, refusing to yield to this order, perpetually asserting the power to recompose it differently. Indeed, if humanism's univocal and imperative meaning transcends the world, content to find in the world (under the coarse features of science and determinism) a *homology* of the external Law that forms its basis (see these terms), Nietzscheanism and anarchism's multitude of meanings (see *perspectivism* and *point of view*) are immanent to the world. They are the world's direct expression, the infinite expression of the infinity of its *possibilities* (see this term). In other words, what humanism reproaches Nietzsche with is not accepting the immutable return of things (the much-misunderstood "eternal return of the same"), but, on the contrary, wanting to "modify," to "transform," to "change" this order of things through this eternal return of the same, this eternal return of that which exists:[1] to exchange what was and thus what is for what returns, in a ceaseless movement in which, as Deleuze says, return itself *is* "the being of becoming."[2] Humanism reproaches Nietzsche not with denying human freedom, but, on the contrary, in the name of the *necessity* that it expresses (see this term), with affirming humanity's infinite power, since it is able to modify the past itself.

Eternity (see *intimate being* and *eternal return*).

Ethics. Contrary to Marxism and its naive and cynical scientism, as Murray Bookchin[3] emphasizes, anarchism is above all an ethical project that directly engages, in its smallest practices, in judging the value of relations and situations. However, this ethical dimension of the libertarian project is completely unrelated to the moral prescriptions (religious or otherwise) that generally prevail in the societies we know. Anarchism refuses any extrinsic and *a priori* prescription, whether under the title of the Ten Commandments, the Rights of Man, or any other "categorical imperative" aimed at regulating conduct and judgment, which is to be applied to particular situations, justifying a jurisprudence that requires an enormous apparatus of priests, judges, and other committees of *experts*. Libertarian ethics is constituted within the very *interior* of the things, situations, and relations experienced by various *collective beings* (see these terms). It depends entirely on the quality of these situations and

---

1   "It is unethical not to want to acknowledge the past (in which, after all, all 'reasons' and 'obligations' are situated) as what it was, i.e., settled, and to want to change and re-create the historical deed that has already happened" (Löwith, *Nietzsche's Philosophy of the Eternal Recurrence of the Same*, 164).

2   Deleuze, *Nietzsche and Philosophy*, 23.

3   Murray Bookchin, "Theses on Libertarian Municipalism," in *The Anarchist Papers*, ed. Dimitrios Roussopoulos (Montreal: Black Rose Books, 2002), 9.

these relations, their ability or inability to increase the force and autonomy of the beings of which they are the cause or the effect. In this sense, libertarian ethics can be recognized within a much older philosophical tradition: the tradition running from Spinoza to Nietzsche (at least within the so-called Western world).

Evaluation (see *point of view* and *genealogy*). The diversity of the beings and points of view that form the basis of the libertarian project is sometimes perceived, by those malevolent toward or ignorant of anarchist thought, as a mere relativism or a liberalism in which all things are equal since anything is just as valid as anything else (see *equality*). On the contrary, because it is founded on the difference and *singularity* of beings, in which "the smallest becomes equivalent to the largest once it is not separated from its own capacities,"[1] anarchist *equality* (see this term) and the methods of association it makes possible presuppose a continuous evaluation of the emancipatory or oppressive quality of actions, points of view, and standpoints. Contrary to the stance of indifference that some think can be deduced from its pluralism, libertarian affirmation is founded on a perpetual *judgment* of beings and of the quality of their associations. This is a judgment without a court or civil or penal code (see *law/rights*) in which each force, through a "universal jurisprudence,"[2] continually evaluates the quality of the other forces at a given moment, thus evaluating the possibilities and impossibilities of association that they present from the perspective of emancipation.

Event (see *stoppage, repetition,* and *given moment*). Any partial (and thus dominatory) order attempts to control space and time, to order and fix the totality of that which exists, and to anticipate everything that can take place. However, because it is partial and dominatory, it never attains this mastery and must continually allow the new and unforeseen, the surprising and the unmastered, to escape. It is continually punctured by events, both tiny (the dropping of a glass, an exchange of glances) and vast (a war, a revolution) in scale, which are pregnant with the most immediate order and expectations, as well as the most permanent organizations and programs. The event is the other side of dominant orders.[3] It is their involuntary and unavoidable opening to the power of that which exists (which they aspire to dominate) and to the possibilities that reality contains (which they strive to master in vain). The event, whether fortunate or unfortunate, each time singular and indefinitely repeated in its

---

1   Deleuze, *Difference and Repetition,* 37 (trans.: modifications my own).

2   Gilles Deleuze, *The Fold: Leibniz and the Baroque,* trans. Tom Conley (Minneapolis, MN: University of Minnesota Press, 1993), 67.

3   For a libertarian analysis of the concept of the event, cf. *L'Effet Whitehead,* ed. Isabelle Stengers.

singularity, is the most constant, direct, immediate, and positive *experimentation* with the limits inherent to all domination and with the possibility of affirming another order that would liberate the power trapped by this domination. In this sense, it can be thought of as the reverse of the *stoppage* and what it makes possible (see this term). Instead of the vacancy and vacuity opened by the stoppage of social and desiring machines that suspends the existing order (a stoppage that precedes all *revolts*), the event presents the apparently chaotic irruption of another possibility. It constitutes both the form and the content of what *revolt* makes possible, the manifestation of the anarchic power that this revolt claims both to liberate and to order (see *positive anarchy* and *more than oneself*).

Experience/experiment [expérience] (see *intuition* and *practical sense*). As the most common use of the word allows us to understand, the word *expérience* has two meanings. In its more recent, erudite sense, *expérience* ["experiment"] indicates that rather specific scientific operation that aims, by means of that equally specific filter that is the laboratory and through selection, reduction, and purification, to fix and determine a certain number of objective and determining facts, identically reproducible, subject to a limited number of the most general possible laws, and which, through the voice of the scientists, then attempts to regiment and organize our lives.[1] In its ordinary sense, *expérience* ["experience"] is, on the contrary, always subjective and singular, since it indicates the way in which a collective being can "try, feel, live in its own person."[2] Because it proclaims an absolute *subjectivism* (see this term), anarchism recognizes only this second sense and demands that those who use it in the first sense make explicit, for themselves and for others, the singular quality of the subjective forces that motivate them and that produce the scientific and technical *arrangements* (see *experts*).

Experts (scientists). Experts claim to be neutral and objective, describing and defining realities to which they are *external*. This pretense of neutrality and objectivity places them unambiguously on the side of *domination* (see this term), specifically because they hypocritically attempt to mask the nature of the *desire* that animates them[3] and to subject reality to forces external to it. As

---

1 I refer here primarily to the work of Bruno Latour and, regarding the logic of this type of experiment and the conditions of its invention, to Steven Shapin and Simon Schaffer, *Leviathan and the Air-Pump: Hobbes, Boyle, and the Experimental Life* (Princeton, NJ: Princeton University Press, 1985).

2 Émile Boutroux, *William James,* trans. Archibald and Barbara Henderson (New York: Longmans, Green, and Co., 1912), 47.

3 See Michel Foucault, *History of Sexuality, vol. 1.*

Deleuze says concerning the Hegelian and utilitarian character of the social sciences, "in this abstract relation, whatever it is, we always end up replacing real activities (creating, speaking, loving etc.) by the third party's point of view on these activities: the essence of the activity is confused with the gains of a third party, which he claims that he ought to profit from, whose benefits he claims the right to reap (whether he is God, objective spirit, humanity, culture or even the proletariat…)."[1]

Expression (see *symbols/signs*). Expression is opposed to *representation* (see this term). In libertarian practice, signs, symbols, discourses, and theories are the *direct* expression (see this term) of the forces that produce them. They are required neither to play the role of "intermediary" (see *direct action*), nor to claim to speak in the name of other forces from which they are distinct. They can speak for themselves (in art, philosophy, and science, in particular), but they do so as their own *autonomous* forces (see this term), without ever claiming to substitute themselves for anyone or anything other than themselves (see *anti-speciesism*).

Exterior/interior (external/internal, extrinsic/ intrinsic) (see *plane of reality, selection*, and *power of the outside*). Anarchism rejects any *bond* of exteriority (see *social bond*), whether this bond takes the form of subjection or – in what seems to be the inverse case – the form of negation and dialectical relations. Libertarian emancipation corresponds to a necessity that is internal to beings, to the intrinsic power that pushes them to go to the limits of their capacities (i.e., *beyond their limits* [see this term]), and thus it corresponds to the very particular methods of association that liberate this power and that this power makes possible. The distinction between interior and exterior is, however, far from coextensive with the difference between domination and emancipation.

If emancipation comes from the interior of beings, in the form of an *affirmation* of what they are capable of, this interior is nothing but (in Deleuze's phrase) a "selected exterior."[2] It is only a *fold* of the outside, which, from a certain point of view, with a certain quality of force, implicates the totality of that which exists – the power of being, the *power of the outside* (see this term), i.e., a power without an outside (see *monad*). The exteriority of the bonds of domination – an exteriority related to the order of this domination – is thus opposed to a completely different exteriority, an exteriority that must be called internal to itself since it embraces all that is: the absolute exteriority of emancipation, the exteriority of the power that it contains, the destructive exteriority

---

1   Deleuze, *Nietzsche and Philosophy*, 74.

2   "The interior is only a selected exterior, and the exterior, a projected interior" (Deleuze, *Spinoza: Practical Philosophy*, 124).

of *revolt, refusal, rupture,* and *insurrection,* when emancipatory forces affirm another possible world that would embrace the totality of existence, a recomposition of the totality of that which exists (see *stoppage, analogy*).

On the contrary, it would be illusory to think that domination is only external to the beings that it captures in its nets. The exteriority of the bonds that it imposes is only due, so to speak, to its need to separate forces from what they are capable of and to repel or repress the power of that which exists (other than itself), so as to maintain the limited and particular order that it imposes on reality. But to these limits, which are indeed external, corresponds a labor that operates within the collective beings that this order needs for its reproduction: a labor upon the internal quality of these beings, a labor of selecting the forces, desires, and wills that constitute them at a given moment (see *planes of reality*). It is to this condition – this internal subjection of the beings to a certain quality of forces and desires, a constraint that Étienne de la Boétie calls voluntary servitude[1] – that the dominant orders owe their capacity to impose themselves as a particular order, to separate the forces that they subjugate from what they are capable of.

---

1 Étienne de La Boétie, *The Politics of Obedience: The Discourse of Voluntary Servitude,* trans. Harry Kurz (Montréal: Black Rose Books, 1997).

F

Federalism (see *association*). Federalism, in libertarian discourse, defines the way in which the various emancipatory forces associate with one another. Federalism always associates forces that are different (if they were the same, they would merge and thus would no longer need to associate) (see *differences* and *indiscernibles*). This difference is not numerical and quantitative (the "same" distributed in space: a group plus a group plus a group; a company plus a company plus a company equals a battalion, etc.) but qualitative. Each of the associated forces is singular in its composition. The methods of association, the nature of the forces associated, and the resultant of their association define the emancipatory quality of this association. The condition that determines its libertarian character lies in the enjoyment of *autonomy* and the absolute right to disassociation on the part of the forces constituting the association, as well as the forces by which the constitutive forces are themselves constituted (which are themselves associations), etc.

Feedback [*rétroaction*] (see *identity* and *herds*). Concept suggested by the ethnologists Jean-Loup Amselle and Elikia M'Bokolo to define the way in which the identities and divisions defined by an oppressive order are subjectively taken up by human beings, transformed into lethal and negative subjectivities.[1]

Focal point (focalization) (see *union, direct action, given moment,* and *nodes of forces*). In *De la Justice*, Proudhon explains how "all the relations of things and of society" come "to be reflected and combined" within the "focal point" of the

---

1   Jean-Loup Amselle and Elikia M'Bokolo, *Au cœur de l'ethnie: Ethnies, tribalisme et État en Afrique*, 2nd ed. (Paris: Éditions La Découverte, 1999).

"soul" and the "self."[1] In various ways, this power of focalization applies to all *collective beings* or types of *subjectivity* (see these terms). Each being focalizes the totality of that which exists, from a certain point of view and through a certain description or evaluation of that which exists. It is in this sense that Proudhon can explain that each collective being constitutes a "particular society" and Nietzsche, in a manner very close to that of Leibniz, can write that "the smallest detail involves the whole."[2] One can thus understand why the libertarian movement is never afraid to be in the extreme minority, even sometimes (wrongly or rightly) to link transformation to an action as solitary and misunderstood as an *attentat* (see *terrorism* and *propaganda by the deed*). As opposed to a mastery of the whole, inevitably producing forms of conformism and a mass membership that is for the most part superficial (as was undoubtedly partially true for the libertarian movement itself in Spain), anarchism proposes the power of *situations*, collective arrangements, and actions that are local and thus capable of concentrating the energy of the possibilities contained within a given milieu and then propagating this energy across the totality of that which exists (see *active minorities*, *core*). Historically, the *affinity* group and especially the *union* (in the revolutionary syndicalist conception) have constituted the principal focal points of libertarian action. It is in this sense that the union could be conceived of by Pelloutier as the "laboratory of economic struggles" or by Griffuelhes as the alchemical crucible of the *social revolution* (see this term), in which, like the "stonecutter" working his stone or the "ore extractor" seeking his metals, the "proletarian," by means of his own "practical experiments" and "preparation[s]," "utilizes the forms of action available to the movement…, extracts them, excavates them."[3] It is in this sense also, on the part of Simondon this time, that it is possible to say that the libertarian union, like the labor chambers of the First International, the Bakuninian secret societies, affinity groups, chemical preparations, *attentats*, or the brain itself, is to be conceived of in the form of a "tension of information," an "arrangement capable of modulating much greater energies."[4] In a

---

1   Proudhon, *De la Justice*, 3:162.

2   Proudhon qtd. in Jean Bancal, *Proudhon: pluralisme et autogestion*, vol. 2, *Les Réalisations* (Paris: Aubier, 1970), 41; Nietzsche qtd. in Michel Haar, *Nietzsche and Metaphysics*, trans. Michael Gendre (Albany, NY: SUNY Press, 1996), 127. One is not surprised to find this idea in the work of Gabriel Tarde, when he explains "that *everything is a society*, that every phenomenon is a social fact" (*Monadology and Sociology*, 28).

3   Griffuelhes, *Le Syndicalisme révolutionnaire*, 10.

4   Simondon, *L'Individuation psychique et collective*, 53-54. Regarding the brain, cf. Gabriel Tarde, for whom the brain is a "node of forces," which transmits "impulses" that "come from afar and are intended to travel afar" (Milet, *Gabriel Tarde et la philosophie de l'histoire*, 172), or the technological neo-monadology of Joseph Déjacque: "Just as, with its calories of heat,

"pre-revolutionary" context – "a state of supersaturation…in which an event is very close to occurring, in which a structure is very ready to spring up" – it then becomes capable of "traversing, animating, and structuring a varied domain, increasingly varied and heterogeneous domains," of "propagating itself" through them (see *propaganda by the deed* and *transduction*), and of drawing forth an entirely new world.[1]

Fold (see *direct action, power of the outside, subject, intimate,* and *intimate being*). A concept borrowed by Deleuze from baroque thought in order to think the various forms of subjectivity.[2]

Force (collective force, collective being) (see *resultant, focal point, subject, subjectivity,* and *arrangement*). As Émile Pouget explains, "Force is the origin of every *movement* and every action, and, of necessity, it is the culmination of these. *Life* is the exercise of force, and without force, there is only oblivion. Nothing is made manifest, nothing is materialized in its absence."[3] The concept of force occupies a central place in libertarian thought. Anarchism is opposed to three illusions: 1) the illusion according to which the human being and humanity are (by their essence) radically separated from nature, from the things and beings that surround them, which it must appropriate and instrumentalize; 2) the illusion according to which this humanity and this human being must be thought in terms of a juxtaposition or a collection of *a priori* identical "individuals" – self-contained, homogenous, and endowed with like attributes of (instrumental) reason and liberty (free will); 3) the illusion according to which human action depends on "ideas," on a purely ideal representation of reality. For anarchism, the human being and humanity are not distinct from the reality through which they move and in which they are embedded. Like this reality of which they form a part, the human being and humanity are composites of forces – physical, organic, psychological, ethical – that command all the ideas that we are capable of having. The individual is a composite of forces, as Proudhon expresses when he says that "the living human being is a

---

steam condenses in the brain of the locomotive and constitutes what one could call its soul, in the same way, within the human body, the boiling of our sensations, condensing from the vapor in our cranium, constitutes our thought and drives all the electrical force of our intelligence, turning the wheels of our corporeal mechanism" (*À bas les chefs!*, 193).

1 Simondon, *L'Individuation psychique et collective*, 53-54.

2 See Deleuze, *The Fold*, as well as *Foucault*, trans. Seán Hand (Minneapolis: University of Minnesota Press, 1988), in particular the chapter "Foldings, or the Inside of Thought (Subjectivation)."

3 Émile Pouget, *Direct Action*, 23 (trans.: modifications my own).

group."[1] "Beings" (with their subjectivity) do not exist in themselves. They are the unstable and changing resultants of an infinity of possible combinations of the forces that compose them and with which they are associated. The quality of a will and the signification of a proposition or a statement do not exist in themselves; rather, they depend on the *arrangement* of the forces that produce them. Libertarian practice does not consist in judging propositions, wills, and beings in isolation, but in always referring them back to the associations or *collective arrangements* (see this term and *genealogy*) that produce them, where things can be changed and where it is possible to experiment with other associations, other arrangements, and other collective beings containing wills and propositions that are both stronger and freer.

Fractiousness (see *collective reason* and *balancing of forces*). The libertarian movement is often reproached for its ceaseless quarrels, in which the anarchy that it calls for so often, and in such an apparently negative way, displays its disorganizing effects (see *stoppage*). This propensity of the libertarian movement for disputes and quarrels is mainly due to the ambitiousness of its projects and the difficulty of implementing the practices and logics corresponding to them (see *ends/means*). Fractiousness testifies simultaneously to this weakness and this ambitiousness. Often present in everyday life as well as in the most political debates, fractiousness is not only the more or less *psychopathic* affirmation (see this term) of the autonomy of the forces that constitute any association or collective being. It is also the manifestation of the way in which anarchism conceives of the development of a common project (see *collective reason* and *common notions*) in relation to the *balancing of forces*. In the libertarian conception of collective action, any *point of view* is always the expression of a force, the discursive face of a force that, in its ambition and its singularity, quickly and necessarily causes the affirmation of contrary forces and points of view. It is within this play of oppositions and differences that the libertarian movement attempts – through a continuous testing and evaluation of the quality and the arrangements of the forces involved – to construct a world without domination, capable of liberating all the power that reality contains.

Free will (see *freedom*). The self-serving illusion of the current order, which, in reducing the abstract powers of an abstract freedom to the fiction of individual freedom, separates the ensemble of collective forces from what they are capable of. Human individuality is forced (by morality, education, law, and language) to deny the composite and changing forces and desires within itself that constitute it (see *subjectivity*), to deny the *more-than-oneself* that enables it to recompose both itself and a radically different world (see *individuation, choice,*

---

1   Proudhon, *Philosophy of Progress*, 23 (trans.: modifications my own).

subject, and *balancing of forces*). At the same time, human individuality is expelled from itself and its own capacities, radically subjected to an order that attempts to mold it exclusively according to its own presuppositions,[1] bending it entirely to its own injunctions and demands. Through free will, the human being is made *responsible* for its own acts (before God, the law, society) and thus culpable for all of the forces and desires that actually constitute it as a *subject* (see this term), which it is always forced to repress, to experience as realities external to itself – dangerous, diabolical realities that it must reject and refuse, despite the fact that they constitute the only means of its emancipation. From the doctrine of original sin to the nothingness of the Sartrean consciousness, along with Descartes's *Cogito*, Kant's categorical imperative, and the rights inscribed in contracts and markets, free will is one of the principal sources of despotism. It is Bakunin who most clearly formulates the position shared by the majority of anarchist theorists: "There is no such thing as free will…Free will is an impossibility, a nonsense, an invention of theology and metaphysics, that leads us directly to divine despotism, and from celestial despotism to all the authorities and tyrannies of the earth…"[2] "Materialism denies free will and ends in the establishment of liberty; idealism, in the name of human dignity, proclaims free will and, on the ruins of every liberty founds authority."[3]

Freedom (see *necessity, power, free will, slavery/freedom*, and *desire*). The freedom championed by anarchism has nothing to do with the abstract and illusory *free will* preached by all moralizing and authoritarian discourses. Nor has it anything to do with the void of the "for-itself," the "nihilating rupture," this obligation to be free that the philosophy of Sartre imposes on it.[4] In libertarian thought, freedom and power go together.[5] Freedom stems from the power of that which exists. Every power is a freedom and every freedom is a power: a power that is not cut off from its own possibilities. In this sense, anarchist freedom is synonymous

---

1 But also by *selection* (see this term) of what can correspond to this order in the human being, embodying it, empowering it, consenting to it.

2 Bakunin, *Œuvres complètes* (Paris: Champ libre, 1982), 8:439-40.

3 Mikhail Bakunin, *God and the State* (New York: Dover, 1970), 48.

4 Jean-Paul Sartre, *Being and Nothingness*, trans. Hazel E. Barnes (New York: Citadel Press, 2001), 415. It is undoubtedly here also that libertarian thought distinguishes itself radically from the thought of Cornelius Castoriadis and his totally Sartrean conception of an abstract emancipation thought in a dualist manner (through the distinctions between the instituting and the instituted, autonomy and heteronomy), in the manner of a creation *ex nihilo*. For an overall picture of Castoriadis's conceptions, see Gérard David, *Cornélius Castoriadis, le projet d'autonomie* (Paris: Éditions Michalon, 2001).

5 "The word *libertas* comes from *libet, libido*, i.e., passional instinct (hunger), drive, *spontaneity* [see this term]" (Proudhon, Économie, 2863 [73]).

with *necessity* (see this term). As Proudhon writes concerning this potential singular-collective force that is the *people* (see this term), "What philosophy, after immense work, discovered from its long speculations, namely the identity and homogeneity of contrary terms – freedom and necessity, for example, which it expressed by the proverb, *summa libertas, summa necessitas* – comes to its realization in the people. In the *intimate* experience of the people [see this term], the identity of these two aspects of life, freedom, and necessity, [constitute a given that is] positive, essential, organic, like will in man, like attraction in matter."[1]

Friends of our friends (see *affinity, putting to death, Daoism, solitude,* and *analogy*). Because it is a stranger to all exteriority (see *exterior*), anarchism refuses the mechanical game of politics in which it is always a matter of defining others, locating them in a place and a space (see *localism*), and classifying them as friends or enemies on the chessboard of power so as to conquer or defend them, depending on one's interests and strategy. Like Nietzsche, anarchism endorses the philosophers' friendship of which Derrida speaks: "We are first of all, as friends, the friends of *solitude*, and we are calling on you to share what cannot be shared: solitude."[2] Because libertarian friendship rests on *affinity* and on the *direct* bond between beings (see these terms) – an affinity internal to what constitutes them and a relation without *mediation* – it refuses any instrumentalization or logical deduction. From a libertarian point of view, the friends of our friends are not inevitably our friends, and their enemies, in a given situation and a given moment, may well be our friends on another *plane of reality*, from another *point of view* (see these terms). Thus, anarchism is ill-suited for politics understood as a game of power, for it proclaims a very different politics: the "great politics" of which Nietzsche spoke, a politics without exteriority, a politics without power or domination.

Fugitive (fleeting) (see *life, becoming, movement, event,* and *given moment*). A concept Bakunin uses to characterize the intimacy of beings (see *intimate being*), this living reality from which the libertarian movement seeks to recompose another world. For anarchism, as for Nietzsche, there is no reality in itself that would be immutable and essential, inaccessible and structural, on which phenomena or existing realities, reduced to mere appearances, would depend. There is no hinterworld, which, like God, would only serve to justify the permanence and the obligatory nature of the current order. As Bakunin demonstrates, the reality of beings is identified entirely with phenomena and "appearances," to the extent that even the *intimate being* (see this term) is precisely "the least essential, the least internal, the most external side, and at once,

---

1   Proudhon, Économie, 2866 [9/2].

2   Jacques Derrida, *The Politics of Friendship,* trans. George Collins (London: Verso, 2006), 35.

the most real and the most transitory, the most *fugitive* of things and beings: it is their immediate materiality, their real individuality [see *individuation*], such as it is presented to our senses."[1] Only the traps of language and *representation* (see this term) can make us believe in the permanence of a reality that they shackle and confine. The libertarian movement itself is not spared from these traps: it is perpetually tempted to transform its history into quaint, sepia-tinted images, its living reality into institutions, its experimentation into dogmatic formulas from which one would then be required to deduce life and practice (see *hagiography* and *theory/practice*).

Even the revolutionary syndicalist or anarcho-syndicalist experiments, which had the most success in realizing the greatest diversity and openness in their practices, do not always escape the traps of representation, the mechanisms of a dominatory order that constantly strives to reduce the complexity and richness of life to simplistic, disembodied representations. It is undoubtedly the great merit of Murray Bookchin that he has demonstrated both the originality as well as the fragility and the fleeting, temporary, and circumstantial character of the libertarian workers' movements.[2] This is in their nature as *movements* (see this term), interstitial and fugitive "moments" in the sense of Deleuze's "lines of flight," moments when everything seems possible because of their difference from (and indifference to) as much as because of their opposition to an order and logic both historical and economic that, in themselves, in no way guarantee human emancipation, the emergence of another world based on justice and freedom per se (see *stoppage*). And it is in this sense, as Bookchin argues and as an attentive analysis of the various revolutionary syndicalist experiences allows us to see, that the libertarian workers' movements never corresponded to the Marxist and structural conception of social classes (see *class*). The force of the libertarian workers' movement (as is undoubtedly the case for any movement of an anarchist character) was always transductive (see *transduction*), whether rooted in work relations or in the "decomposing agrarian strata" that Bookchin felicitously names the "transitional classes"[3] (issuing from the rural world or immigration, for example), or, when it was linked to older and more lasting professional environments, benefitting from the variations, holdovers, sidesteps, or deviations that are to be found in any milieu, even the most stable, the most inclined to define themselves entirely in terms of the order that constitutes them. We can

---

1   Bakunin, "Considérations philosophiques," *Œuvres* 3.393. It is in this sense that libertarian thought may be seen to intersect with Whitehead's analyses, for which the nature of the beings is identified with "transitory concretions," "events," "fluid monads." On this point and on the links between Whitehead and Simondon, cf. Anne Fagot-Largeault, "L'individuation en biologie," in *Gilbert Simondon: Une Pensée de l'individuation et de la technique*, 19-54.

2   Bookchin, "Theses on Libertarian Municipalism," 9-22.

3   Ibid. 19.

find a striking example of this transductive, circumstantial character of the libertarian workers' movements – fleeting but always recurring in new forms – from
the twofold perspective of time and space, history and geography, in the brief but
intense adventure of the Industrial Workers of the World in America.[1] We can
find it in the brief history of the watchmakers of the Jura Federation, as described
by Marianne Enckell, which was in effective existence for less than a decade.[2]
However, we can also find it in France, in the First International's four or five
years of peak activity at the end of the Second Empire; in the unique but fleeting
history of the Bourses du Travail, 25 years later, from 1895 to 1901; or, in yet
another way, from 1901 to 1908, in the seven revolutionary years of the General
Confederation of Labor (CGT), before French revolutionary syndicalism began
to explicitly abandon its hopes of radical transformation in the wake of the events
of Villeneuve-Saint-Georges.[3] Even the Spanish libertarian workers' movement,
despite its seemingly long duration, would also require a very fine analysis of
the several moments of its existence, the shifts and splits that led it, from one
struggle and transformation to another, to the tragic confrontation of 1936. We
must offer a variety of examples and concrete analyses of this sort. Revolutionary
syndicalism and anarcho-syndicalism, like the anarchist movement considered
as a whole, never had the essentialist unity and permanence that their titles so
readily evoke in the representations and the imaginary of those who employ
them. Generally very minoritarian experiments, the libertarian movements were
only ever the expression of moments and forms of existence that, far from being
inscribed within the history of capitalism – even dialectically – or within the
history of the working class – even when magnified by historiography – instead
assert themselves *against* this history, within its gaps, in what escapes it, as another possibility, another present. They are the emancipatory affirmation of another
composition of that which exists, arising from the momentary and fugitive character of things and beings of which Bakunin spoke, in which living reality gives
itself over to life, because life itself is "fugitive and momentary" and because it
alone "can and indeed always does encompass all that lives, that is to say, all that
is passing or fleeting."[4]

---

1   On the IWW, see Larry Portis, "Les IWW et l'internationalisme," in *De l'histoire du mouve-
    ment ouvrier révolutionnaire* (Paris: Éditions CNT-RP/Nautilus, 2001), 49-67.

2   Marianne Enckell, *La Fédération jurassienne: les origines de l'anarchisme en Suisse* (Lausanne:
    La Cité, 1971).

3   Translator's note: as Kenneth H. Tucker explains, "The 1908 deaths of several workers at
    strikes at Draveil and Villeneuve-Saint-Georges were blamed by many within the CGT
    on the radical rhetoric of the syndicalist leadership," which found itself purged from with-
    in and persecuted from without (*French Revolutionary Syndicalism and the Public Sphere*
    [Cambridge, UK: Cambridge University Press, 1996], 24-5).

4   Bakunin, "Considérations philosophiques," *Œuvres*, 3:395.

G

Genealogy (see *evaluation*, *point of view*, and *judgment*). As Gilbert Simondon demonstrates, collective beings are always more than what they are because they contain forces that partake of the *apeiron* or the *charge of nature*, making them able to *go beyond their limits* (see these terms). Every point of view, every standpoint, every act can thus be traced back to the forces of this otherness internal to the being of which it is the subject, forces that determine the quality of this point of view, this standpoint, and this act.[1] It is the *evaluation* of this quality that the term "genealogy" indicates. Evaluation and genealogy go together, and it is in this sense that Deleuze can explain how "genealogy means both the value of origin and the origin of values. Genealogy is as opposed to absolute values as it is to relative or utilitarian ones."[2]

General assembly (see *direct democracy*).

General (and insurrectionary) strike (see *Great Evening*, *nonviolence*, *war*, and *insurrection*). The revolutionary syndicalist and anarcho-syndicalist formulation

---

1 Although, unlike Proudhon or Nietzsche, Simondon tends to quickly refer any form of individuation (collective force, in Proudhon's vocabulary) to the *apeiron* and the indeterminate, like Proudhon and Nietzsche, he does not overlook the "compound" character of any individuation, which is compounded from a multiplicity of other individuations, as Muriel Combes demonstrates (*Gilbert Simondon and the Philosophy of the Transindividual*, trans. Thomas LaMarre [Cambridge, MA: MIT Press, 2013], 22). At the same time, the "indeterminate" itself is such only "in relation to the individuated being," and thence to the "modalities" of the being, for the knowledge of which Simondon only notes that the "concepts are lacking" (Simondon, *L'Individuation psychique et collective*, 204) – concepts that we find in Proudhon or Nietzsche.

2 Gilles Deleuze, *Nietzsche and Philosophy*, 2.

of the popular idea of the *Great Evening* that served for some time, before the war of 1914-1918 and mainly in France, as a slogan for broad sectors of the working class. In assembling the entirety of the producers, who are themselves federated by trade, industrial sector, and company, syndicalism defines a particular *plane of reality* (see this term) that traverses the totality of human realities – that of *labor* (see this term). When everyone ceases to work, the producers stop the reproduction of the economic and social machine, creating by this *stoppage* (see this term) the conditions for a radical transformation of the existing order, the conditions for the *passage to the act* of all emancipatory forces. The originality of the project of the general strike undoubtedly lies in its capacity to renew the insurrectionary and warlike dimension of the 19th century movements of revolt within a collective expression that is generally nonviolent, as it traverses most human activities at a given moment and in a given context. In this sense, the idea and project of the general strike are not at all limited to a particular period or human configuration, such as that of labor. They constitute the first act of any collective revolt, the prelude to the emergence of any other possibility.

Generosity (see *implication*). The *affirmation* of a collective force able to *exceed its own capacities*. In libertarian thought, only generosity – i.e., the power of a force unconfined by external or internal limits (see *balancing of forces*) – can be the basis of an altruism and an opening to the other not founded on guilt and an external morality.

Gesture (see *tools/weapons*, *plastic force*, and *action*). An important notion from everyday language that, in its plurality of senses, its link to the body, its essential character as "movement," and its frequent ethical and aesthetic dimensions ("beautiful" and "ugly" gestures, etc.), is one of the rare words that makes it possible for us to grasp the conditions for the emergence of beings (in an exception to the usually reductive effects of language). The philosopher and mathematician Gilles Châtelet, following Jean Cavaillès, further highlights the richness of the concept of gesture in the domain of physics and mathematics, this instance in which "being is glimpsed smiling," when thought no longer fears "to position itself at the outposts of the obscure, looking upon the irrational not as 'diabolical' and resistant to articulation, but rather as the means by which new dimensions come into being."[1] As the linguistic expression of *action*, of its creative power, and of all emancipatory experiences (from *propaganda by the deed* to the Makhnovshchina), "the gesture is not substantial: it gains amplitude by *determining* itself [see *determination*]…The gesture is not a simple spatial displacement: it decides, liberates, and suggests a new modality

---

1   Châtelet, *Figuring Space*, 10 and 3.

of 'moving oneself'…The gesture is elastic, it can crouch on itself, leap beyond itself…The gesture envelops before grasping and sketches its unfolding long before denoting or exemplifying: already domesticated gestures are the ones that serve as references;…a gesture awakens other gestures…"[1]

Given moment (see *situation*, *event* and *focal point*). Émile Pouget explains how, thanks to the "unparalleled plasticity" of "direct action," "organizations actively engaged in the practice" can "live in the present with all possible combativity, sacrificing neither the present to the future, nor the future to the present."[2] The libertarian conception of the given moment should not be confused with the militaristic and mechanistic concept of the "conjuncture" or "present situation" in Leninism.[3] Against a mechanical and external vision of the action of forces – give me a lever (the Party) and a fulcrum (the conjuncture), and I shall move the world, thought Lenin[4] – in which an external agent can manipulate and exploit their *resultant* for his own benefit, libertarian thought and practice opposes the internal dimension of a reality that is in "the heat of the moment," the "unparalleled *plasticity*" of which Pouget and Proudhon speak (see *plastic force*),[5] the *species activity* and *univocal being* of Nietzsche and Deleuze, the "unitary spirit" of Gustav Landauer.[6] The given moment as it is constituted within the ceaseless flux of situations and arrangements of forces, *focuses* and repeats *possibilities*, different each time, which are neither the symbol nor the example of anything else. These possibilities, associated with the being itself at this moment or in this *situation* are the *expression* of this being and its *singular*

---

1   Ibid. 10.

2   *Direct Action*, 13.

3   Vladimir Ilyich Lenin, *Revolution at the Gates: A Selection of Writings from February to October 1917*, ed. Slavoj Žižek (London: Verso, 2002), 24, 21.

4   Translator's note: Colson paraphrases Lenin's *What Is to Be Done*, in which Lenin in turn paraphrases the "well-known epigram" of Archimedes ("Give me a place to stand on, and I can move the earth"): "Give us an organisation of revolutionaries, and we shall overturn the whole of Russia!" See T. L. Heath, ed., *The Works of Archimedes with the Method of Archimedes* (New York: Dover Publications, 1953), xix, and Vladimir I. Lenin, *Essential Works of Lenin: "What Is to Be Done?" and Other Writings* (New York: Dover Publications, 1987), 150.

5   Pierre-Joseph Proudhon, *De la Création de l'ordre dans l'humanité* (Paris: Rivière, 1927), 421.

6   "A degree of high culture is reached when the various social structures, in themselves exclusive and independent of one another, are filled with a unitary spirit" (Gustav Landauer qtd. in Martin Buber, *Paths in Utopia*, trans. R.F.C. Hull [Syracuse, NY: Syracuse University Press, 1996], 53 [trans.: modifications my own]). (Translator's note: see also Gustav Landauer, *Revolution and Other Writings: A Political Reader*, trans. Gabriel Kuhn [Oakland, CA: PM Press, 2010], 129.)

point of view on the totality of that which exists, are what libertarian forces attempt to discover, develop, and pursue. In this way, the given moment can be identified with "the historic opportunity" of which Hélène Châtelain speaks in connection with the Makhnovshchina, the Ukrainian anarchist insurrection of 1917, this "moment when historical space" comes to "coincide with the free and open geographical space" of the plains surrounding Gulyai-Polye.[1]

God (see *nature*). An illusory *resultant* of the totality of *collective forces*, insofar as these are separated from what they are capable of, thus becoming incapable of understanding what makes them act and the nature of the effects of this *action* (see these terms). God is transformed from a resultant into a first principle. Thus, it is transformed from an imaginary and delusory expression of the power immanent to the forces that give it meaning into a transcendent power that reacts upon these forces to order them, unify them, and subject them to the very real power of priests and other representatives of collective power, to the authoritarian and oppressive yoke of relations of domination.

Good/bad [bon/mauvais] (see *good/evil*).

Good/evil [bien/mal] (see *hierarchy*). Anarchism rejects any distinction between good and evil, these two prescriptive categories that inevitably refer to a transcendent authority (God, the State, the categorical imperative) charged, like God in Eden or in the Sinai, with dictating to human beings what they must do: where lies the good, where lies evil ("thou shalt not eat of that apple!," "thou shalt honor thy father and thy mother!"). As Giorgio Agamben demonstrates, good and evil are not external to one another, in a relation where any extension of the good would reduce or suppress the share reserved for evil.[2] To this *external* relation (see this term), anarchism opposes an internal relation in which evil and good are only two internal and subjective evaluations of the modalities of existence of beings and the relations through which they associate. This is a relation in which, this time in the vocabulary of Gilbert Simondon, the evaluating *subject* is more than *individual* (see these terms) since it opens onto the outside (*apeiron*) that it contains in itself, onto the "innermost exteriority" of which Agamben speaks (see *collective*).[3] It is also in this sense that the anarchist conception runs parallel to that of Spinoza. In place of good [*bien*] and evil [*mal*], anarchism asks what is good [*bon*] and bad [*mauvais*] for such-and-such a being in such-and-such a situation. What is good (or positive) is what increases the power of a being; what is bad (or negative) is

---

1   Hélène Châtelain, Radio Libertaire, Fall 1993.

2   Agamben, *The Coming Community*, 13 et passim.

3   Ibid. 15.

what decreases it. Each being decides for itself the possibility of evaluating this positivity and this negativity through experience. An increase in the power of a being is expressed in the form of a feeling of *joy*, a reduction in the feeling of *sadness*. Good and bad are thus entirely *immanent* to the experiences of beings.

Good sense (see *common sense*).

Government (see *self-management, particular*, and *private/public*). An old notion of the 19th century that serves to indicate the State ("If truly happy you would be/the government has got to go!"[1]), but that, at the same time, by its maritime etymology (from the Latin *gubernare*, to steer by the rudder [*gouvernail*]), makes it possible to think the *autonomy* and the mutual *dependence* of all *collective beings*. This is expressed in the idea of "governing oneself" and thus the possibility of "being governed" by others. It is in this sense that Gustave Courbet argues that any private person (see *particular* and *private/public*) – i.e., any being existing at a given moment – is a government. This is because, in libertarian thought, each collective being is equally equipped, by virtue of what constitutes it (see *equality*), with the absolute prerogatives of autonomy and free choice, which the defenders of the current order reserve solely for the State's sovereignty. From the libertarian point of view, as Courbet puts it, the Government (in the traditional sense of the term) is thus itself merely a "particular" individual (so to speak) making the exorbitant claim to subject all other private individuals from whom it draws its power to its authority.[2] It is also in this sense that Whitehead can say of Descartes, contemplating from his window the hats and coats worn by phantoms (in his "Second Meditation"[3]), that he is then "a particular, characterized only by universals," while at the same time, "every so-called 'universal' is particular in the sense of being just what it is, diverse from everything else" (see *indiscernibles*).[4]

---

1 Translator's note: refrain from "Faut plus d'gouvernement" ("No More Government"), a song by François Brunel, a militant café waiter, ca. 1899.

2 See Gustave Courbet, letter to Bruyas, October 1853, qtd. in James Henry Rubin, *Realism and Social Vision in Courbet and Proudhon* (Princeton, NJ: Princeton University Press, 1980), 15.

3 Translator's note: in the "Second Meditation," Descartes muses about "how prone my mind is to error," reflecting that, for instance, "were I perchance to look out my window and observe men crossing the square, I would ordinarily say I see the men themselves...But what do I see aside from hats and clothes, which could conceal automata?" (22). See Descartes, *Meditations on First Philosophy*, trans. Donald A. Cress (Indianapolis, IN: Hackett Publishing Co., 1993).

4 Alfred North Whitehead, *Process and Reality* (New York: Free Press, 1978), 48-49.

Great Evening [*Grand soir*] (see *general strike* and *revolution*). When we read of working-class militants in the days before 1914 running to the window at the least noise from the street in the belief that the revolution had broken out, we can begin to understand the force of the idea of "the Great Evening."[1] Michael Löwy aptly describes the libertarian workers' movement at the turn of the century as having a messianic dimension.[2] For a few decades, broad sectors of the labor movement expected that strikes and confrontations with the State (revolts, riots, and various transgressions) would culminate in a radical transformation of the existing world, a total recomposition of the order of things in which Justice and Freedom would assert their power amid the debris of a world heretofore captive to oppression, lies, and domination. This messianic vision of a radical transformation of all that exists – a messianism without a messiah, completely independent of the religious institutions existing at the time in Europe (Jewish and Christian) – should not be confused with the idea of *revolution* that it also radically transforms, nor even with the slogan and project of the *general strike*, its revolutionary syndicalist and anarcho-syndicalist expression (see these terms). The concept of the Great Evening undoubtedly manifests the greatest difference in comparison with the traditional idea of revolution, in three ways: 1) by refusing to identify social transformation with a mere political alteration, a change at the top of the State, on the model of the French Revolution and its republican, Blanquist, and Marxist-Leninist extensions; 2) by refusing the division of revolutionary labor between, on one side, the masses charged with toppling the old government and, on the other side, an enlightened and educated political vanguard tasked with reconstructing, in the form of a dictatorship, a new form of public legitimacy, a new State; 3) by refusing to tie the movement of transformation to a more or less long-term strategy and to stifling, instrumentalized organizational forms (parties, unions, and other mass "organizations" specializing in this or that aspect of life, firmly subordinated to the tactical and strategic direction of the Party). The Great Evening, like the totality of the libertarian projects of which it was the expression at a *given moment*, maintains a particular relationship with space and time.

To begin with, time: in its popular form, as well as its mystical and religious forms,[3] the Great Evening expresses the radical and general character of the transformations of which reality is capable in the domain of time. Indeed, contrary to the *Revolution* and what one might believe about it, the temporal radicality of the Great Evening is not tied to the future, to changes yet to come

---

1   Unpublished memoirs of Laurent Moulin, secretary of the Metalworkers' Union of Chambon-Feugerolles (Loire).

2   Michael Löwy, *Redemption and Utopia: Jewish Libertarian Thought in Central Europe: A Study in Elective Affinity*, trans. Hope Heaney (Stanford, CA: Stanford University Press, 1992).

3   On this point, see Löwy, *Redemption and Utopia*.

that exist in the present only as a "utopian" promise, that are guaranteed by the conquest of Power, thus entrusting this Power with the responsibility for giving it a reality in the future – someday, later on ("Communism," the withering away of the State, etc.). The temporal radicality of the Great Evening is always tied to an anteriority and an accumulated power: an anteriority or a *past* (see this term) that merges with the present (see *repetition* and *eternal return*) because it characterizes the actual state of things; an emancipatory power capable of effecting the transmutation of which the Great Evening is the final demonstration. Whereas the revolution is thought as a starting point – the point of departure for a transformation to come – the Great Evening is thought as an outcome: the outcome of a transformation that has already been realized.

Secondly, space: because it encompasses the totality of that which exists – from the minuscule to the vast – in the absence of any hierarchy or utilitarian articulation of one aspect of reality with respect to another, the transformation expressed in the idea of the Great Evening is an *immediate* transformation (see this term) in which each situation and each moment contain the totality of the transformations called for by this conception of revolution (see *focal point*, *active minorities*). Every struggle, every crack, every rift, every sidestep is in reality a *repetition* and the *expression* (see these terms) of the final explosion. As Émile Pouget explains, "the day to day struggle" and the "task of laying the groundwork for the future" are neither "contradictory" nor dependent on a plan or a strategy that has been thought from the outside. Each "passing moment" devoted to *struggle* and *revolt* (see these terms) is lived in such a way as to "sacrific[e] neither the present to the future, nor the future to the present" (see *ends/means*).[1]

"Come the dawn of the Great Evening!" As this humorous phrase implies, the Great Evening is at once an evening and a morning, a twilight and a dawn, the immediate transmutation of the existing order, where, in its cracks, another possible world can be sensed, present even now at the heart of things.

Groups (groupings) (see *intimate, collective being*, and *union*).

Guilt (see *ressentiment, reaction*, and *responsibility*). Guilt is the obverse or hidden face of *ressentiment*, in which a relation of domination is internalized from the dominant point of view, justifying, from this position, a never-ending expiation. A negative force, but one which contains its own satisfactions or benefits, guilt authorizes a subtle mixture of power, persecution, submission, and domination that is opposed to all emancipation. A historical example of successful culpabilization: Christianity.

---

1 Émile Pouget, *Direct Action*, 13.

Guilty party [*responsable*] (see *power*). "*Au poteau!*" ("To the whipping post!") This old war cry expressing the *ressentiment* of bankrupt shopkeepers and shareholders or veterans in the first half of the 20th century could serve as the slogan for any of the extreme right-wing movements of this century: the desire to find the "guilty parties [*responsables*]" who are to blame for one's own ills – the "Rich!," the "Spics!,"[1] the "Jews!," the "Freemasons!," the "Huns!," the "Decadents!," the "Others!" – to drag them before the courts, or better yet, to render "justice" oneself, cutting their throats with one's own hands and, in their blood, (temporarily) drowning one's own impotence and fury at understanding nothing of what one experiences, due to the the misfortune of being only what one is, of not being more beautiful or wealthy, of being in bad health, aging, and having to die. As Bernanos wrote, having learned something of it from experience, "The wrath of the Stupid fills the world."[2] Indeed, "whipping posts," "firing squads," and massacres in the clearing of a wood done for the cause or in the name of public safety are not a monopoly of the extreme right, nor even of the identity wars that are always stirred up anew, whenever possible, by the idiots who hurl themselves at one another, at "the other," whether that be one's neighbor of the day before or a nameless transient. Whipping posts and political assassinations are just as readily produced, in terms apparently more cold and scientific, by a good part of the revolutionary left of the past century: in Russia, in China, and in all parts of the world where the "bourgeois," "sons of the bourgeois," "wives of the bourgeois," "petty bourgeois," "kulaks," "enemies of the people," "opportunists seemingly of the left but actually of the right," "counter-revolutionaries," and other "lustful vipers" had to pay with their lives, *en masse* and anonymously, for their supposed "objective" and "collective" responsibility for the economic disasters, famines, and catastrophes that actually existing socialism, like capitalism, never ceased to produce. Because it refuses any morality, any summons in the name of an extrinsic or transcendent code that claims to dictate who one is and what one is to do, libertarian ethics rejects the notion of responsibility along with its grand procession of guilt, trials, judges, prosecutors, psychologists, professors, priests, pedagogues, and other dispensers of "lessons."[3] Libertarians can engage

---

1   Translator's note: In French, *métèque*, a cognate for the obsolete English word "metic," is an all-purpose derogatory term for "foreigners," sometimes likened to such offensive American English epithets as "wop" or "dago."

2   Georges Bernanos, *A Diary of My Times*, trans. Pamela Morris (London: Boriswood, 1938), 30. (Translator's note: Bernanos, a conservative Catholic author, recorded his disillusionment with the Spanish Falangist movement in this 1938 book. According to Seth D. Armus, "[t]he wrath of the stupid was what he saw in Spain" [*French Anti-Americanism (1930-1948): Critical Moments in a Complex History* (Lanham, MD: Lexington Books, 2007), 139.])

3   This "lesson" is always a knowledge (beaten into one) and a "grading [*correction*]," both in

in concerted actions over long periods of time, requiring a great deal of effort and self-control. What binds them together always partakes of the nature and the quality of the action undertaken, the reasons for which each of those involved choose to pursue it and to accept the *constraints* this entails, which are then transformed into *necessity*. It is in this sense that one can speak of *trust* (see these terms). But the perpetuation of these bonds and the commitment that they presuppose is never founded on an extrinsic morality, a code of correct conduct that attempts to fix the framework (legal or otherwise) of a common action, independent of the nature and modalities of this action. This is why, in a libertarian process, any one of the associated forces can always break off its association with the others and reclaim its independence or, if it is denied this right, if higher imperatives are invoked, imperatives that are *transcendent* with respect to the action undertaken, it can revolt. Likewise, obviously, each force can choose not to join those who demonstrate too much flightiness to sustain their participation in a collective action of any duration.

Since it rejects this logic of responsibility [*responsabilité*] in its very constitution, the libertarian movement rejects it just as much in relation to those against whom it fights. Libertarian violence (see *revolt, insurrection, war/warlike*) is always tied to the respective circumstances and positions of the parties in confrontation at a given moment and in a given situation or context. The enemy it fights against or (sometimes) kills is always an enemy with regard to its position at that moment, but certainly not because it is to be held responsible for a political or social choice imagined as some intangible essence (see *movement*). It is true that, in Spain or elsewhere, libertarian struggles were often accompanied, afterwards or alongside the movements of *revolt* and *insurrection* (see these terms), by executions and "settlings of accounts" (priests, bosses, landlords) – aftereffects of the violence of a domination too long borne. Whatever their justification and whether they were called for before or after the fact, these "executions" in themselves, having no direct relationship to the immediate situation other than to reverse the positions of torturer and victim, are radically contrary to the dynamics and logic of libertarian emancipation. They merely demonstrate once more that the position of the dominated is in no way the guarantee of emancipation, that *revolt* and *insurrection* can always turn into *vengeance, ressentiment,* and the "settling of accounts," corrupted or contaminated by the relations of domination that gave birth to them, the very relations that they attempt to destroy but end up reproducing in another form (see *affirmation* and *emancipation*).[1]

---

the lofty and trivially violent senses of this word.

1   On this libertarian ethic and the controversies to which it can give rise, even under the worst conditions of a civil war, see the remarkable texts published by ACL in connection with Simone Weil and Louis Mercier-Vega in *Présence de Louis Mercier: Actes du Colloque autour de Louis Mercier, Paris, 1997* (Lyon: ACL, 1999).

Hagiography (see *theory/practice, common notions,* and *collective reason*). A sacred (or pious) account of history, false and oppressive, to which the libertarian movement is no stranger, as is too often demonstrated by the slogans and images to which it appeals when it refers to the past. Any practice, any experimentation contains its own meaning and value, indissociable from the internal *forces* and *desires* that it arranges together [*agence*] at a given moment. The processes of association that give birth to the most powerful and thus the freest beings correspond to this encounter of the wills and forces belonging to each collective being, internal to each of them (see *freedom*). But for such an association to have an emancipatory character, it must not be captive to any external narrative or representation (see *direct action*), which are the sure symptoms of a relation of oppression, domination, and disempowerment. Because it is always enacted in the present moment within which the forces are acting, this refusal of *representation* (see this term) is also opposed to any external reconstruction of the past as a finished and dead reality. Only the internal actualization and repetition of past meanings and wills – their recovery as an *other* that is always actual – can take on force and meaning within an emancipatory movement and project. The otherness of beings or arrangements perceived as belonging to the past is thus no greater than that of present beings or arrangements. Although an association with these past beings and arrangements is distinctive (as any association is), this does not introduce any difference of nature that would partake of the false inevitability that relations of domination generally attach to the idea of the past (see *eternal return*). It is in this sense that Bakunin can affirm the eternity of the intimate being of his friend Nicolas Stankevich (see *intimate being, eternity*) and that Jean Tardieu can evoke the return of the act of a blacksmith riveting the railings of a balcony: "But the blacksmith is still close by, and if I tap with a key the iron which he beat in the past, I can still hear in its unsullied sound, surging from the depths of centuries of crime, the cry of his effort and his triumph."[1] It is in this sense that Gilbert Simondon can regard as eternal or eternally present the "desperate, anonymous gesture of the slave in revolt,"[2] not as a mere image – passed down for posterity in the form of a didactic tableau or narrative, for example – but "as a transductive being" (see *transduction*), as an experience that has left its mark within the "milieu" from which it emerged and took its meaning, the annihilation of which would "presuppose the annihilation of the medium [*milieu*] as well."[3]

Herd (see *mass* and *multitude*). A violently pejorative term, as one readily discovers in Nietzsche as well as in libertarian discourse, used to denounce *conformism* (see this term) and the subjective acceptance (see *feedback*) of the roles, functions, and affiliations (class, gender, nationality, religion, etc.) defined by the existing order.

Heteronomy (see *autonomy*, *nomos*, and *nomad*).

Hierarchy (see *leader*, *equality*, *differences*, *limits*, and *balancing of forces*). Within anarchist thought, this is an important and ambiguous concept, requiring us to distinguish between an *extrinsic* hierarchy (see *constraint*) – oppressive, dominatory, and violently resisted by the libertarian movement – and, on the other hand, an *intrinsic* hierarchy (see *necessity*) – inherent in the manner in which the libertarian movement conceives of its own development and reality. Anarchism is opposed to extrinsic hierarchy, that vertical and pyramidal organization of reality in which some collective beings, in an external manner, are subjected to others, given a status and position defined in an abstract and general way on a vast scale of command underpinned by relations of domination. But it is also opposed (and with the same determination) to a false equality, every bit as extrinsic (what Proudhon calls "communism"), in which, for the same reasons of status and position, all beings, like slaves or atoms, are equal, but only under the self-serving and external gaze of the law, the State, God, the party, the program, and those who speak on their behalf.

---

1   Jean Tardieu, *The River Underground,* trans. David Kelley (Newcastle upon Tyne, UK: Bloodaxe Books, 1991), 141-143.

2   Simondon, *L'Individuation psychique et collective*, 105.

3   Ibid. 102. (Translator's note: for further explanation of Simondon's notion of "transduction" as "the ways and means by which the operation of individuation is carried out…so that a modification is carried forward (transducted)," see David Scott, *Gilbert Simondon's* Psychic and Collective Individuation: *A Critical Introduction and Guide* [Edinburgh: Edinburgh University Press, 2014], esp. 77-80.)

An apparent paradox of libertarian thought: against these extrinsic, oppressive hierarchies, anarchism does not posit the formal equality of the marketplace or the courts, nor the communism of the barracks, but another kind of hierarchy – a hierarchy *intrinsic* to the beings' composition, which operates in two ways: 1) through a continuous, delicate evaluation of the quality of collective forces and the possibilities of their association, not in a binary way – in terms of *good* or *evil*, black or white – but in terms of the perpetual variation of the *power* of each relative to the others within a given *situation* (see these terms); 2) through the differentiation of beings, which needs further explanation.

Anarchism affirms the *singularity* of beings and thus their *difference*. In this sense, the collective forces found within any given situation or *plane of reality* (see this term) are never equal, and every force or association (for a task or action that is always just as singular) necessarily induces a positive hierarchy, internal to this force, this task, or this action. This positive hierarchy manifests in the constitution of a new collective being in which some components more than others impart a certain skill, quality, taste, energy, and power, which arise simultaneously from their capabilities at a given moment and from the momentary or lasting nature of the task, action, or association. This is demonstrated by even the smallest experience of collective action (doing the housework, paying the bills, struggling, speaking, holding meetings, singing, etc.). As Bakunin explains, "At the moment of action, in the midst of the struggle, the roles are naturally distributed in accordance with everyone's aptitudes, evaluated and judged by the whole collective."[1] This hierarchical ordering within any kind of collective being of the forces that comprise it at a given moment, this "complex mode of association" of which Proudhon speaks, in which "between one man and another in society, or between one faculty and another in the same individual, there is an infinite difference,"[2] does not constitute a *limit* for this being (see this term) or a necessary evil (from a utilitarian, extrinsic point of view). As a libertarian ordering, it is intrinsic to this being, constitutive of its possibilities, and it generates, for the forces that produce it in associating with one another, the kind of intense pleasure that the bass guitar often produces in accompanying a particularly eloquent saxophone solo, or the satisfaction one experiences when participating in a meeting with a competent and effective facilitator.

However, this hierarchical ordering intrinsic to the forces that constitute a being at a given moment never takes place automatically, and just because a task, an action, or a form of association is proclaimed to be libertarian in its

---

1   Bakunin, *The Political Philosophy of Bakunin*, 259.

2   Pierre-Joseph Proudhon, *What Is Property?*, trans. Benjamin R. Tucker (New York: Dover, 1971), 242, 238-239.

goals and functioning does not mean that it is safe from two distinct risks: on the one hand, that of reproducing within itself the extrinsic hierarchies that it was to supplant, and on the other hand, that of the will to domination inherent in any force and thus the risk that one of its own constitutive forces may try to subject the others to its own will, its own point of view, its own desire. Traditional divisions (as between, for example, men and women, manual and intellectual, young and old, etc.) and practices of submission to extrinsic authorities continue to operate within the actions that seem to be the most peaceful and free (see *discipline, self-discipline,* and *responsibility*). It is not rare to see some collective force (an individual, a body or institution, a secretary, secretariat, or commission), with a great show of modesty (see *servants of the people*), reveal heretofore unsuspected predispositions, attempting to extend its prerogatives over ever-wider domains, trying to perpetuate them through violence, law, or all kinds of lofty rationales, and transforming itself into a despotic power. Therefore, the continuous evaluation of how forces are hierarchically ordered – of their emancipatory or oppressive quality in a given situation and within a given arrangement – requires a great deal of finesse and attention to detail and the tiniest relations (see *anti-authoritarian*). Moreover, this especially requires a great readiness to rebel, an acute sense (and a *warlike* sense; see this term) of *revolt*, insolence, and irony, so as to be capable of *refusing* (see these terms) any ossification[1] and externalization of whatever hierarchies might happen to be necessary at a given moment, for a given task, and in a given context.

More generally, in light of the experience of the anarchist movement, the libertarian character of relations between forces – their ability, when they bring their differences into association, to liberate all the power (and thus all the freedom) that reality contains – depends on three broad conditions:

1.   First of all, libertarian *law* (see *law/rights* and *direct democracy*). The collective forces that associate for a given action or in a given arrangement invent or implement certain (formal or informal) working rules to counteract the effects of the existing order in the unfolding of this action as well as in the (short- or long-term) functioning of this arrangement: rotation of tasks, revocability of delegates, rigorous report-back sessions, modes of membership, the use of *statistical* tools, methods of decision-making, etc. Bound up with a form of *law* that one can describe as libertarian, these shared rules constitute, along with the *collective reason,* an important dimension of the anarchist project and

---

1   Bakunin speaks of the danger of differences becoming "petrified" (Mikhail Bakunin, *The Basic Bakunin: Writings, 1869-1871,* ed. and trans. Robert M. Cutler [Amherst, NY: Prometheus Books, 1992], 126).

the mode of social composition of which it is the expression, but on one condition: that they are always closely tied to the changing reality of the relations of which they are only the provisional expression and codification. As the willed and formalized yet also immediate and revocable expression of an association – kept as faithful as possible to this association's inner balance and the wills animating it – these explicit rules, which aim to prevent the internal reproduction of an extrinsic, dominatory hierarchical ordering, are always liable to change, like the hierarchy they oppose, either into forms that serve the extrinsic order or into instruments of power for a hegemonic will. By reinforcing the internal logic of the collective beings with a body of regulations and written or oral procedures, the rules that libertarian associations make for themselves are constantly in danger of metamorphosing into institutions *analogous* (see this term) to the suffocating molds by which the extrinsic order imposes its relations of domination. This is why they must immediately be *balanced* by a second and a third condition.

2. The second condition is the *autonomy* of forces (see this term). However well a collective force may be integrated into a larger power, associating with still other powers, this force must always preserve its ability, first of all, to constantly evaluate the quality of the relations that link it to other forces and the way in which these relations affect its own power, and secondly, to break off these relations whenever it deems this necessary (a drummer joining a new band, a union breaking away from its federation, etc.). And it is obviously with regard to this ability, within the collective being under consideration as well as within each of its components, that the libertarian character of an association may be assessed. Thus, a libertarian collective force must maintain its ability to recognize, on the terrain of laws and customs, the right of each of its constituents to secede or to contest some given relation or situation within this association. Furthermore, it especially must construct and balance itself (see *balancing of forces*) such that this autonomy arises as a matter of course, because it results from this construction and this balance, and such that any dispute or dissent is immediately understood (if not supported) by all the other forces heretofore associated.

3. The final condition is the multiplication of relations of association across equally varied *planes of reality*. The *singularity*, the difference, and thus the *anarchy* of collective beings affect all beings without exception, whatever their size and strength, from the infinitely small to the infinitely large. The development of a shared emancipatory movement and the will to make it coincide with the totality of that which exists do not at all imply the homogeneity or conformity of the various relations and forces that compose it, neither in the movement's

impetus nor in the ends of its action, on the assumption that it will come to embrace the totality of that which exists (see *plane of immanence*). On the contrary, they imply, from beginning to end, a multitude of practices and forms of association, each demanding, at a given moment, equally distinctive qualities and thus an equally distinctive hierarchical ordering of forces. Loving, thinking, struggling, planning, feeling, seeing, creating, etc. – all these practices give us only a rather feeble notion of what is enabled by the power of that which exists, of the diversity of possibilities that this power opens up. To each possible practice correspond just as many different possible compositions and hierarchical orderings of forces, selecting qualities and competences that are equally diverse and varied. Thus, each collective force or being discovers the possibility of going to the limit of its capacities (i.e., going beyond the *limits* [see this term] imposed on it by the dominant order) by experimenting with what each association, each plane of reality, has permitted for its own development by selecting the forces and qualities that seem best suited for a stronger affirmation of its potential power. Deleuze defines this libertarian manner of conceptualizing hierarchy, which could be called an anarchic proliferation of hierarchies, interconnected and ever-changing hierarchies of the largest and the smallest forces alike, in this way: "There is a hierarchy which measures beings according to their limits, and according to their degree of proximity or distance from a principle. But there is also a hierarchy which considers things and beings from the point of view of power: it is not a question of considering absolute degrees of power, but only of knowing whether a being eventually 'leaps over' or transcends its limits in going to the limit of its capacities, whatever their degree" (see *limits* and *balancing of forces*).[1]

Hinterworld (see *fugitive*).

History (see *hagiography* and *eternal return*).

Homology (see *analogy*).

Horizontality (see *base*).

Humanism (see *power of the outside*).

---

1   Deleuze, *Difference and Repetition*, 37 (trans.: modifications my own).

Idea (see *propaganda by the deed* and *collective reason*). The anarchist Idea (always written with a capital letter) is not an *ideal*, a *utopia*, or an abstraction. It is neither a program nor a catalogue of regulations or prohibitions (see *anti-something*). Rather, it is a force common to all beings (see *direct action, plastic force*) that expresses the totality of the *possibilities* (see this term) that all these beings contain. It is a living force (see *life*) that, in certain circumstances, takes us outside of ourselves, warranting this definition given by Paul Brousse during his days as an anarchist: "The Idea shall be manifested, not on paper, not in a newspaper, not in a painting; it shall not be sculpted in marble, carved in stone, nor cast in bronze: having come to life, in flesh and blood, it shall walk before the people."[1] It is a perceptible force that sometimes, like love, seizes us in the deepest parts of ourselves. As Joseph Déjacque writes, "The Idea is a lover who, in her impetuous embraces, bites you to make you shout and does not let you go for a single moment, breathless and exhausted, except to prepare you afresh with more ardent caresses. To court her, one must be, if not great in knowledge, at least bold in *intuition* [see this term]."[2]

Ideal (utopia) (see *idea*). The ideal is often used to characterize anarchism. It should be noted that this really concerns *anarchism* and not *anarchy*, an everyday reality of which none can be in doubt. The error is twofold, however. If libertarian thought is always on the side of anarchy and of the evident

---

1   *Bulletin de la Fédération jurassienne* (August 5, 1877); see Paul Brousse, "Propaganda by the Deed," trans. Paul Sharkey, in *Anarchism: A Documentary History of Libertarian Ideas,* vol. 1, *From Anarchy to Anarchism (300 CE to 1939),* ed. Robert Graham (Montréal: Black Rose Books, 2005), 151.
2   Joseph Déjacque, "Qu'est-ce qu'une utopie?" (1859), in *À bas les chefs!,* 134.

and disturbing vulgarity of its disorder, but also, consequently, on the side of the *superabundance* and *indefinite prodigality* of nature of which Bergson and William James speak (see *apeiron*),[1] the ideal, whether anarchist or not, may well drape itself in lofty conceptions, in ritually purified sacred histories (see *hagiography*), in grand notions of the justice, truth, beauty, and purity that are to come. In the present, however, the ideal never fails to procure for itself an extremely concrete and ordinary body – a simplified and repetitive body of priests, theorists, codes, ready-made images, clichés, obligations, and constraints – that is proportional, in its viciousness, pettiness, and sleaziness (quite real this time), to the grandeur of the ideals it claims. Any rebel of reasonably consistent *intuitions* can only turn away in the greatest *repugnance* (see this term) from any ideal and all idealism.

Identity (see *collective force, resultant, differences, feedback, classification,* and *indiscernibles*). The subjective and objective form of collective beings, very often illusory, that seeks to cement their existence (in particular through family, religion, and the State) so as to reproduce a hierarchical and dominatory order. How do we invent emancipatory identities and forms of subjectivity? Anarchism attempts to answer this question in two ways: 1) by denouncing the poverty, simplicity, and reductive violence to which existing identities subject the reality of our lives by limiting these identities to a few *homologous* or homogeneous categories (sex, citizenship, ethnicity, party, individuality, age, religion, social origin, etc.); 2) by affirming the infinite diversity and the continually changing character of possible identities and the equally infinite possibility of continuous experimentation with new ways of *composing* these identities.

Ideomania (see *point of view*). A fetishized, autonomized point of view, detached from its conditions of production, intent on applying itself as it is, absolutely, everywhere and in all circumstances. Ideomaniacs are the curse of the libertarian movement.

Idiosyncrasy (see *temperament*).

Imaginary (see *ideal, possibility,* and *monad*). The imaginary is often associated with what does not exist: an insubstantial daydream that distracts us from hard and pressing realities. On the contrary, because it refuses to separate or oppose realities and ideas – as well as to autonomize representations, whether in the domain of signs or of images – libertarian thought considers

---

1   Bergson, *The Creative Mind: An Introduction to Metaphysics*, trans. Mabelle L. Andison (New York: The Philosophical Library, Inc., 1946), 249

the imaginary in all its forms (dreams, reveries, fantasies) to constitute an important manifestation of that which exists and of the *possibilities* (see this term) that reality contains. As an expression of the implications of "individual" and collective consciousnesses (see *monad* and *subjectivity*), the imaginary relates closely to the bodies of the beings that produce it (see *gesture* and *brain*). This is why the imaginary is never a projection into the future of that which does not yet exist, but, on the contrary, the actual expression of the infinite *possibilities* that reality contains right now. And it is in this sense that Paul Hazard can hear Leibniz say, "[T]he man who had studied the largest number of pictures of plants and animals, of drawings of machines, of descriptions or plans of houses or fortresses, who had read the greatest number of ingenious romances, listened to the greatest number of strange narratives – that man would possess more knowledge than his fellows, *even though there were not a grain of truth in all that he had heard, read, or seen depicted* [emphasis my own]."[1] It is also in this sense that Whitehead can write that "any item of the universe, however preposterous as an abstract thought, or however remote as an actual entity has its own gradation of relevance…in the constitution of any one actual entity."[2]

Immanence (see *transcendence*, but also *outside/inside*). Anarchism is an absolute immanentism. For libertarian thought, everything that takes place is internal to things, beings, and their encounters with one another. Nothing comes from an external source (God, State, Laws, Ideas, Constitutions); everything comes from within, from an interior unlimited in its possibilities, which Bakunin calls *Nature* (see this term).

Immediate. An important notion in the libertarian vocabulary. Immediacy refers both to space and time. Libertarian action takes place instantaneously and without *mediation*. It refuses to be subordinated to more or less remote objectives (see *ends/means*) and, at the same time, to entrust and submit its diffusion and the relations of association that it entails to a mediation or representation that, from its perspective, can only cut it off from its possibilities (see *direct action*).

Imperceptible (see *life*).

Imperative mandate (see *direct democracy*).

---

1 Paul Hazard, *The Crisis of the European Mind: 1680-1715*, trans. J. Lewis May (New York, NY: New York Review Books, 2013), 217-18, emphasis my own.
2 Whitehead, *Process and Reality*, 148.

Implication (altruism) (see *other* and *outside/inside*). Anarchism rejects in disgust the altruistic, hypocritical, and external morality that claims to obligate beings to forget themselves in order to care for others, entrusting the task of imposing such a coercive program to an inevitably external guarantor and supervisor (Law, State, Church, superego, etc.). Genuine care for others comes about, first of all, through "the care of the self" as a "rule coextensive with life."[1] In other words, one does not discover an interest in others externally, by denying oneself, but on the contrary, within the inmost recesses of that which constitutes us, through implication, because every being is implicated in others, for better or worse, and because every being implicates all the others in itself (see *monad*). From a libertarian point of view, generosity alone can be the foundation of a genuine altruism. However, generosity always comes from the interior of beings, from an unpremeditated and spontaneous force (see *action, direct action*), the aptly named "initial impulse [*premier mouvement*]" produced by their implication in that which exists. In this sense, anarchism is close to the thought of Leibniz, to the conception of a world based on the spontaneity of beings, a world in which everything comes from within, an implicated world constitutive of space and time: space, since each being contains every other possible being in itself, and time, since each moment contains all the others, and since, from a libertarian point of view, the future is inevitably implicated in the present (see *ends/means*).

Implicit (see *fold*).

Impotence/powerlessness [*impuissance*] (see *lack* and *alienation*). As is clear from the word and its most current sense, impotence is the state of any collective being when it is separated from its own capacities.

Impulse (see *force, power, body, spontaneity,* and *entelechy*).

Indefinite (see *definition, unspecified, limitlessness of the limited,* and *apeiron*).

Indeterminacy/Indeterminate (see *stoppage, subject, anarchy, apeiron,* and *limitlessness of the limited*). Because it constantly attempts to transform more into less, to separate forces from what they are capable of, the existing order, in its negation of all that is not itself, conceives of the indeterminate in the form of *lack* or non-existence, the vague and the dubious: an adolescent or immature uncertainty with regard to the roles, professions, functions, and attributes proposed by society; the vacuity of lazy and dreamy types, when, deprived

---

1   Michel Foucault, *The Hermeneutics of the Subject: Lectures at the Collège de France 1981-1982*, ed. Frédéric Gros, trans. Graham Burchell (New York: Picador, 2006), 247.

of utility, these people, without doing anything, await a possibility or events to which the social machine denies any value or reality (see *stoppage*). In its libertarian usage, indeterminacy yields another meaning. If it is clearly opposed to *determinism*, it is not the opposite of *determination* (see these terms). Indeed, whereas determination expresses the power of collective beings, the indeterminate constitutes its source or condition. However, this concerns the indeterminate in the primary sense of the term, a power not yet "determined" by the external order, not yet subjected to the yoke and the limits of a given order. This is indeterminacy in the sense of *possibility* and the *apeiron* (see these terms), the "reality of the possible" in the sense that philosophers like Gilbert Simondon and Gabriel Tarde give to these words, this power of being that each *collective force*, each *subject*, contains in itself, which enables it to go *beyond its limits* and to compose an entirely new or different world.[1]

Indignation (see *revolt* and *repugnance*). An *intimate*, violent, and total perception of injustice, of the failure to respect the autonomy of beings, of their unacceptable submission to desires and ends that are not their own, imposed on them by others. Intuitive, ethical, and without measure, indignation is not at all personal or "interested" (in the utilitarian sense of the term). Always singular or circumstantial in its conditions of appearance and origin, it is not primarily or solely born from the feeling of being oppressed or instrumentalized or from the effects of this oppression or instrumentalization, but from the outrage that the absence of justice constitutes in itself. This outrage is felt for oneself as well as for others, oneself also being an other, in a perception that embraces the totality of being, since any reduction in power is, potentially, a reduction in my own power. Through indignation, as through the feeling of *anguish* (see *power of the outside*), each collective force accedes in a single leap (see *intuition*) to the totality of that which exists – this totality that it contains in itself and that makes it sensitive to all beings, to all the relations that may unite them. At the same time, it accedes to the fundamental significance of the damaged and damaging totality that rejects and oppresses forces, cutting them off from their possibilities, and it accedes to the absolute and general possibility of another and radically different possible world. As an *affirmative* moment, indignation stands at the origin of *revolt*. In the brief moment of its positivity (see *stoppage*), indignation provides revolt with its initial impetus, before which moment revolt does not produce, even briefly, the positive effects of its own *affirmation*. Indignation is indeed always fleeting or interstitial. When it becomes an enduring presence, cultivated for its own sake, losing sight of the totality that animates it in the first place, it inevitably changes into either an

---

1   On the difference between libertarian indeterminacy and the meaning that other authors, such as Claude Lefort, give to this word, see *stoppage*.

empty posture or a narrow *ressentiment* (see this term), inevitably inventing an enemy or a scapegoat (see *guilty party*).

Indiscernibles (see *singular, monad, equality, federalism, differences, entelechy,* and *identity*). A principle of Leibniz's philosophy according to which two real beings always differ by characteristics internal to that which constitutes them, not by their positions in time and space (see *localism*). Following Leibniz, libertarian thought refuses to base the identity of beings on mere numerical difference (atoms of matter, individuals of a crowd or a mass, "cells" or "sections" of a political organization) or an organic difference (the body with its head, its members and its various organs, the watch with its various cogwheels and gears), and at the same time, it denies that human identity, which is completely different in nature, is of a "personal" order (see *person*), tied to the human being's consciousness of itself (see *ego*). As Pierre Guenancia emphasizes, all of Leibniz's reflections on identity "are driven by the concern to restore the difference that gives each thing in the universe its *raison d'être* – i.e., its reason to be itself rather than another [see this term]."[1] From this point of view, "the identity of the human person is a particular case, a higher degree in the hierarchy of beings according to the complexity of the identity of the individual substances; it is a kind of amplification of the unity of each *thing* [see this term], each of them forming a *species infima*, each individual forming a species unto itself."[2] One finds this position in Proudhon, when he explains why "[t]he living human being is a group, like the plant or the crystal, but to a higher degree than those others; it is all the more alive, sensitive, and sentient to the degree that its organs, secondary groups, are in a more perfect agreement with one another, and form a more extensive combination."[3] In this sense, the identity of a thing does not depend on "the permanence of the limits that separate and distinguish it from all the others, its individual substance being perceived only from the outside, like that of a thing simply located in a place, a tenant [*locataire*] of the place that it occupies," so that "to identify a thing comes down to locating it, knowing where it is, being able to single it out" (see *localism*).[4] Identity is "inherent in things."[5] A position that Bakunin explains as follows: "Each thing contains its *own* law, i.e., its particular mode of development, existence, and action, within itself [emphasis in original]."[6]

---

1   Pierre Guenancia, "L'identité personnelle entre Locke et Leibniz," *Perspectives sur Leibniz,* ed. Renée Bouveresse (Paris: Vrin, 1999), 154.

2   Ibid. 154. (Translator's note: a *species infima* is a category of one, a class to which only one member belongs.)

3   Proudhon, *Philosophy of Progress,* 23 (trans.: modifications my own).

4   Guenancia, "L'identité personnelle entre Locke et Leibniz," 153.

5   Ibid.

6   Bakunin, "Considérations philosophiques," *Œuvres,* 3.352-354.

Individual (see *collective force*, *individuation*, *multitude*, and *subject*). In external representations of the libertarian movement, anarchism is often identified with individualism. Socialism (and its authoritarian and communist alternative) would be on the side of the collective, anarchism on the side of the individual. This handy but simplistic opposition is contradicted by all libertarian experiences (the Spanish revolution, the Makhnovshchina, anarcho-syndicalism, etc.), as well as by anarchist theory itself. Anarchism refuses the false distinction between the individual and the collective. Within anarchism's conception of reality and its possibilities for transformation, any individual (contrary to the etymology of this word) is a collective; any collective, however transitory it may be, is itself an individual. Thus, an infinity of individuals or *subjectivities* (see this term) are possible.

Individuation (see *subject*). Following Gabriel Tarde, anarchism refuses to substantialize beings, to regard individuals "as original sources, as absolutely primary givens." It requires, on the contrary, treating them as "emergents,"[1] or, in the vocabulary of Proudhon this time, as *resultants* (see this term and *anarchy*). But it is Gilbert Simondon who provides the most developed theory of a conception of being as *becoming*, a theory in which individuals are always more than what they are (see *genealogy* and *limitlessness of the limited*), because they are the resultants of a ceaseless process of *individuation*. All production of given individuals (individuation) comes from a limitless content that wells up within each of them in all of its power, without any relays or intermediate phases. While the history of evolution can be retrospectively articulated in terms of discrete stages, *collective* or *social* individuation is not therefore, for example, the product of psychic individuation, which would be the product of biological individuation, itself the product of physical individuation. Each of these individuations can be located within the others as, each time, they remobilize the totality of the power of that which exists by returning to the origin of the being, by a "recommencement," as Simondon says.[2] Thus, a new individuation can emerge, a radically new individuation that is neither the consequence of the preceding ones nor their destruction (by substitution), but that instead takes place through an originary return to the power and the tensions that reality contains, which no preceding individuation could either exhaust or resolve (see *eternal return*).

Instinct (see *spontaneity*, *power*, *vital* and *entelechy*). A concept frequently employed in the anarchist vocabulary of the 19th century, but in the primary sense of *force* and *desire*, impulse and excitation. Contrary to the way in which it is

---

1   See Milet, *Gabriel Tarde et la philosophie de l'histoire*, 154.

2   Simondon, *L'Individuation psychique et collective*, 192.

ordinarily conceived, in libertarian thought, instinct is in no way related to the *determinism* of heredity. Even if it is closely (though not exclusively) linked to living beings, the term "instinct" really serves to denote manifestations of the *spontaneity* or *freedom* (see these terms) – i.e., the *power* – that, at a *given moment*, in various forms and to different degrees, characterizes any collective being, whatever it may be.

Insubordination (see *war/warlike* and *insurrection*). An important notion in the anarchist vocabulary that serves to express, from the interior (not always without naïveté or grandiloquence), the attitude and libertarian character of emancipatory forces. At the same time, in a narrower sense, it serves to indicate the consistent practice of the refusal of military institutions and of the horrors of war produced by States and other institutions of power.

Insurrection (see *war* and *general strike*). The military aspect or (more precisely) the *warlike* dimension of the experience and imaginary of the libertarian revolts, from the 19th century to the (chronologically atypical) collective experiments of the Spanish revolution of 1936, including the important Makhnovist movement. Despite being stigmatized, sometimes for its macho [*viriliste*] connotations (see *virility*) and sometimes because of the growing and dubious hegemony of certain tendencies advocating *nonviolence* (see this term), insurrection nonetheless constitutes if not an essential concept of libertarian thought, then at least the most direct and apt expression of *revolt*, as well as of the polymorphic character of projects and movements with a libertarian dimension. Dazzling and spectacular in the great movements of collective revolt, insurrection and its warlike or aggressive dimension act within the totality of the relations constitutive of that which exists, from the vastest to the tiniest, from popular uprisings to the sometimes imperceptible revolt demanded by the immediate relations of labor, love, and the intimate aspects of individual life.

Integral pacifism (see *war*). A particularly repugnant example of *ideomania* (see this term and *repugnance*) in which, in reaction to the horrors of the World War I, a certain number of libertarians adopted the pacifist slogan of the CGT vis-à-vis Nazism in 1938: "Better servitude than war!" – a servitude that indeed led several of them to become dedicated servants of the French State and Nazism.

Interior (internal) (see *exterior/interior*, *planes of reality*, and *power of the outside*). Anarchism refuses all bonds of exteriority, synonymous in its eyes with constraint and domination. For anarchism, everything takes place within the interior of beings, in their capacity to include the exterior in that which constitutes them, and thus to compose more powerful and freer beings.

Interior world (see *intimate being*).

Interval (see *Daoism, midst of things*).

Intimate (intimacy, intimate circle) (see *affinity, active minorities, core, subjectivity, union,* as well as, on another register, *science, life, fugitive, intimate being*). A philosophical concept that Bakunin uses to define (among other things) the nature of the secret "circles" that he attempted to constitute throughout his revolutionary activities. Bakunin has often been reproached for his childish taste or mania for secrecy and secret societies, but only by those who lack an understanding of the true nature of the libertarian movement and project, and thus the manner in which the Bakuninian "intimate circles" are their best expression. Bakuninian intimacy reveals three meanings which are, so to speak, "intimately" linked:

- First of all, it concerns an emotional reality, founded on the *elective affinities* (see this term) between a number of "friends," "allies," or "companions." This is a harmony in which shared "ideas" (see *common notions*) are merely the expression of a proximity of temperaments, sensibilities, and relations to the world. This greater or lesser intimacy defines a series of nonconcentric "circles," narrower or wider according to the intensity of the relations through which they are constituted. A steelworkers' union circa 1900 is an intimate circle with a certain breadth and intensity that always tries to attract new members, breaking down into constituent circles (sections organized by trade, by workplace), with an internal life and a power to expand beyond itself depending mainly on the intensity of the largely informal, hidden, or implicit innermost circles (which Monatte will attempt to think through the concept of the *core*). These can be based either on a shared project and beliefs (membership in an anarchist, Blanquist, or Allemanist[1] group, for example) or quite simply on an affinity rooted in a shared family or region, a common history (shared neighborhood, shared primary school, shared apple pilfering), etc.[2]
- Bakuninian intimacy is thus coextensive with the existence of particular and distinctive individualities or, in the vocabulary of Bakunin as well

---

1   Translator's note: Allemanist: following the leadership of Jean Allemane (1843-1935), a radical socialist and veteran of the Paris Commune.

2   On this intimacy, see Limousin's role in the formation of the Lyonnais construction workers' unions, Jean-Luc de Ochandiano, *Formes syndicales et luttes sociales dans l'industrie du bâtiment: Une identité ouvrière assiégée, Lyon (1926-1939)*, Diss., Université Lumière Lyon II, 1996.

as Proudhon, of the *collective forces* for which this intimacy defines the greater or lesser reality of their existence. This collective force, variable in its power, can correspond to the "individual" in the usual sense of this term, but it generally indicates smaller or larger ensembles of human and nonhuman beings (a mason and his trowel, Jewish artillerymen of the Makhnovist army with their guns), the "intimate" ensembles belonging to some particular place or culture (the Armenian, Jewish, Tatar, Ukrainian, or Georgian anarchist groups of Odessa before 1914, for example[1]), not at all corresponding to the limits of the body and "individual" biology as such.

- Bakuninian intimacy finally reveals a third meaning, which is more strictly philosophical and which Lalande is not wrong to call "dangerous."[2] The word "intimate" indicates the internal, the private, and the secret, as opposed to the external, the explicit, and the public. For Bakunin, as well as for revolutionary syndicalism and anarcho-syndicalism later on, a recomposition of the world in which we live cannot achieve the height of its power and scope by means of communication, nor through transparency or openness [*dépli*], which permit signs, experts, psychologists, and oppressive institutions to unfurl their nets, to deploy all their powers of subjection and domination. It is to be achieved by concentrating and withdrawing into one's innermost recesses [*le repli sur soi*], through the constitution of a multitude of internal forces, forces that are literally explosive (see *energy*) and that are alone capable of dynamiting and recomposing the old world.

Intimate being (Eternity) (see *subject, intimate*). Concept proposed by Bakunin to define the reality and the subjective and singular dimension of beings. For Bakunin, the "intimate being" (which one could identify with "the most intimate essence of being" that Nietzsche speaks of as characterizing the *will to power*[3]) is not that false interiority of the metaphysicians, profound and inaccessible, from which everything supposedly arises. For Bakunin, "[t]here really exists in all things a hidden aspect or, if you like, a kind of intimate being that is not inaccessible, but that eludes the grasp of science. It is not at all the intimate being of which M. Littré and all the metaphysicians speak, which

---

1   See Michaël Confino, "Idéologie et sémantique: le vocabulaire politique des anarchistes russes," in *Cahiers du monde russe et soviétique* 30.3-4 (Jul.-Dec. 1989): 255-284.

2   Lalande, "intime," in *Vocabulaire technique et critique de la philosophie*, 1:394.

3   Nietzsche, *Nachgelassene Fragmente* 1888, 14 [80], in *Writings from the Late Notebooks,* ed. Rüdiger Bittner, trans. Kate Sturge (Cambridge, UK: Cambridge University Press, 2003), 247 (trans: modifications my own).

constitutes, according to them, the in-itself of things and the why of phenomena."[1] For Bakunin and libertarian thought, the "intimate being" is really an "internal world" that children, for example, acquire to the extent and degree that "*will* is born in them" and that they achieve a "beginning…of empire over themselves."[2] But this *internal world* is merely a fold of the outside, and it "expresses itself" entirely through the totality of the relations that beings maintain with the external world, "these multiple, often elusive relations that pass unobserved most of the time."[3] For Bakunin, "intimate being" does not refer to a mysterious essence that grounds things and beings; "[i]t is, on the contrary, the least essential, the least internal, the most external side, and at once the most real and the most transitory, the most *fugitive* of things and beings: it is their immediate materiality, their real individuality, such as it is presented to our senses alone, which no mental reflection could grasp, nor which any word could express."[4] And it is very precisely because of this apparent superficiality and externality – where, as Deleuze says with regard to Foucault, the "inside" is "more profound than any inner world" since it is also an "outside…farther away than any external world"[5] – that the intimate being of beings can attain *eternity*, to the very extent that "it is not an intimate being at all that is not completely expressed in the sum total of its external relations or its actions upon the external world."[6] And it is in this sense that Bakunin can affirm the eternity of the intimate being of Nicolas Stankevich, a friend of his youth:[7] "I had in my youth quite a dear friend, Nicolas Stankevich. His was truly a brilliant nature: a great intelligence accompanied by a great heart. And yet this man did not accomplish or write anything that could preserve his name in history. Is this, then, an *intimate being* [emphasis in original], who disappeared without a word [*sans manifestation*] and without a trace? Not at all. Stankevich, although he was the least pretentious and least ambitious being in the world – or perhaps precisely because of this – was the living center of a group of young people in Moscow, who for several years lived, so to speak, on his intelligence, his thoughts, his soul. I was among this number, and I, to some extent, regard him as my creator…His intimate being was completely expressed [*manifesté*] first of all in his relationship with his friends and then with all those who had

---

1   Bakunin, "Considérations philosophiques," *Œuvres*, 3:393.

2   Ibid. 3:387.

3   Ibid.

4   Ibid. 3:393.

5   Deleuze, *Foucault*, 96.

6   Bakunin, "Considérations philosophiques," *Œuvres*, 3:390.

7   On this point, cf. Alain Thévenet, "La trace de Nicolas Stankéwitch," *Réfractions* 1 (Winter 1997).

the good fortune to come near him."[1] From Bakunin to us, the intimate being of Nicolas Stankevich, this fold or smile of being, thus continues to be present in the world and to act on it.

In a manner very close to Bakunin's, Gilbert Simondon relates this eternity of things and beings – whether the "desperate, anonymous gesture of the slave in revolt" or the genius of a "book of Horace"[2] – to the fact that any individual is always more than itself, both in what constitutes it as a subject (see *apeiron*) and in the fabric of the "milieu" that is "associated" with its individuality. This is the fold or configuration of being in which Nicolas Stankevich's interior world expressed itself, this mark or *symbol* (see this term) of the singular "resolution" that this individual constituted at a given moment for the becoming of the being in its totality.[3] In this sense, one can also say – with Simondon this time – that any individual is eternal "not as a substance, subject or substantial body, consciousness or active matter" but "as a transductive being" (see *transduction*) that has left its mark on the "medium" from which it emerged, the annihilation of which would require us to "presuppose the annihilation of the medium [*milieu*] as well."[4]

Intuition. It is understandable that some have linked revolutionary syndicalism to Bergson and particularly to the role that he assigns to the concept of intuition. Libertarian intuition comes from within *collective beings* (see this term), from the deepest recesses of that which constitutes them (see *intimate, monad, interior, Idea*). It is intuition that governs relations between beings and their potential to join together, constituting a more powerful being. Intuition governs our most immediate and significant relations but also the capacity to consider the reasons to join or not to join with so-and-so (see *analogy, affinity, repulsion,* and *repugnance*). Intuition is not only a gift inherent to each collective being (as a resultant of the mode of composition specific to this being). It also supposes the accumulation of a great deal of experience with relations between collective forces, an art of good and bad encounters.

Irrational (see *direct action, raison d'être, common concepts,* and *collective reason*). A polemical notion used by the current order to indicate all that escapes its

---

1 Bakunin, "Considérations philosophiques," *Œuvres,* 3:389. On Bakunin's youth and intellectual formation, cf. Benoit-P. Hepner, *Bakounine et le panslavisme révolutionnaire: cinq essais sur l'histoire des idees en Russie et en Europe* (Paris: Rivière, 1950).

2 Simondon, *L'Individuation psychique et collective,* 105.

3 "The Individual…is the expression of a resolution. He is…the complementary symbol of another reality, the associated medium [*milieu*]" (Gilbert Simondon, *L'Individu et sa genèse physico-biologique* [Grenoble: Millon, 1995], 62).

4 Simondon, *L'Individuation psychique et collective,* 102.

influence. For libertarian thought, everything is rational, since each being, each event, each situation has its own *raison d'être*, obeys its own law. This is why Bakunin can affirm that "each *thing* [see this term] contains its *own* law, i.e., its particular mode of development…within itself,"[1] and Proudhon can write that "every kind of error, every aberration of judgment or equity, only takes place under the terms of the same laws of reason that it hides."[2] Libertarian thought does not oppose truth to error. It substitutes for this false distinction the perpetual evaluation of the quality of beings and of the force produced by their associations. It does not oppose *good* to *evil* (see these terms). In place of these two reductive concepts, which are supposed to order the world, it posits the ceaseless play of *powers* (see this term) and their capacity to promote (or not promote) the existence of an emancipated world, to do (or decline to do) all that they are capable of.

---

1   Bakunin, "Considérations philosophiques," *Œuvres*, 3:352-354.

2   Proudhon qtd. in Pierre Haubtmann, *Pierre-Joseph Proudhon: sa vie et sa pensée (1808-1849)* (Paris: Beauchesne, 1982), 243.

J

Joy/sadness (see *good/bad*).

Judgment (see *evaluation, practical sense, repugnance,* and *law/rights*). In libertarian thought, the concept of "judgment" has two meanings. As something *external* and *transcendent* – i.e., when it appeals to a third party (State, Judge, Spiritual Director, Expert, etc.) – it is one of the great means by which the current order perpetuates its domination. However, as something *internal* and *immanent* to collective beings, mobilizing the totality of that which they are and of which they are capable, it aptly defines their ability to continually assess the emancipatory quality of their internal relations, as well as of the relations that they develop with others, and thus of the worlds in which they can deploy their power.

Justice (see *equality, autonomy, indignation,* and *balancing of forces*). An immanent perception of the radical autonomy of collective beings, of the *respect* that this autonomy requires, and of the balancing that it presupposes. By means of its autonomy and the possession in itself of all that exists (see *subject*), each being is the equal of all others. Thus, by the *affirmation* of that which constitutes it and its free *association* with others, it is enabled to *go to the limits of its capacities*.

Justification (see *rendering of accounts* and *utilitarianism*). Justification is the reverse of justice. Justice is both respectful and *intimate*, impersonal and internal to things, beings, and situations. Justification is, on the contrary, intrusive, indiscreet, and despotic toward those it catches in its nets. At the same time, it is completely external to the beings whom it so efficiently summons, pins down, and implicates in its trials and confessions, to whom it lends a subjectivity that is compelling and effective and yet, simultaneously, entirely untrue, entirely caught within the traps of language and social interactions. Justification, whether in its mundane or its religious sense, always presupposes the existence of an external and higher authority (God, the Party, the Courts, or the Others) before which we must justify ourselves, rendering an account of our actions, our thoughts, and our being, measuring them against the yardstick of a compulsory externality that we must beg to recognize us, to define that which we are (see *master/slave*). Anarchists refuse all justification, for themselves as well as for others. The *evaluation* of a collective being and of the quality of its association with other collective beings (in terms of *emancipation* or increase in *power*) is always internal to this being and its associations, immanent to that which they are at a *given moment*. It thus takes place through *collective reason* and *common notions* (see these terms).

L

Labor/work (see *war/warlike* and *tools/weapons*). Historically, anarchism has long been identified with the relations of production, with manual laborers' status as "producers," and with the various forms and experiences of the labor movement. In contrast to the Marxist predilection for metaphysics and abstraction, the libertarian movement attended especially closely to the concrete and immediate dimensions of working-class life and to the emancipatory possibilities that arise from within it. However, the most visible characteristic shared by the libertarian workers' movements of the last two centuries should not mask the great diversity of these movements, nor, above all, the originality of an emancipatory project that never confines itself to just one given condition or identity, a project that connects them all on the basis of what each renders possible with a view toward emancipation. This originality is attested to by the very singularity of those multifarious experiences, which are each time different and vary so widely across time and place as to resist all generalization. It was Proudhon who contributed the most to illuminating the emancipatory potentialities of the various working classes of the second half of the 19th century, as well as the nature and relations of labor in that same period. But he also did much to render possible an escape from an extrinsic vision of the libertarian workers' movements and a sacred and hagiographic history of these movements, as well as from an ahistorical valorization of manual labor and the "producer" identified with it, which too often encumber libertarians' minds and imaginations.

While Proudhon defines labor as "the *plastic force* [see this term] of society," while he indicates that it is "one and identical in its domain [*plan*]" and "infinite in its applications," this is true only and precisely "in its domain" – "like creation itself," Proudhon adds[1] – i.e., insofar as it stems from a power that

---

1   "Labor, one and identical in its domain [*plan*], is infinite in its applications, like creation

131

goes far beyond what is usually meant by "labor," particularly labor as it is practiced within the framework of the existing order. In this sense, on the basis of the power that makes it possible, labor itself escapes from the *determinism* (see this term) that imprisons it and transforms it into slavery. From the force that it contains arises a much broader field of creative activity, which is expressed by love, by *war* (see this term), by art ("man is a worker, i.e., a creator and poet"[1]) or any other human activity on the particular plane on which it deploys itself. From a certain perspective, the perspective of creative *power*, work can be regarded as a specifically human activity.[2] However, from another perspective, the perspective of the limits of the *plane of reality* within which this labor unfolds and, especially, of the constraints and limits that imprison its power (constraints and limits stemming not immediately from the relations of domination over its current forms but from the very essence of the laboring activity; see *tools/weapons*), work can also be regarded as a prison within which human collective forces are in no way distinct from the determinism that governs all animal species. As Proudhon writes, "[I]f, as is impossible, nature had constituted man as a purely industrial and sociable animal…, he would have fallen, from the very beginning, to the level of the animals whose destiny is entirely determined by association;…living in pure community, our civilization would be a cowshed."[3] In this sense, the Proudhonian critique of work and the social relations that so closely depend upon it anticipates the contemporary critique of work and, more particularly, of the way in which Marxism, in over-valorizing work, conceives of emancipation. As Gilbert Simondon demonstrates, like Proudhon, work and the sociality that accompanies it are not at all the species trait of humanity and its capacities, as opposed to what Marxism affirms. For Simondon, work, such as it is conceived by Marx, does not differ from the cooperation of bees and ants. It is a "species" sociality, concerned only with a living *individuation* as a "mode of conduct with respect to an environment." "Understood as a living thing in the world, [human beings] can associate in order to exploit the world," but only as a living thing, just like all the other animal species. "Labor exists at the biological level as exploitation of Nature; it is the reaction of humanity as a species, a species *reaction* [see this term]."[4]

In other words, in libertarian thought, what usually serves to define human species being – the opposition to nature through labor – does not constitute its specifically human dimension, merely its membership in the living world,

---

itself" (Proudhon, *De la Justice*, 3:89).

1   Proudhon, *Système des contradictions économiques*, 2:361.

2   "Thus man, alone among the animals, works, gives existence to things that nature…does not produce," ibid.

3   Proudhon, *La Guerre et la paix*, 31-32.

4   Simondon, *L'Individuation psychique et collective*, 189 and 191.

along with all other animal species, in the closed and repetitive form of a "community" and a "civilization of the cowshed." Contrary to the old anthropology that it rejects, libertarian thought grounds the power of human subjectivity in its capacity to open itself up to *nature*, to the *other* in one's self, to the *outside* that constitutes it (see these terms), which its specialization as a species pushes it to fight against and to subject to the limits of its *determinisms* as a living species. In other words, from a libertarian point of view, one could say that the specificity of human existence lies in its capacity to open itself up to the non-human, to leave behind the pseudohumanity of the hive or the cowshed, the "animal farm" so aptly described by Orwell. It resides in the human capacity to always return to the *indeterminate*, the *preindividual* (see these terms) and, thus, to found the possibility of new forms of subjectivity. As Simondon once again writes, "Nature is not the opposite of humanity."[1] Human power consists precisely in the possibility of returning to nature, to being in its totality, the possibility of remobilizing the totality of the forces of the *apeiron*, the *reserve of being*, the *charge of nature*, the *limitlessness of the limited* (see these terms).

Laboratory (see *experiment, experts,* and *science*)

Lack (see *desire, appetite, power,* and *master/slave*). The identification of desire with lack, absence, and deprivation – from Christianity to psychoanalysis – has played an essential role in the subjection of beings to a damaging and oppressive order. In place of a conception based on the negative – in which desire, inevitably placed under the sign of *ressentiment* (see this term), exists only through the absence of its object, through castration, in which every force is separated from its own capacities (see *virility*) – libertarian thought substitutes an identification of desire with *power, plenitude, superabundance,* and *generosity* (see these terms). It is true that in both cases desire is deprived of an object: in the first case because desire has been alienated in a vanished or impossible object from which it is irremediably separated, and in the second case because desire has no need of external objects to exist, because it draws everything from itself (see *monad*). Yet these two forms of absence are one another's antipodes. Whereas in the theory of desire as lack, the encounter with the other becomes impossible, the libertarian conception of desire and its power continuously make possible an encounter with the totality of other collective forces on a

---

1   Ibid. 196. It must be recalled that, for Simondon as for libertarian thought, "Nature" is synonymous with being and its power. Bakunin formulates this position as follows: "[n]o revolt is possible on the part of man against what I call universal causality or universal Nature; the latter envelops and pervades man; it is within and outside of him, and it constitutes his whole being. In revolting against this universal Nature, he would revolt against himself" (Bakunin, *The Political Philosophy of Bakunin*, 91).

certain *plane of reality*, since these forces are also subjective beings, each one of which potentially contains the others within itself as seen from a certain point of view (see *appetite*). Any encounter and any difference, as long as they can avoid the traps (dialectical or otherwise) that external shocks and confrontations never fail to present, may then serve as the occasion (see *event*) that reveals to each being the infinite power that it contains, the occasion for it to exceed its own limits and to do all that it is capable of (see *balancing of forces* and *contradictions*).

Law/rights (contracts, conventions) (see *hierarchy* and *autonomy*).[1] The libertarian conception of law has nothing to do with the absolute power, the autonomy, the logical coherence, and the external character of the Law [*la Loi*], whether it comes from God, the State, or the so-called "general will" (Rousseau's "social contract"). For anarchism, as Proudhon writes, "each power," "each force," "contains its own law," the "right [*droit*]" to *do all that it is capable of*.[2] Such a conception is already present in Max Stirner ("What you have the *power* to be you have the *right* to"[3]), and we find it in Émile Pouget when he explains that "Direct Action is workers' might applied to creative purposes: it is the might that gives birth to new rights, producing social law!"[4] In libertarian thought, law is immanent to collective forces and, like them, it is manifold in its sources and manifestations – a conception that Bakunin formulates as follows: "Each thing contains its *own* law [*loi*], i.e., its particular mode of development, existence, and action, within itself [emphasis in original; see *entelechy*]."[5] Experimental and intuitive, libertarian rights are coextensive with the power of beings, with their methods of *association* and *disassociation* (see these terms). A constitutive element of these methods – what George Gurvitch calls "act-rules" – is to always refer to a justice internal to collective forces, as "technical procedures for the formal statement of a preexisting law that validates the conventions themselves."[6] Instead of conforming to a single transcendent source ("sovereignty"), it depends on a plurality of primary sources (*collective forces*), "generative centers of law," "autonomous sources of law," corresponding to the great diversity of experiments in the association and composition

---

1   Translator's note: in French, *droit* can mean both "right"/"rights" and "law," although French also possesses the cognate *loi* ("law").

2   Proudhon, *La Guerre et la paix*, 133.

3   Stirner, *The Ego and His Own*, 247.

4   Pouget, *Direct Action*, 23 (trans.: modifications my own).

5   Bakunin, "Considérations philosophiques," *Œuvres*, 3:352-354.

6   Georges Gurvitch qtd. in Jean Bancal, *Proudhon, pluralisme et autogestion*, vol. 1, *Les Fondations* (Paris: Aubier-Montaigne, 1970), 130.

of forces.[1] As the expression of the relationships between forces and of the conflicts and solidarity that characterize them, libertarian law more specifically helps to express and produce (together with *collective reason* [see this term]) the balance between contrary interests at a given moment, the balance of necessary antinomies (see *balancing of forces*). Under the various forms of contracts, conventions, regulations, customs, courts of honor, arbitration, and pacts, and contrary to all the juridical sciences, it produces what we might call "law [*droit*] without laws [*règles*]."[2] In this sense, the libertarian concept and practice of law are close to the baroque thought of Leibniz in which one no longer asks "what available object corresponds to a given luminous principle, but what hidden principle responds to whatever object is given, that is to say, to this or that 'perplexing case,'" but instead of "a case being given," one invents the principle, so that Law is transformed into "universal Jurisprudence."[3]

Leader (see *boss* and *hierarchy*). An English term that makes it possible to distinguish the preeminence that a collective being may sometimes acquire in a given situation or within a given action from that of *bosses* (see this term). The latter are solely defined by the status or violence that they impose on other collective forces from the outside.

Liberalism (see *neoliberals* and *utilitarianism*).

Life (fugitive) (see *intimate, immediate,* but also *vital/vitalism*). Anarchism often makes reference to "life." This life should not be understood in the biological sense generally given to this word. In libertarian thought, it is at the same time synonymous with *force* and *affirmation* (see these terms), but also partakes of the *fugitive*, ephemeral, and *intimate* character (see this term) of the realities from which the libertarian project attempts to develop and construct another world. Bakunin best formulates the originality of the meaning that the libertarian movement gives to the term "life": "[o]nly life…is in connection with the living and sensible but elusive and inexpressible aspect of things." "Science concerns itself only with shadows…The living reality escapes it and gives itself

---

1   On this point, cf. Antoine Garapon, "L'Idée de droit social: Georges Gurvitch," in *La Force du droit, panorama des débats contemporains*, ed. Pierre Bouretz (Paris: Esprit, 1991), 215-228. (Garapon is evidently unaware of the overwhelmingly and explicitly Proudhonian inspiration of the "originality" of Gurvitch's analyses.)

2   Ibid. 222. (Translator's note: this phrase could also be rendered as "rights without rules.")

3   Deleuze, *The Fold*, 67. Jean Bancal, in characterizing the Proudhonian conception of right, speaks of "acts of jurisprudence" (*Proudhon, pluralisme et autogestion*, 1:130). For a contemporary libertarian approach to law, cf. also Ronald Creagh, "Au-delà du droit," in *Réfractions* 6 (Winter 2000).

only to life, which, being itself fugitive and temporary, can and indeed always does encompass all that lives, that is to say, all that is passing or fleeting." "Such, then, is the nature of this intimate being that really remains eternally inaccessible to science. It is the immediate and real being of individuals as things: it is the eternally momentary, the fugitive realities of the eternal and universal transformation."[1]

Limitlessness of the limited[2] (see *apeiron, more than oneself, plastic force, anarchy,* and *possibilities*). An essential notion of Chinese *Daoism* (see this term). It can be found in Western libertarian thought and even more particularly in Gilbert Simondon, who uses it to characterize the power of being and its capacity to produce an infinity of possible *collective beings*. It is through this "limitlessness of the limited" that one can understand the way in which Gilles Deleuze defines *equality* as the capacity of collective beings to *go to the limits of their capacity*, i.e., "beyond their external limits," limits imposed on them by an oppressive order, but especially (in associating with and confronting others) their inner limits (see *balancing of forces*), insofar as any collective being is always more than what it is, more than its present individuality (see *more than oneself* and *individuation*).

Limits (see *power, interior, equality,* and *balancing of forces*). In a strange phrase, Deleuze explains how *equality* (see this term) does not lie in the conformity of beings but in the ability of each of them to go "to the limit of its capacities," which is to say, Deleuze immediately adds, beyond its own "limits."[3] In light of a common sense formed by centuries of domination, how can that of which a being is "capable" exceed its physical, intellectual, sexual, and other "limits" – what are so aptly named "thresholds of incompetence" – imposed by an order that castrates and crushes us? Here, undoubtedly, resides the profound originality of libertarian thought and, by contrast, the equally profound myopia of the world in which we live. In libertarian thought, there are two possible definitions of collective beings: first, an *external* definition in terms of limits and places occupied (see *differences* and *localism*), causes and effects, dependence with respect to a whole; on the other hand, an *internal* definition in terms of force, power, and desire.

---

1   Bakunin, "Considérations philosophiques," *Œuvres*, 3:394-395.

2   Translator's note: I have borrowed the phrase "limitlessness of the limited" from Jonathan R. Herman's translation of *Reden und Gleichnisse des Tschuang-tse*, Martin Buber's translation of the *Talks and Parables of Chuang Tzu*, LI ("The Place of Tao"), in *I and Tao: Martin Buber's Encounter with Chuang Tzu* (Albany, NY: SUNY Press, 1996), 63. It seems a reasonable way to translate into English Colson's French expression, *illimité dans la limite*, more literally "unlimited within the limit."

3   Deleuze, *Difference and Repetition*, 37 (trans.: modifications my own).

For libertarian thought, limits are indeed boundaries that externally (but also internally; see *balancing of forces*) fix, frame, and define an infinite inner power that is irreducible to these limitations and to the order upon which they are founded. This is an inner power that stems from the *apeiron* (the indeterminate) of which Anaximander spoke (see *direct action*) or, in contemporary philosophy, what Gilbert Simondon calls the "preindividual," this more-than-oneself that each individuality contains and that continually authorizes the emergence of new, vaster, and more powerful individualities (see *subject*). Not only can any collective being depart from its current "limits" (in order to assassinate somebody or to give its life for that somebody, for example), but it is precisely in going beyond those limits, in composing relations with other forces in other circumstances, in thus giving rise to new beings, that it discovers its potential to realize all of its potentialities, to "do all that it is capable of."

Localism (see *monad* and *indiscernibles*). A pejorative term (both within and outside of the libertarian movement) that stigmatizes anarchists' frequent tendencies to disperse their efforts amid a profusion of struggles and groups (often tiny and inward-looking), to act where they are and according to what they are at a *given moment*, within the narrow limits of their immediate environment and particular concerns. In fact, for them, there is no question of limiting their possibilities for action and their perceptions of things solely to their own individuality. This dubious critique (see *individual*), which generally does nothing to prevent the recurring fragmentation of the libertarian movement, actually expresses a deep ignorance both of the reality of this movement and of the emancipatory logic that animates it, of which "localism" is one of the principal manifestations. Indeed, the "locale" should not be confused with the "site" to which the dominant order seeks to reduce it, so that each thing would have its place (house, communist cell, workplace, city, sex, "identity" card, etc.) within the *limits* (see this term) defined by the whole, thus requiring a pyramid of increasingly broad coordinating authorities charged with synthesizing and harmonizing the smaller, subordinate authorities – subordinate because they are smaller (town, county, region, nation, United Nations; cells, sections, federations, central committee; etc.). As Jean-Clet Martin demonstrates,[1] the "local" is "a *point of view* upon the whole [see this term]." Leibniz explained this through the example of the city: "Each urban complex presents itself as a set or a 'block.' It designates a *finite* grouping of elements, of cataloged, numerable buildings. On the other hand, what will necessarily exceed the enumeration of elements is the *infinite* figure of possible perspectives that this city could offer

---

1   Jean-Clet Martin, "Of Images and Worlds: Toward a Geology of the Cinema," trans. Frank Le Gac and Sally Shafto, in *The Brain is the Screen: Deleuze and the Philosophy of Cinema* (Minneapolis, MN: U. of Minnesota Press, 2000) 64, 62, 73 (trans.: modifications my own).

us depending on the point of view from which one considers it [emphasis my own]." "There is thus an expansivity to the *local* not covered by the extension of the *global*, an expansion of perspectives the immensity of which does not have to do with the extended space of the site [emphasis in original]." "A space is born that is not reducible to exteriority; instead of condemning us to see things from the outside, it clarifies them from within." (see *interior, monad*). Ultimately, it becomes possible to construct "a new intersubjectivity."[1] Far from being an obstacle to the development of the libertarian movement, localism is its precondition, the precondition for a true *federalism* (see this term) founded on the multiplicity of points of view.

Locking horns [*Prise de têtes*] (see *point of view, exterior/interior*, and *monad*). A colloquial expression for those useless confrontations (often after dinner) in which it is a question of being right, a matter of honor, of saving face, of having the last word, when nobody listens to anybody else anymore but only tries to make points in arguments that each would be hard-pressed to remember two hours later. These confrontations generally involve a few individuals – usually two, who are often men (although women can also manifest the macho hypersensitivity [*la susceptibilité virile*] that generally fuels this type of dispute) – before an increasingly quiet audience, the existence of which they eventually forget. This ridiculous and useless struggle to come out "on top" (aptly expressed in the image of one "head" being "locked" with another "head") must not be confused with the discussions that are brought about and necessitated by differences in *points of view* (see this term), which are inevitably animated, sometimes vehement. In the latter case, discussion and confrontation mobilize convictions or beliefs (in the sense that Gabriel Tarde gives to this concept) that arise from the very being of each protagonist, such as it has been able to compose itself up to this point, and touch the most intimate part of what constitutes them. Thus, they are not just a matter of superficial vanity, the locking of horns (or of "heads"). In this kind of encounter, on the contrary, the head is seized [*prise*], but by issues that arise from within things, within oneself and others. Paradoxically, it is exactly in these often intense, sometimes dramatic situations – in which acts emerge from the most profound part of oneself, rather than from a superficial and public image of that self – that a true (and rare) encounter can finally take place between these beings and bring about their transformation.

---

1   Ibid. 64, 73; Jean-Clet Martin, *L'Image virtuelle, essai sur la construction du monde* (Paris: Kimé, 1996), 32.

Main front/second front (see *militant, organization, platform and platformism,* as well as *friends of our friends*). An old military and political distinction that attempts, from the outside, to establish a hierarchy of struggles and causes, subordinating some of them to others. This distinction was mainly used by authoritarian parties and revolutionary organizations, but also, at times (albeit without much success), it was used by certain libertarian organizations fascinated by their seeming effectiveness. Because it affirms the absolute independence and *autonomy* of emancipatory forces, anarchism both refuses any hierarchical organization of struggles and revolutionary forces and affirms their freedom of association and the free determination of their reasons to struggle.

Manual/intellectual (see *death, midst of things,* and *theory/practice*). Because it long developed within the labor movement, anarchism is strongly marked by an anti-intellectual tradition. One can thus highlight the paradox of a movement violently critical of all theory, the militants of which nonetheless have often demonstrated an immense thirst for knowledge. This can be seen from the eclecticism and the encyclopedic character of even the smallest of the workers' libraries that has survived the vicissitudes of history.

Eager for culture, science, and knowledge, but judging with Proudhon that "the idea is born from action and not the action from reflection,"[1] anarcho-syndicalist and revolutionary syndicalist militants reject theoretical and scientific formations (sociology, psychology, physics, biology, etc.) that attempt, from the outside, to dictate what they are and what they want, as well as to define the frameworks and the limits of what is possible and what is not. In libertarian thought, emancipatory knowledge is never external to that of which it speaks

---

1 Proudhon, *De la Justice,* 3:71.

and the collective being that produces it. It is only from the interior of beings and the relations that they establish among themselves – the relations that make them possible – that a science not linked to domination can emerge. Because it contains the totality of that which exists, any *force* or *situation* is capable of enunciating the meaning of this totality, but only from a certain *point of view*, from what constitutes it as a force or a situation at a given moment. It is here that the paradox of the libertarian position resides: inwardly possessing the totality of the meaning of things, having the right to refuse any external determination or definition, but being unable to express this totality of meaning or only being able to express it from a limited point of view, through an inner *tension*, through the non-coincidence with itself of a singular force possessing in itself a power and a meaning that, in order to unfold itself or be explicated, depends on an infinity of other forces and their capacity, in joining, to give rise to other more powerful and thus more clear-sighted beings (see *collective reason*).

This non-coincidence or, in the vocabulary of Simondon, this "dephasing" internal to every form of *individuation* is constitutive of their existence as *subject* (see this term). This is at the heart of the libertarian project, of the aspiration of beings to another possibility, as well as of the methods of *association* and *disassociation* capable of realizing this other possibility. But it is also at the heart of the relations between practice and theory, between manual and intellectual labor. If, from a certain point of view, each force, each situation, each activity contains in itself the totality of the meaning and power of that which exists, the expression of this totality is not required to merely wait for the effects of an emancipatory recomposition of collective beings that has yet to arrive. Due to this inner tension between its capacities and the bounded singularity of its present existence, it is possible for each force, each situation, each activity, right now, to call upon the great diversity of past experiences and points of view (conversely, see *hagiography*). Each force has the possibility to discover, through what is generally called culture – i.e., through words, texts, gestures, musical notes, strokes of the paintbrush, numbers, etc. – a corollary external to the lived totality it inhabits at a given moment (see *tradition*). In this relationship between the symbolic resources of past experiences and the lived experiences of the present, in the capacity of the latter – originating in its innermost being and the tension that characterizes it – to mobilize the power and the meaning of the former, it is no longer a question of external bonds or of any claim on behalf of either party to express the truth of the other. It is only, so to speak, a matter of enabling a direct encounter between different modalities in order to express the totality of that which exists. Like Proudhon and Simondon, anarchism conceives of this internal and direct relationship, for better or worse, between present and past experiences, between present and past situations (insofar as these are perceptible through words and other cultural codes), through the concept of *analogy* (see this term).

Mass (masses) (see *conformism*, *herds*, and *multitude*). "The masses," "the broad working masses," "the masses of the people," "the broad masses," "the mass line," "go to the masses," "demands of the masses," "the masses are not yet awakened," "the masses have a potentially inexhaustible enthusiasm for socialism" (Mao),[1] the "masses" as the "raw material [sic]" of politics,[2] etc. From Marx to the Italian extreme left, including Lenin and Mao Zedong, the concept of "mass" (the mere title of which should be enough to make the most obtuse conformists quiver with indignation) constitutes the exact expression of authoritarian communism, the blind manifestation of the arrogant and terrifying idiocy of its pretensions.

From fascism and Nazism to communism, it cannot be denied that the masses are a tragic invention of the 20th century. The *people* of the 19th century – this concept of the people, ambiguous in its revolutionary potentialities,[3] but which the revolutionary syndicalists and anarcho-syndicalists had believed themselves able to transform (taking the conditions of the working class and labor as a starting point) into complex and differentiated emancipatory forces – are then lastingly transformed into anonymous and undifferentiated masses. This occurred first in the muddy trenches of World War I, in which a million men learned how to lose all singularity or difference and to strip life of all value. Then it occurred amid the riotous and bloodthirsty crowds of the right-wing and left-wing revolutions of Moscow, Rome, or Berlin, among the armies assembled for *labor* and *war*, and in the flawless ballets of the great "mass" ceremonies held for the glory of the race or the class and of the leaders who are their incarnation, before wisely returning to obedient and honest mass consumption in stadiums, housing projects, and supermarkets.

Master/slave (see *dialectic*). Anarchism refuses the trap of the master-slave dialectic (see *emancipation*). With Nietzsche and in the sense that he gives to these words, anarchism is always and without hesitation on the side of masters and not of slaves. The emancipatory point of view is that of a master and not of a slave: the dominated, in radically liberating themselves by revolting

---

1   Mao Zedong, *Quotations from Chairman Mao Tsetung* (Peking: Foreign Languages Press, 1972), 122, 40, 122, 128, 122, 128, 124, 123-124, 126, 121.

2   Étienne Balibar, *Masses, Classes, Ideas: Studies on Politics and Philosophy Before and After Marx*, trans. James Swenson (New York: Routledge, 1994), 144-145, 186. Antonio Negri, *The Savage Anomaly: The Power of Spinoza's Metaphysics and Politics*, trans. Michael Hardt (Minneapolis, MN: University of Minnesota Press, 1991), 84.

3   On the acute perception of this ambiguity of the revolutionary potentialities of "the people" in 19th century libertarian thought, cf. Alain Pessin, "Proudhon et les contradictions du peuple," in *Peuple, mythe et histoire*, ed. Simone Bernard-Griffiths (Toulouse: Presses Universitaires du Mirail, 1997).

against the bonds that affix them to an external force, *affirm* their new *power*, becoming their own master (see these terms) and breaking through the boundaries imposed by domination. Here and from this point of view, one can understand why the libertarian workers' movement, insofar as it corresponds to the movement of differentiation of the strong and the masters of which Nietzsche speaks, was historically always so radically foreign to Marxism (a variant of Hegelianism) and to its conception of the class struggle.[1] Indeed, in the anarcho-syndicalist or revolutionary syndicalist conception – as opposed to what is often asserted – the working class, considered from the point of view of its emancipation, is not initially or mainly defined by the class struggle or the struggle that opposes it to the State and the bourgeois. Its revolutionary power primarily depends on its capacity to constitute itself as an autonomous, independent power, possessing all the services and institutions necessary for its independence. For anarcho-syndicalism and revolutionary syndicalism, the working class must first of all secede in a radical way, must have nothing more in common with the rest of society. In the discourse belonging to the libertarian dimension of the labor movement, this movement of differentiation bears the name (crystal-clear from a Nietzschean point of view) of "worker separatism." The workers' movement must "separate" itself from the rest of society. This is what Proudhon explains in his posthumous book *De la Capacité politique des classes ouvrières*: "The separation that I recommend is the very condition of life. To distinguish oneself, to define oneself, is to be; just as to merge and be absorbed is to lose oneself. To break away, a legitimate secession, is the only means we have for affirming our rights…May the working class, if it takes itself seriously, if it pursues something more than fantasy, remember: it must before all else leave behind its tutelage, and…from now on, act exclusively by itself and for itself."[2]

In this way of seeing things, the class struggle is not absent, but it is no longer a dialectical relation in which "the moribund society" of which Jean Grave speaks[3] (the society that the workers' movement refuses) always threatens to trap those who fight against it in a lethal and anesthetizing vise by obliging them to accept shared rules of combat and to adopt forms of struggle belonging to the order that this movement wants above all to negate and destroy. For the libertarian workers' movement, the strike, as the privileged expression of class struggle, consists of two things: 1) it is a perpetually repeated founding

---

1   Cf. Daniel Colson, "Nietzsche and the Libertarian Workers' Movement," trans. Paul Hammond, in *I Am Not a Man, I Am Dynamite: Nietzsche and the Anarchist Tradition*, eds. John Moore and Spencer Sunshine (Brooklyn, NY: Autonomedia, 2004), 16-17.

2   Proudhon, *De la Capacité politique des classes ouvrières* (Paris: Rivière, 1924), 237.

3   Jean Grave, *Moribund Society and Anarchy*, trans. Voltairine de Cleyre (San Francisco: A. Isaak, 1899).

act, an always singular and circumstantial "conflict" that breaks the former bonds and boundaries (see *direct action*). It is a rupture that, through the multiplication of partial conflicts and by means of its very movement, decisively contributes to the transformation of the worker's very being.[1] 2) It is the way in which workers "educate themselves," "harden themselves," and prepare for "movements" of increasingly "general" scope, until the final explosion of the general strike.[2] In this multitude of partial struggles, the workers' associations can certainly give themselves immediate objectives and make agreements, but these objectives are always secondary and these agreements always provisional. Because of what constitutes them as revolutionary forces, they do not aim at any "reasonable" compromise as defined by the framework through which it was reached or at any "satisfaction" that could be obtained from the economic and social order, which would be subject to that order's limitations. Even and especially when they sign agreements, the workers do not put themselves in the position of petitioners. They are content to obtain a portion of their "rights" temporarily, while waiting to obtain them in full, free and clear, with no "guarantors" other than themselves. If the workers ask for nothing, it is because they have no desire for the old world, which they want to abolish and which they scorn and ignore. Their revolt is a pure affirmation of the forces and the movement that constitute them, and it is only in a derivative way that they are constrained to fight against the reactive and reactionary forces that oppose this affirmation. They ask nothing of anyone, but demand everything from themselves, from their own capacity to express and develop the power that they contain. Their relationship with the external world is at once a relation of *selection*, of affirmation, and of the recomposition of that which exists:

- a selection, from within the existing order, of the means necessary for the affirmation of this new power;
- the assertion of the right to one day occupy the totality of social space through a radical transformation of the bourgeois order, as well as of values, morals, economics, and politics;
- a recomposition of the totality of that which exists.

Victor Griffuelhes formulates this project as follows: "The working class, having nothing to expect from its leaders and masters, denying their right to govern, pursuing the end of their reign and domination, organizes itself, groups itself, gives itself associations, sets the conditions for its own development, and thereby studies, reflects, works to prepare and establish the sum of the guarantees and rights to be conquered. Then it settles on the means of

---

1 Griffuelhes, *Le Syndicalisme révolutionnaire*, 11.
2 Yvetot, *A.B.C. syndicaliste*, 11.

ensuring this conquest, borrowing them from the social environment, using the modes of action that this social environment contains, rejecting all that attempts to make the worker into a subjected and governed being, always remaining the master of its own acts and actions, the arbiter of its own destiny."[1]

Matter (see *God*, *State*, and *analogy*). Because it proclaims a radical monism, anarchism denies any separate and transcendent existence to "mind," "reason," or "thought." However, like Bakunin and in a sense close to that of Whitehead's analyses, it just as vigorously refuses to turn "matter," in a symmetrical or *analogous* manner, into a new divinity: "For us, matter is not at all this inert *substratum* produced by human abstraction," and "it is not this uniform, formless, and abstract matter of which positive philosophy and materialist metaphysics tell us"; rather, "it is the real ensemble of all that is, of all existing things, including the sensations, minds, and wills of animals and human beings. The generic word for matter thus conceived would be Being, the real Being, which is at the same time a *becoming*: i.e., the movement always and eternally resulting from the infinite sum of all the particular movements down to the infinitely small, the totality of the mutual actions and reactions and ceaseless transformations of all the things that appear and disappear in turn [emphasis in original]."[2]

Mediation (see *midst of things*, *Daoism*, and *direct action*). Anarchism always begins from the *midst of things*, where all becomes possible again, where beings can enter into genuinely emancipatory relations from the interior of what constitutes them, by *affinity* and in relations of *analogy*. The midst of things is very precisely the reverse of mediation: in the latter, a third party or some other channel of communication presumes to serve as an intermediary that separates forces or benefits from their separation so as to impose its own existence, fixing in place the beings it pretends to unite, enclosing them in their defined roles, reducing the infinite power of otherness that these beings contain – a power that it both damages and exploits – to its own role as intermediary. Anarchism refuses any form of mediation, whether it takes the form of the middleman (between producer and consumer), the priest (between humanity and God), the union representative (between the workers and the owners), but also that of the friend who wishes you well, the organization that has its demands, the role that imposes its duties, the absurdity of the laws and commandments that are supposed to give meaning to life, etc.

---

1   Griffuelhes, *Le Syndicalisme révolutionnaire*, 19-20.

2   Bakunin, "Considérations philosophiques," *Œuvres*, 3.345 and 3.347. For a contemporary critique of the concept of a permanent and continuous matter and of its catastrophic effects on "the various systems of pluralistic realism," see Alfred North Whitehead, *Process and Reality*, 78 et passim.

Midst of things [*milieu des choses*] (see *manual/intellectual*, but also *direct action*, *theory/practice, common sense*, and *Daoism*). Anarchism often manifests a violent rejection of intellectuals and theory. This attitude – linked to what was, for a long time, the working-class character of the libertarian movement – is in many respects questionable, but it also constitutes the negative side of an important theoretical proposition: the refusal of any transcendence, any all-encompassing system that claims, from the "heights" of its external perspective, to know and define the *raison d'être* and the meaning of each person and thing. From a libertarian point of view, science, in its pretensions to truth and objectivity, which it has developed over three centuries, is the analogue (see *analogy*) of capital, the State, and religion. For anarchism, any knowledge or signification can only emerge in the midst of things, in the midst of *immediate* relations (see this term), relationships immediately perceived by the forces that experience or undergo them. This perception of immediately lived relations requires, on the one hand, a local knowledge [*savoir propre*] that simultaneously consists in practice and experimentation and, on the other hand, in a specific theoretical development with a pedigree as ancient as that of totalizing and dominatory science, a science and a theoretical direction that, following Deleuze and Guattari, one might call "minor" or "nomadic."

Milieu (anarchist milieu).[1] Generally a pejorative or deprecatory expression in the discourse of *organizations*, serving to designate any individuals or forces of libertarian content that reject the traps and limitations of these organizations. The "milieu," sometimes compared to a nutritive or indigestible "sludge," a more or less consumable resource, could then be imagined as a kind of goldfish bowl or aquatic environment [*milieu aquatique*] in which revolutionary fish would find the resources necessary to their historical mission (finding voters, recruiting demonstrators, taxing resources, etc.), a "goldfish bowl" that counter-revolutionary institutions would mainly be interested in draining or controlling. In the libertarian project and its thought, on the contrary, the milieu (see *midst of things*) constitutes the only space, the only reality in which an emancipatory recomposition of that which exists can take place through self-organization, developing from itself the totality of the forces and concerns necessary for this emancipation.

---

1 Translator's note: the most commonly used equivalent expression in English (since the 1960s, at least) is really "the anarchist scene." However, the connotative baggage of this metaphor (with its suggestions of spectacle, performance, looks and the gaze, etc.) gives rise to quite different reflections than those pertaining to the loan word "milieu." For a more in-depth consideration of the anarchist scene/milieu in a U.S. context, see Laura Portwood-Stacer, *Lifestyle Politics and Radical Activism* (London: Bloomsbury Academic, 2013).

Militant (see *war/warlike*). An ill-considered term (see *organization*, among many other terms), borrowed from military language and used to define a particular category of collective beings who choose the emancipation of all as their primary *raison d'être*. The military connotation of this word is hardly fortuitous. It directly expresses the quite often authoritarian character of the groups and organizations that proclaim their "militancy." Anarcho-syndicalism preferred to speak of *active minorities* (see this term), an interesting attempt to try to think the ways in which an emancipatory movement can develop.

Mobility (see *milieu, movement,* and *becoming*).

Monad (see *possibility, localism,* and *indiscernibles*). In *De la Justice dans la Révolution et dans l'Église*, Proudhon explains, in connection with freedom, how it is time to return to the monadology of Leibniz in a new context, a monadology finally freed from the divine mortgage [*hypothèque*]: "Monadology was for Leibniz nothing more than an hypothesis [*hypothèse*]: it is now a question of making it a truth."[1] Against the illusory and dominatory claims of the whole to determine the parts (see *limits*), Leibniz affirms the sole existence of an infinity of singular, individual beings irreducible to any *external determination* (see these terms): monads. From a certain *point of view* that belongs to each of them, each monad includes and expresses the totality of that which exists. In this sense, Proudhon declares, "Man is a worker, in other words a creator and a poet" because he "produces from the depths of himself" and "lives from his inner being."[2] The monads have neither doors nor windows, Leibniz tells us,[3] because their relation is an *internal* relation (see this term and *affinity, intimate*), which pertains to the quality of the world that they "inter-express."[4] This is a

---

1   Proudhon, *De la Justice,* 3:400. Gabriel Tarde renewed this attempt 35 years later, in 1893, with his *Monadology and Sociology.*

2   Proudhon trans. and qtd. in Rubin, *Realism and Social Vision in Courbet and Proudhon,* 113-21.

3   Leibniz, *The Monadology,* trans. Robert Latta (Oxford: Clarendon Press, 1898), 219: "The Monads have no windows, through which anything could come in or go out." This permits some, quite wrongly, to make monadology the justification of modern individualism, this individualistic "egoism" with which libertarian tendencies are so often reproached, this "narcissism, exclusive concern for oneself, the cult of independence, the sacrifice of the social" (Alain Renaut, *The Era of the Individual: A Contribution to a History of Subjectivity,* trans. M. B. DeBevoise and Franklin Philip [Princeton, NJ: Princeton University Press], 136-137) (see *individual, implication,* and *autonomy*).

4   Deleuze, *The Fold,* 81 (trans.: modifications my own). Translator's note: here, Conley's translation says that the monads "express one another," but this clearly does not capture the dimension of the original French expression, "s'entr'expriment," that Colson intends here, an expression that, just a page earlier, Conley translates as "expressed among each other."

world that, with the disappearance of the divine postulate, becomes multiple and thus obliges us, as Tarde says, to conceive of a "renewed monadology." This would allow us to think of monads as no longer "mutually external," of monads able to "open" onto others from the inside, "penetrat[ing] one another reciprocally,"[1] themselves becoming an "internal cause of diversity"[2] and thus selecting, among the infinity of possible worlds, that which is appropriate for their full flourishing (see *possibilities*).[3] And it is in this new meaning that the Leibnizian monad, rid of the hypothesis of God, allows us to understand the cry that Arshinov hurls before the proletarians of the world shortly after the crushing of the Makhnovshchina: "Proletarians of the world, look into the depths of your own beings, seek out the truth and realize it yourselves: you will find it nowhere else."[4] In this sense, it also helps us to understand how Louise Michel, after the manner of the misogynist Proudhon (see *multiple*) and in a similar movement of thought, can grasp the *intimate* relation between "the total emancipation of women" (who, "from one end of the earth to the other…form a whole, each group, even each woman") and the artistic activity "which shall one day, perhaps even soon, be the spirit of humanity!" all in the context of a general emancipation in which "[a]ll who arise unite with one another, complement one another like the notes of a chord," since "everything is possible in the movement of beings and groups that are folded together, swept up together…, without even realizing it," but which "harmonize and coalesce with one another like the nebulae from which worlds are formed."[5]

Monism (pluralism) (see *nature*). Anarchism is a radical monism. It admits no distinction or hierarchy between body and soul, mind and matter, or humanity and nature (*dualism*). As Proudhon emphasizes, the human composite does not differ in any respect from any other composite, from anything else that

---

Neither would "express *to* one another" seem adequate to Colson's conception, as it would imply a more conventional notion of something being communicated from one monad to another. Mark Lester and Charles Stivale translate the same expression in Deleuze's *The Logic of Sense* as "inter-expressive" (New York: Columbia Press, 1990), 177.

1 Tarde, *Monadology and Sociology*, 26.

2 Maurizio Lazzarato, postface to *Monadologie et sociologie*, Gabriel Tarde (Paris: Les empêcheurs de penser en rond, 1999), 116.

3 On this neo-monadology or neo-baroque, deriving from Whitehead this time, cf. Deleuze, *The Fold*, 81.

4 Peter Arshinov, *History of the Makhnovist Movement*, trans. Lorraine and Fredy Perlman (Detroit: Black and Red, 1974), 261.

5 Letter addressed to the Fédération féministe des Arts et Métiers, March 22, 1902, in *Louise Michel: Je vous écris de ma nuit: correspondance générale, 1850-1904*, ed. Xavière Gauthier (Paris: Les Éditions de Paris, Max Chaleil, 1999), 689.

nature composes, except in degree of power: "The living human being is a group, like the plant or the crystal, but to a higher degree than those others; it is all the more alive, sensitive, and sentient to the degree that its organs, secondary groups…form a more extensive combination."[1] And with the Deleuzean Spinoza, anarchism can affirm: "one Nature for all bodies, one Nature for all individuals, a Nature that is itself an individual varying in an infinite number of ways."[2] However, along with Whitehead this time, anarchism refuses, on the one hand, to privilege a primary reality, whether it is called *nature, substance, God,* or *matter* (see these terms), and, on the other hand, to oppose a "monistic universe" to a "pluralistic universe."[3] For libertarian thought, monism and pluralism coincide.

More than oneself (see *subject, monad, apeiron, balancing of forces, anarchy, power of the outside,* and *event*). "*I* is an *other*," said Rimbaud.[4] We harbor the other within ourselves, not in the manner of a double, a brother, a guardian angel, or a soul, but as *anarchy*, as the *indeterminate* totality of being, as the *reserve of being* or the *limitlessness of the limited*, in the words of Gilbert Simondon and, before him, the immense *Daoist* tradition (see this term). This limitlessness of the limited authorizes human beings to open up to all the possibilities that reality contains, to discover, through association with others, the power that they contain and thus to allow the free expression of the totality of that which exists. One can understand nothing of the originality of anarchist thought if one does not grasp the sense of the libertarian paradox that wants the fully emancipated human being to be, as Proudhon affirms, simultaneously the part and the whole, both "what is greatest in nature" and "the summary of nature, all of nature."[5] It is between the *apeiron* or *anarchy* – the indeterminate power contained by all beings (physical, biological, psychic, social) – and *positive anarchy* – an ordered and determined expression of the power of being – that human emancipation emerges, that the capacity emerges for human beings to express the totality of that which exists, both by rebelling against all forms of domination and by experimenting with new associations. In this sense, Gilbert Simondon writes that if "the domain of psychological individuality…exists as something superimposed on the physical and biological domains, it is not inserted between them, strictly speaking, but *joins them and partially includes*

---

1   Proudhon, *Philosophy of Progress*, 23 (trans.: modifications my own).

2   Deleuze, *Spinoza: Practical Philosophy*, 122.

3   Whitehead, *Process and Reality*, 96.

4   Rimbaud, "Lettre à Paul Demeny," 15 mai 1871, in *Poems,* trans. Paul Schmidt (New York: Alfred A. Knopf, 1994), 275.

5   Proudhon, *De la Justice*, 3:175.

them even while it is located within them [emphasis my own]."[1] Also in this sense, Proudhon says that "man – multiple, complex, collective, evolutionary – is an integral part of the world that he attempts to absorb."[2] Furthermore, "in any organized...being, the resultant force is the freedom of that being, so that the more this being, whether crystal, plant, or animal, approximates the human type, the greater will be its freedom."[3] Finally, because human beings are multiple, complex, collective, and evolutionary, it is always possible for them to increase, through the richness of their associations and creations, the power and thus the freedom that they contain, to fully express the power and freedom of being.[4]

Movement (becoming) (see *life* and *fugitive*). In the current vocabulary of anarchism, the word "movement" is used as an alternative to the biologizing and misleading concepts of *organization* (see this term). In place of "organizations" (libertarian or otherwise), "movement" posits a common reality that is simultaneously open within its limits, diverse in its components, and, above all, entirely engaged in the becoming of forces and beings. It is in this last usage that the concept of movement plays an essential theoretical role in libertarian thought. *Anarchy* (see this term) proclaims not only multiplicity but also *becoming*, ceaseless change, the refusal of any tidy arrangement, which can only be that of the cemeteries or the violence of the dominant ("nobody move!"; "everything in its place!"). In this sense, the idea of movement is closely related to that of *action* (see this term), an overall philosophical conception that Bakunin clarifies as follows: "in *nature*, all is *movement* and *action* [see these terms]: to be means nothing more than to do. All that we call the *properties* of things – mechanical properties, physical, chemical, organic, animal, human – are merely various modes of action...from which it follows that each thing is real only insofar as it...acts...This is a universal truth that admits of no exceptions and that applies even to those inorganic things that are seemingly the most inert, to the simplest bodies as well as to the most complicated organizations: the stone, the chemical atom, as well as the man of genius and all things intellectual and social [emphasis my own]" (see *life, fugitive*).[5] The repose of cemeteries, military parades, or entomologists' display cases (see *classification*) constitutes no more than an oppressive and dominatory fiction because, "in

---

1   Simondon, *L'Individuation psychique et collective*, 152.

2   Proudhon, *De la Justice*, 3:409.

3   Ibid. 3:433.

4   "In man himself, free will manifests itself all the more energetically as the elements that generate him by their community are themselves developed in power: philosophy, science, industry, economy, law" (Ibid.).

5   Bakunin, "Considérations philosophiques," *Œuvres*, 3.384-385.

nature, strictly speaking, there is not a single point that is ever at rest, since at every moment, in the least infinitesimal fraction of each second, each is agitated by a ceaseless action and reaction. What we call immobility, a resting state, is only a crude appearance, an entirely relative concept."[1] We find this same notion in the work of Gabriel Tarde, when he shows how "rest is only a special case of movement," a movement "indefinitely" slowed down.[2] This notion is also to be found within the project of revolutionary syndicalism, in the writing of Victor Griffuelhes, for instance, when he explains how "syndicalism is the movement of the working class that wants to arrive at the full possession of its rights in the factory and the workshop."[3] Indeed, contrary to Marxism, the libertarian workers' project always refused to essentialize or substantialize working-class identity (even dialectically) and to subject what it was capable of, fleetingly, at a *given moment* and in specific *situations* (see these terms) to the laws of historical materialism. Griffuelhes clarifies this notion, too often ignored by those who later declared their allegiance to revolutionary syndicalism or anarcho-syndicalism (see *hagiography*), in a particularly illuminating way when he wonders about the attitude that revolutionary syndicalists must adopt toward "workers who are imbued with religious ideas or who trust in the reformist values of the ruling classes."[4] An obvious Marxist answer was popularized by the famous Comintern anthem: "[Y]our place is here, my friend!/ March along in the workers' united front/You're a worker until the end!"[5] On the terms of this response, it suffices to replace the Christian or reformist label with another label, that of "worker," a label that is held to be anterior or more determining because it is supposed to emanate from the base of the social and economic structure. Instead, Griffuelhes opposes a very different conception of working-class struggle. If revolutionary syndicalism does not have to reject Christian and reformist workers, Griffuelhes tells us, it is not first of all because they are "workers"; on the contrary (or in a different or paradoxical way), it is because it is always a good idea to carefully distinguish between "movement and action on the one hand, the working class on the other."[6] In the eyes

---

1   Ibid. 384.

2   Tarde, *Monadology and Sociology*, 40; Jean Milet, *Gabriel Tarde et la philosophie de l'histoire*, 159.

3   Griffuelhes, *Le Syndicalisme révolutionnaire*, 2.

4   Ibid. 3.

5   Bertolt Brecht and Hanns Eisler, "The United Front Song," trans. Ernst Busch, in *The Undying Flame: Ballads and Songs of the Holocaust*, ed. Jerry Silverman (Syracuse, NY: Syracuse University Press, 2002), 6-8.

6   "If it rejected them, this would be to confuse different factors with one another: movement and action on the one hand, the working class on the other" (Griffuelhes, *Le Syndicalisme révolutionnaire*, 3).

of revolutionary syndicalism, as opposed to what is sometimes believed, belonging to the working class does not guarantee anything, precisely because workers can be "Christians" or "Socialists" (see *class*). Emancipatory differentiation does not operate in the context of the prevalence or rank of *identities* (see this term), the context of things-in-themselves and things-for-themselves in which working-class identity and its so-called emancipatory virtues would be obtained through propaganda, stereotypes, emotions, constraints, and conformism. It operates in the context of "action" and "movement," which alone are able to act on things and labels, to scramble their points of reference and their limitations, to engage "workers," "Christians," "socialists," "anarchists," but also "masons," "steelworkers," and "pastry cooks," or "Greeks," "Germans," and "Spaniards" in a process that gives itself a different set of ambitious objectives, since it attempts to transform the workshop, the factory, and the entire society, and thus to abolish the working-class condition (see *nomad, nomos*). And as if it were necessary to hammer home this essential idea – not only of the superiority of syndicalist movement and action over working-class identity and its representations, but of the difference in their natures – Griffuelhes quickly reiterates the point: "Syndicalism, let us repeat, is the movement, the action of the working class; it is not the working class itself."[1]

Multiple (see *identity, subjectivity*, and *planes of reality*). One never knows what a being is capable of given time and given the multitude of possibilities it carries at a *given moment* (for *good* and *bad*), which remain for *events, situations, encounters*, and *associations* to disclose or leave hidden. This unpredictability pertains not only to the future of this being or even only to its present, where anything can happen at any time, as it is said and as any experience with love or friendship demonstrates.[2] It also pertains to this being's past, which, even after this being has disappeared, always has a future, in multiple ways, through the traces or imprints that it has left on the becoming of things (see *intimate being, eternity*, and *eternal return*). This is why one should never judge a being externally (see *hagiography*), under the illusion of permanence, from the standpoint of the identity bestowed on it by a given order's crude categories and classifications, or from a circumstantial point of view that, through myopia or *ideomania*, would fail to open up to the infinity of the possibilities and significations that this being contains, preventing it from going beyond its own limits (see *balancing of forces*, but also *guilty party*). It is in this sense that the misogynist Proudhon can nonetheless enable us, a century and half later, to

---

1 Ibid.

2 See Nathalie Sarraute, *Over Nothing at All*, trans. Philippa Wehle, in *France: Plays by Marguerite Duras, Nathalie Sarraute, Michel Vinaver, Gildas Bourdet, Enzo Cormann, Jean-Claude Grumberg* (New York: PAJ Publications, 1986), 43-62.

think and perceive the nature and the value of women's emancipatory movements, as well as the affirmation and meaning of their most radical feminist currents. In the same way, his anti-unionism and his radical condemnation of strikes did not prevent him (for many reasons, both good and bad) from inspiring some of the most impressive aspects of the thought and action of the revolutionary syndicalist and anarcho-syndicalist currents (see *theory/practice*).

Multiplicity (see *one*). Opposed to the one, understood in the current sense of a first principle or foundation. It is here that the specificity and the great originality of the anarchist movement is to be found: it not only conceives of the one by way of the multiple, the common by way of the different, but it also refers this way of thinking to that which exists, saying that this corresponds to an entire dimension of reality, as well as to its maximal conditions of possibility and development. Consequently, it attempts to foster a general movement of emancipation based on this multiplicity, based on the absolute singularity and *autonomy* of the forces that compose it. Following Proudhon and Antonin Artaud, it is undoubtedly Deleuze who provides the best definition of the anarchist project: "*anarchy* and unity are one and the same thing, not the unity of the One, but a much stranger unity that can only characterize the multiple."[1]

Multitude (see *mass*). The word "multitude" can be used in two radically different ways. In libertarian thought, "multitude" (without an article) refers to *anarchy*, the multiple and different, to the potentially limitless composition of beings from a proliferation of singular forces and subjectivities. In the dominant thought – from liberalism to Marxist communism – "*the* multitude" (with the article) is thought in the form of a great number of like individuals, which may agglomerate or accumulate in an equally undifferentiated *mass* – that rather particular power of sameness and quantity so necessary for successful demonstrations and revolutions, for electoral or marketplace victories. Certain revolutionary currents of Marxist inspiration continue to invoke the multitude in the second sense of the term. Quite wrongly, they refer this invocation to Spinoza, specifically to his political writings. But as even observers the least inclined to disparage Marxism have demonstrated, the concept of the multitude, completely absent from the *Ethics*, has a generally negative sense in this philosopher's political writings.[2] And if one absolutely had to relate it to Spinoza's major concepts, it would not be in order to think a coming revolution, an *a posteriori* emancipation in which human beings, supposedly liberated from their original *charge of nature*, would agglomerate into a multitude in

---

1   Deleuze and Guattari, *A Thousand Plateaus*, 158 (trans.: modifications my own).

2   See Balibar, *Masses, Classes, Ideas*, 10 et passim.

the arbitrary vacuum of a "political constitution,"[1] their materiality reduced to mere human passions. On the contrary, following Deleuze, one would have to think an *a priori* emancipation, in the profusion of the forces that we contain, forces that never cease to constitute us (see *eternal return*), which Deleuze describes as follows:

> Bodies (and souls) are forces. As such they are not only defined by their chance encounters and collisions (state of crisis). They are defined by relationships between an infinite number of parts that compose each body and that already characterize it as a 'multitude.' There are therefore processes of composition and decomposition of bodies, depending on whether their characteristic relationships suit them or not. Two or several bodies will form a whole, in other words, another body, if they compose their respective relationships in concrete circumstances. And it is the highest exercise of the imagination, the point where it inspires understanding, to have bodies (and souls) meet according to composable relationships.[2]

---

1 Negri, *The Savage Anomaly*, 226.

2 Deleuze, "Preface to *The Savage Anomaly*," in *Two Regimes of Madness: Texts and Interviews, 1975-1995*, trans. Ames Hodges and Mike Taormina (New York: Semiotext(e), 2006), 192. For a critique of Negri's analyses, cf. Daniel Colson, "Anarchist Readings of Spinoza."

N

Natural laws (see *autonomy* and *naturalism*).

Naturalism (see *vital/vitalism*, but also *Nature, power of the outside*).

Nature (see *anarchy* and *plane of immanence*, but also *plastic force, apeiron, species activity, universal causality, chaos, composed unity*, etc.). A traditional and commonplace concept within the libertarian vocabulary, indicating the totality of that which exists, which Bakunin defines as follows: "since I have to use this word Nature frequently, it is necessary to make my meaning clearly understood. I could say that Nature is the sum of all things that have real existence. This, however, would give an utterly lifeless concept of Nature, which, on the contrary, appears to us as being all life and movement. For that matter, what is the sum of things? Things that exist today will not exist tomorrow. Tomorrow they will not pass away but will be entirely transformed. Therefore I shall find myself much nearer to the truth if I say: Nature is the sum of actual transformations of things that are and will ceaselessly be produced within its womb...Call it, if you find it amusing, God, the Absolute – it really does not matter – provided you do not attribute to the word God a meaning different from the one we have just established: the universal, natural, necessary, and real, but in no way predetermined, preconceived, or foreknown combination of the infinity of particular actions and reactions which all things having real existence incessantly exercise upon one another."[1]

Necessity (freedom). Necessity is opposed to coercion. Coercion is always *external* (see this term) and synonymous with oppression and domination.

---

1 Bakunin, *The Political Philosophy of Bakunin*, 53.

Necessity is always *internal* (see this term), and in this sense, it is synonymous with freedom. As Spinoza says, "That thing is said to be free [*liber*] which exists solely from the necessity of its own nature, and is determined to action by itself alone. A thing is said to be necessary [*necessarius*] or rather, constrained [*coactus*], if it is determined by another thing to exist and to act in a definite and determinate way."[1] Such is the position Bakunin takes when he explains, "In obeying the laws of nature…man is no slave, since he only obeys laws inherent in his own nature, which are the conditions for his own existence and which constitute his entire being. In obeying them, he obeys himself."[2]

Negation (see *analogy, contradictions,* and *indeterminacy*).

Neo-Confucianism (see *liberalism* and *Daoism*). In the current efforts of liberal capitalism to subject the totality of that which exists to its order, the *selection* (see this term) of the elements and mechanisms favorable to this world (rationalist, utilitarian, humanist, conventionalist, universalist, etc.) from all existing cultures becomes a major concern. We can see this in connection with Arab thought, for example, in the Moroccan philosopher Mohammed Abed al-Jabri's critique of the taste for the *gnosis* of the Arab East and in his discomfort at the ways in which the irrationalism (see *irrational*) of certain European philosophers often denounced as "oriental" thinkers (Spinoza, Nietzsche) lends new meaning to the mystical traditions of Arab civilization.[3] This is also the case with regard to aspects of Chinese history and culture that have been subjected to a rereading that might be described as "neo-Confucian," which, while sometimes attempting to open up to the strangeness of the other, is generally content to rediscover the clichés of the most oppressive currents of Western philosophy. In France, François Jullien is undoubtedly the most significant representative of this rereading.[4] Western humanism (with Rousseau, who can be summarized in the declaration that "man is human") rediscovers the

1   Spinoza, *Ethics*, Part I, Definition 7, trans. Samuel Shirley, in Spinoza, *Complete Works*, 217.

2   Bakunin, *Œuvres complètes*, 8:201.

3   Mohammed Abed al-Jabri, *Introduction à la critique de la raison arabe* (Paris: La Découverte, 1994).

4   Among the many works of this author, see especially – for what is both closest and furthest from what is said here – François Jullien, *Procès ou création: Une introduction à la pensée des lettrés chinois* (Paris: Seuil, 1989), *Figures de l'immanence: Pour une lecture philosophique du Yi King* (Paris: Grasset, 1993), and, with Thierry Marchaisse, *Penser d'un dehors (la Chine): entretiens d'Extrême-Occident* (Paris: Seuil, 2000). On the importance of this neo-Confucianism in a contemporary Chinese philosophy marked by the West, see Joël Thoraval, "La Chine dans la philosophie: Pensée orientale, pensée occidentale; L'Humanité et ses figures," *Esprit* (May 1994): 5-38.

servitude of Confucian conventions (e.g., Mencius's moral tautologies). In opposition to these, in its own work of selection, libertarian thought proposes the Daoist "freedom of spontaneity," the "unmooring" of which Jacques Gernet speaks.[1] This opposition is especially visible in the ways in which Daoism and Confucianism diverge in their interpretation of the *I Ching*, that founding document of Chinese thought.

A neo-Confucian interpretation of yin and yang rests on a hierarchical duality (that of Heaven over Earth), in a homology according to which humanity can both attempt to "enclose" reality within the reductive assumptions of its thought and, quite rightly, identify the ends of its action with Heaven's role as "initiator"[2] (itself constructed on an imperial model). In this way, this interpretation harbors an incipient will to control and domination,[3] the intent to lock the order of things within the cramped isolation cell of the conscience and its corresponding social, moral, and economic conventions. Because the Daoist conception is *monist* (see this term), indifferent to hierarchy,[4] and in a relation to the world in which all beings ("the ten thousand things" of the *Dao De Jing*) participate in the whole and its movement, it is conducive to an attitude and a conception with obviously libertarian dimensions: rejecting as futile the mastery of the game of distinctions, values, and social positions; continually returning to the "undifferentiated" (see *limitlessness of the limited* and *apeiron*), to the univocity of being, "the Mystery [that] is the first ancestor of the Spontaneous,/the root of the many diversities,"[5] to the "mysterious" source, "the roots of Heaven and Earth";[6] recognizing the "spontaneity" of things by situating human activities within the flows of the existing and of that which causes them to exist. In opposition to a false neo-Confucian mastery, paid for by an infinity of servitudes – rites, social conventions, hierarchies, morals – Daoism can thus propose a single form of "obedience": the obedience of beings "to the [internal] orders of their own nature"[7] as the singular expression of the whole. Such a conception is very close to the opening of Spinoza's *Ethics*: "That thing is said to be free [*liber*] which exists solely from the necessity of its own nature, and is determined to action by itself alone. A

1   Jacques Gernet, *L'Intelligence de la Chine: Le social et le mental* (Paris: Gallimard, 1994).

2   Jullien, *Procès et création*, 184.

3   Ibid. especially chapter 13: "De l'analyse du devenir à sa maîtrise."

4   On this indifference, particularly noticeable in Daoist alchemy, see Isabelle Robinet, *Taoism: Growth of a Religion*, trans. Phyllis Brooks (Stanford, CA: Stanford University Press, 1997), 255-256.

5   Ge Hong, *Baopuzi*, qtd. in Robinet, *Taoism*, 82.

6   Lao-Tzu, *Te-Tao Ching*, trans. Robert G. Henricks (New York: Modern Library, 1993), 60.

7   Joseph Needham, *Science and Civilization in China*, vol. 2, *History of Scientific Thought* (Cambridge: Cambridge University Press, 1991), 582.

thing is said to be necessary [*necessarius*] or rather, constrained [*coactus*], if it is determined by another thing to exist and to act in a definite and determinate way."[1] It is also close to Bakunin, when he explains that "each thing contains its *own* law, i.e., its particular mode of development, existence, and action, within itself [emphasis in original]"[2]

Neoliberals [*libertariens*][3] (see *individual* and *individuation*). Neoliberals should not be confused with the *anarchists of the right* (see this term). Right-wing anarchism amounts to a mere individual attitude, seldom capable of forming a collective movement based on *ressentiment*.[4] On the other hand, neoliberals constitute from the start a collective arrangement of practices and opinions that has no relationship to the *ressentiment* or spirit of loathing peculiar to the anarchists of the right. Gilles Châtelet gives the best definition of neoliberal ideology: "An intellectual current which, often subtly and even playfully, presents submission to the market as the incarnation of liberatory ideas brought to maturity. The market therefore appears as the victory of a type of anarchist ruse on the part of History, completing a peaceful synthesis of all social relations (economic, political, cultural, etc.) understood solely in terms of the particular individual."[5] From the point of view of libertarian thought, the neoliberal *libertariens'* imposture is made evident by two postulates essential to their conception of the world:

---

1   Spinoza, *Ethics*, Part I, Definition 7, trans. Samuel Shirley, in Spinoza, *Complete Works*, 217.

2   Bakunin, *Œuvres*, 3:352-354.

3   Translator's note: *libertariens*, in French, refers to partisans of laissez-faire economics, as opposed to *libertaires* or libertarian socialists. The French word *libertaire*, like its cognates in other European languages (*libertario, libertär*, etc.), is synonymous with "anarchist"; however, in the United States, the English cognate was appropriated in the mid-1960s by the founders of the Libertarian Party, a formation espousing a combination of anti-statism and *laissez-faire* economics. As Murray Rothbard recounts, "'[O]ur side,' had captured a crucial word from the enemy…'Libertarians'…had long been simply a polite word for left-wing anarchists, that is for anti-private property anarchists, either of the communist or syndicalist variety. But now we had taken it over" (*The Betrayal of the American Right*, ed. Thomas E. Woods, Jr. [Auburn, AL: Ludwig von Mises Institute, 2007], 83). The same ideology, imported to France, has received the neologism *libertarien*, but more commonly – in France as in the rest of the world – it is referred to simply as "neoliberalism." For the origins of *libertaire*, see Valentin Pelosse, "Joseph Déjacque et la création du néologisme 'libertaire' (1857)," *Economies et sociétés* 4.12 (1972): 2313-2368.

4   See the case of Céline during World War II.

5   Gilles Châtelet, *To Live and Think Like Pigs: The Incitement of Envy and Boredom in Market Democracies*, trans. Robin Mackay (London: Urbanomic, 2014), 181.

- The identification of the individual as a being without singular qualities, equivalent to all other individuals (see *equality*), radically separate from any force or possibility outside of what is required by the system that produces it and on which it is entirely dependent. The individual is, in this conception, reduced to a mechanical and *external* poverty (see this term), to "free particles" that presuppose and impose the tests of the marketplace, statistics, and the electoral logic of democracies.
- The need for an invisible hand (the modern God), a minimal but ferocious and all-powerful State (the absolute monarch) to enforce strict respect for a pitiless game in which "individuals" – these new Robinson Crusoes, who are as "wild" as they can be in the struggle for profit and success but who, at the same time, as a *multitude* of "contract fodder," the "cannon fodder" of supermarkets, stadiums, and political or religious rallies – "are no more than grains of sand, units of greed, pathetic warring billiard balls, whose every effort to differentiate themselves only bogs them down further in a great equivalence."[1]

Nodes of forces (see *focal point/focalization*). Concept used by Gabriel Tarde, from whose perspective (very close to the thought of Proudhon) "all beings in nature behave as if they were nodes of forces, which seek to enter into combination with other beings, to constitute new, more complex nodes of forces, which then combine with still others, and so on…All beings [are] forces, *appetites* [Tarde also says 'desires'], which seek to join one another."[2]

Nomad (see *war/warlike* and *nomos*).

Nomos (see *war/warlike* and *autonomy*). A Greek word that, in its later career, refers simultaneously to Law, Property, and the division of territory. These are three reasons to refuse a concept that, via the dichotomy of "autonomy" and "heteronomy," comes to infect libertarian thought itself by suggesting that autonomy could consist in refusing an external law in order to give oneself one's own laws, when in fact all law inevitably comes from the outside (see *autonomy*). The captive of States, legislators, and the administrators and guardians of property, the word *nomos* nonetheless has a rather different origin – a nomadic origin, opposed to all law, to all property conceived in the form of a division of spaces and goods (see *localism*). In the beginning, *nomos* and its derivative *nomas* designated spaces without boundaries, unfenced pastures, and the herds that traversed these pastures. As Deleuze and Guattari emphasize,

---

1 Ibid. 55.
2 Milet, *Gabriel Tarde et la philosophie de l'histoire*, 172-173.

[T]he nomadic trajectory may follow trails or customary routes, it does not fulfill the function of the sedentary road, which is to *parcel out a closed space to people,* assigning each person a share and regulating the communication between shares. The nomadic trajectory does the opposite: it *distributes people (or animals) in an open space,* one that is indefinite and noncommunicating. The nomos came to designate the law, but that was originally because it was distribution, a mode of distribution. It is a very special kind of distribution, one without division into shares, in a space without borders or enclosure...[It] is in this sense that it stands in opposition to the law or the *polis,* as the backcountry, a mountainside, or the vague expanse around a city [emphasis in original].[1]

It is in this sense, too, that *nomos* at its origins, before it becomes law, can be compared to Ibn Khaldūn's distinction between *Hadara* as the place of the city and *Badiya* as *nomos,* the outside of the city,[2] or to the *bilad as-siba* of the Berbers, the "rebel country," "rebellious margin," or "fringe of anarchy," "this space refractory to the authority of the State...which knows neither God nor master" of which Hélène Claudot-Hawad speaks in her introduction to a collection of poems by the libertarian Tuareg, Hawad.[3]

Nonviolence (see *violence, war* and *insurrection*). An important tactical concept for the libertarian movement in its struggle against dominatory institutions and forces, which helps to destroy these from within (see *subversion*) and to prevent *revolts* and *insurrections* from themselves adopting the oppressive violence of the dominatory and external relations that they are intended to combat, from turning into new sources of oppression, domination, and relations that are unacceptable from a libertarian point of view. But when it is transformed into a central concept of the libertarian project (see *ideomania*) – organizing the whole of this project around its own demands and its own imaginary – nonviolence always risks vitiating the emancipatory qualities of

---

1   Deleuze and Guattari, *A Thousand Plateaus,* 380.

2   Ibn Khaldūn, *The Muqaddima: An Introduction to History (Abridged),* trans. Franz Rosenthal (Princeton, NJ: Princeton University Press, 1969), 93.

3   Hawad, *Le Coude grinçant de l'anarchie* (Paris: Méditerranée, 1998).

    (Translator's note: See also Georg Gugelberger, "Tuareg (Tamazight) Literature and Resistance: The Case of Hawad," in *The Desert Shore: Literatures of the Sahel,* ed. Christopher Wise [Boulder, CO: Lynne Rienner Publishers, 2001], 101-126 and *Poems for the Millennium,* vol. 4, *The University of California Book of North African Literature,* ed. Pierre Joris and Habib Tengour [Berkeley, CA: University of California Press, 2013], 529-534.)

the movement that animates it, separating it from its own capacities, obliging it to accept and internalize *symbolic* forms (see this term) of domination and violence that are more effective than ever within the current framework of economic and political liberalism.

Objective. The objective is doubly refused by anarchism: in its spatial dimension, when one speaks of an "objective" fact; in its temporal dimension, when one speaks of the objective to be attained. In both cases, it is a question of returning to the old distinction between "objects" and "subjects" in which, under the guise of distinguishing between two hierarchical classes of beings (objects and subjects), one constantly attempts to reduce all that exists to the rank of mere objects, pitilessly subjected to a transcendent and external order in which the only subject tolerated is identified with God and the State. For anarchism, there are only subjects, or rather *subjectivities* (see this term), as variable in what constitutes them (in size, quality, and nature of the beings thus associated) as the infinity of collective beings that reality contains.

Objects (see *tools/weapons*). Because it refuses any dualism, any differentiation based on the opposition between culture and nature, human and nonhuman, in libertarian thought, objects are a component of the world in which we live, like other collective beings, no different in any respect other than their degree of power and *freedom* (or autonomy).[1] In other words, as reflected by the old ethnological concept of the "fetish" and as certain currents in contemporary sociology demonstrate,[2] objects are not neutral and passive instruments, pro-

---

1   "[S]pontaneity, at the lowest degree in unorganized beings, higher in the plants and animals, attains, under the name of freedom, its plenitude in man" (Proudhon, *De la Justice*, 3:403).
2   See, for example, Bruno Latour, "On Interobjectivity," *Mind, Culture, and Activity* 3.4 (1996): 228-245. On the historical and spatial extension of the autonomy and the subjectivity of objects to technical arrangements as temporally and spatially extensive as a 19th-century metallurgical company, see Daniel Colson, *La Compagnie des fonderies, forges et aciéries de Saint-Étienne (1865-1914). Autonomie et subjectivité techniques* (Saint-Étienne: Publications

duced once and for all by an external force of another nature, endowed only with their physical qualities (weight, density, shape, etc.) – instruments that would submissively obey the intentions, the goals, and the injunctions of the masters who conceived them. On the contrary, an object has its own force and quality that stem from the nature of the activity or collective arrangement to which it belongs, as well as from the nature of the situation in which it takes on meaning and to which, in return, it gives meaning and effect. This force belonging to the object acts upon all the collective beings, including human beings, with which the object is associated at a given moment. An anarchist to whom one gives a Kalashnikov, an office, a dress, or a screwdriver, becomes each time another man (or another woman), often with unforeseeable or surprising effects. These effects are not only or primarily due to the social and symbolic meanings of the objects possessed, but also to the force of their arrangement and the way in which this force can take on meaning in the context of human activity.

One (unity) (see *multiplicity* and *anarchy*). Following Antonin Artaud, Deleuze and Guattari explain that "anarchy and unity are one and the same thing, not the unity of the One, but a much stranger unity that can only characterize the multiple."[1] Libertarian thought does not reject the idea of the one. It is content to strip this word of its capital letter and to give it a rather different signification. In a sense close to Whitehead's, anarchism considers that "one" always designates the *singularity* of a being (see *thing*), in the sense of the definite or indefinite articles "a," "an," "the" ("an" angry crowd, "the" Gryffe Bookstore, "the" construction site on strike), the demonstratives "this" and "that" ("this" sunset, "that" angry crowd), or the relative terms "which," "that," "who" ("who" eats today? "how" is this crevice to be opened? "the" soldier "who" deserts). In other words, as Whitehead puts it, "the term *many* presupposes the term *one,* and the term *one* presupposes the term *many*."[2] This is why the anarchist project has been so readily able to recognize itself in the formulation of the delegate from the town of Sète at the international congress at Geneva of August 1882: "We are united because we are divided."[3] This is why it has every reason to recognize itself in Whitehead's remark that "the ultimate metaphysical principle is the advance from disjunction to conjunction, creating a novel entity other than the entities given in disjunction"[4] (see *resultant* and *tension*)

---

de l'Université de Saint-Étienne, 1998).

1   Deleuze and Guattari, *A Thousand Plateaus*, 158 (trans.: modifications my own).

2   Whitehead, *Process and Reality*, 25.

3   Qtd. in Jean Maitron, *Histoire du mouvement anarchiste en France: 1880-1914* (Paris: Société universitaire d'editions et de librairie, 1955),105.

4   Whitehead, *Process and Reality*, 21.

and to endorse the English philosopher's motto: "the self-enjoyment of being one among many, and of being one arising out of the composition of many."[1]

Oppression. The *intimate* and *subjective* perception of a general order in which some collective forces are subjected to the domination of other collective forces – molded, crushed, or denied by them. Subjectively, the feeling of oppression is above all negative, because it is defined and produced mainly by the oppressive order (see *contradictions*). It is always at risk of becoming definitively fixed within this order through *ressentiment*. Only through revolt can the forces experiencing oppression escape from the order that crushes them and subjects them to its own will, bring forth other forces outside of this order, and thereby destroy it and attempt to compose a new world in their turn (see *analogy*).

Order (system) (see *plane of consistency*). A partial and dominatory organization that attempts, through selection and repression, to subject the totality of that which exists to its own particular *raison d'être*. If *anarchism* is the enemy of all order, whatever it be – the "orders" that one receives as commands or the rationales that justify them – it is in the name of an emancipation of the totality of that which exists, of a power of being that would no longer be separated from its own capacities. In this sense, as Bakunin puts it, anarchy can be identified with "the order of life."

Organization (see *movement*). An unfortunate term borrowed from biology to designate *militant* groupings (see this term) and the bond that links them. This crude concept attempts to isolate elements, to treat them on a hierarchical basis (hands/head, bottom/top, etc.), and to subject them to a whole that would assign them their function and value. As *collective forces* (see this term), libertarian groupings (unions, groups properly speaking, or any other kind of association) obey a logic other than that of organization – a logic based on *affinity*, *intimacy*, and *autonomy* (see these terms), without hierarchy or external dependence.

Other (the other) (see *outside/inside* and *power of the outside*). Anarchy and the anarchist are often categorized as disconnection and egoism, an exaggerated affirmation of the individual, the absolute independence of beings, and thus the incapacity to perceive others and, consequently, to accept the rules and the constraints necessitated by cohabitation with them. This superficial interpretation fails to perceive the originality of the libertarian project and its thought. For the anarchist, the other is within oneself. It is by opening up to this other that one contains in oneself that it is possible to open onto other

---

1   Ibid. 145.

collective forces and, at the same time, to refuse the dominatory, blind, and limiting exteriority of the bonds that the existing order attempts to impose on us. For libertarian thought, opening to the other does not take place through a denial of oneself – the denial of selfishness and the acceptance of the external shackles that bind us to others – or obedience to roles and functions that are supposed to necessitate the sacrifice of our selves (see *subject*). On the contrary, for anarchism, opening up to the other is made possible by the will to *go to the limits* of what constitutes us: the limits of our desires, of the power that we possess, of this otherness that we contain and that alone can open us up to others, necessitating a relationship with them – an internal relationship, entirely inherent in the reality of collective beings – by means of an increase in power. This effective discovery of the other in ourselves generally takes place in the context of "an exceptional situation" (see *stoppage* and *event*), "the illumination of an exceptional event," "presenting from the outside the aspects of a revelation," as Simondon puts it – and as Nietzsche's Zarathustra demonstrates with the corpse of the tightrope walker fallen from his high wire, from whom the crowd turns away, since it has just lost the only function and *raison d'être* that the existing order recognized in it. But it is only by immediately withdrawing into oneself – like Zarathustra in his cave, far from the Procrustean bed of communication – that one can find a new relation with others, an emancipatory relation (see *solitude*).[1]

Outside/inside (see *exterior/interior, power of the outside*). The apparent paradox of anarchism could be formulated as follows: while it refuses all relations of externality – which are inevitably linked to domination – instead always affirming the primacy of the autonomy of beings, the primacy of their capacity for establishing relations from the interior of that which constitutes them (see *intimate, affinity, intuition*), anarchism just as vigorously rejects their pretense of wishing to be sufficient unto themselves. It rejects the *self-sufficiency*, necessarily dominatory, that inevitably leads beings (at the price of considerable suffering, misfortune, and oppression) to want to master the totality of that which exists within their own organizations, their own discourses, their own practices, within the *planes of reality* on which they unfold themselves, and thus within the inevitably limited forms of their individuality (see *individuation, totality/totalitarianism, ideomania*). In opposition to this self-sufficiency that

---

1   Friedrich Nietzsche, *Thus Spoke Zarathustra*, trans. Adrian Del Caro (Cambridge, UK: Cambridge University Press, 2006), 12 et passim; Simondon, *L'Individuation psychique et collective*,155 et passim. For an approach to the way in which Leibnizian monadology makes it possible to think this relationship between interior and exterior, the external other, as well as the other within oneself, cf. especially the allegory of the "baroque house" that Deleuze proposes in *The Fold*, 4 et passim.

leads to war – the external conflict of all with all – and domination, anarchist *autonomy* and the *will* or the *determination* that animate it are entirely directed toward the outside, toward the other, as what alone is capable (from a certain point of view and through particular methods of association) of increasing their power. This increase in power is not accomplished externally, by an addition of forces, but internally, by revealing the power and the *otherness* that each being contains within itself (see *monad, balancing of forces, more than oneself*). Since, according to Deleuze's formulation, the "inside" is only a "fold" of the outside – the "outside" is entirely inside beings, it is at the same time outside and inside – it is always ready to deploy its power within that which exists at a given moment, provided that these beings detach themselves from themselves, from the limited character of their present individuality, provided that they open, in joining with others, to the *indeterminate* that constitutes them as *subjects* (see this term), thereby forming freer and more powerful individualities.

P

Particular (see *government, universal, base,* and *private/public*). A 19th century libertarian notion employed in the sense nearest to its common usage. Indeed, as opposed to what its etymology and thus its scholastic sense might indicate, the "particular" refers neither to a part of a whole (see *localism*) nor to the concept of a particle or atom, but to the absolute singularity of the *collective beings* existing at a *given moment*. In this sense, each thing or being is particular and thus "a" particular, in the sense in which one speaks of an "odd sort" [*drôle de particulier*] or a "wild card" [*drôle de numéro*], implying that the cards themselves are wild [*lorsque les numéros prennent eux-mêmes la tangente*].[1]

Passage to the act (see *direct action, propaganda by the deed, anarchist chemistry,* and *symbols/signs*). The psychiatrist Gaëtan Gatian de Clérambault opposed "the two major kinds of delusions, ideational and active."[2] On one side, "a paranoid-interpretive ideal regime of significance": the delirium of Judge Schreber, who acts crazy, who believes himself to be pregnant with God's baby, but who continues to manage his money wisely. On the other side, "a passional, postsignifying subjective regime": the delirium of the sisters Christine and Lea Papin, for example, who seem to be perfectly proper maidservants and who abruptly, savagely assassinate their mistresses, or that of the rural farm laborers who suddenly "pass to the act," as it is said, and kill their bosses or set fire to haystacks and granges.[3] Deleuze and Guattari are not wrong to demonstrate how, while

---

1   Translator's note: the French word *particulier* means both "particular" and "an individual" – meanings activated, in various ways that are difficult to capture, in the wordplay closing this entry.

2   Deleuze and Guattari, *A Thousand Plateaus*, 121.

3   On the passage to the act of the rural arsonists, cf. Regina Schulte, *The Village in Court:*

they are generally understood on the register of the individual, via psychiatry (see *subject*), these two deliriums can also be related to classes or collective situations. The former relates to a bourgeois or dominant class, "[a] class with radiant, irradiating ideas (but of course!)," masters of signs or just inscribed in their order and profiting from these signs. The latter relates to a dominated class, subjected to the violence of the effects of this order in reality and reduced, in its impotence, "to linear, sporadic, partial, local actions."[1] However, with Michel de Certeau this time, and as opposed to Deleuze and Guattari, we can refuse to reduce these local and sporadic actions – in which actions substitute for ideas, acts for signs – to a mere "line of flight," a mere "passional" outburst, "authoritarian" and violent, within the dominant symbolic order.[2] Beyond their "linear" and asocial madness and violence, beyond or beneath their most extreme forms, passages to the act can also be related to a whole spectrum of "tactics," from the most imperceptible to the most violent. They can be collective or individual, but they are always deliberate, variegated, and continuously repeated. If metaphysics itself, with Nietzsche and Kierkegaard, can "be put into motion," "[made to] act, and [made to] carry out immediate acts,"[3] the passages to the act – beyond their "linear" and asocial madness and violence, beyond or beneath their most extreme forms – can also be related to an "to an "art of the weak" that "operates in isolated actions, on a case-by-case basis." This art of "seiz[ing] on the wing the possibilities that offer themselves at any given moment entails a different relation to time and space, taking advantage of "the cracks that particular conjunctions open in the surveillance of the proprietary powers" (see stoppage). Passages to the act reveal the dominant symbolic order's inability to control the totality of that which exists.[4] This is why, in *propaganda by the deed* and in the *direct action* of libertarian syndicalism and anarcho-syndicalism, passages to the act take on meaning, even in their most extreme dimensions, within an overall revolutionary project that aims to substitute another relation between signs and forces, words and things, significations and affects for the dominant order and the snares of the particular symbolic order that it deploys. This is a project in which, as Émile Pouget writes, "Direct Action, the manifestation of the workers' strength and determination, shows itself in accordance with circumstance and setting, through acts

---

Arson, Infanticide, and Poaching in the Court Records of Upper Bavaria, 1848-1910, trans. Barrie Selman (Cambridge: Cambridge University Press, 1994), 25-78.

1   Deleuze and Guattari, *A Thousand Plateaus*, 120-121.

2   On this point, see ibid. 121 et passim.

3   Deleuze, *Difference and Repetition*, 8.

4   See de Certeau, The *Practice of Everyday Life*, 37 (trans.: modifications my own). On this point also see Daniel Colson, "Anarcho-syndicalisme et pouvoir," in *Anarcho-syndicalisme et luttes ouvrières* (Lyon: ACL, 1985), 19 et passim.

that may well be very gentle, just as they might as easily be very violent," since there is no "form specific to direct action."[1]

Past (see *tradition*). "No more tradition's chains shall bind us!"[2] With this phrase, the anthem of the International, generally more felicitous in its other verses, attempted to pay tribute to the strength of the working class at the end of the 19th century and its feeling of its own power to imminently bring about – through its *will* alone (see this term) – another world. But it perpetuated the revolutionary and *voluntarist* illusion (see this term) of the communist and other regimes of the future ("dictatorships of the proletariat"), for which the totality of that which exists is reduced to the status of a blank slate upon which the party and its leaders, armed with Science and all the powers of the State, purport to inscribe the radiant future of the people. The libertarian conception of time is of an altogether different nature. The libertarian movement observes a multiple and qualitative time that corresponds to the duration belonging to each collective being and to the relations of composition, recomposition, and decomposition that increase, decrease, or destroy their power to act (see *eternal return*). If it were necessary at all costs to transpose libertarian duration onto the linear register of Marxist historical materialism, one would have to speak of *a priori* and *a posteriori* [*d'aval et d'amont*]. Anarchism, no less than Marxism, calls for a radical transformation of that which exists, but for anarchism, this coming transformation is not *a posteriori*, in the vacuity, the arbitrariness, the utopia of power and voluntarism. It is *a priori* (an *a priori* that is always present), in the infinity of *possibilities* (see this term) that reality contains, where human experimentation unfolds itself on a "*plane of immanence* or *of consistency* [see this term], which is always variable and is constantly being altered, composed and recomposed, by individuals and collectivities."[3]

Patriarchy (see *class* [*sexual*]).

People (see *mass* and *multitude*). A more or less mythical concept, which served throughout the 19th century (and beyond) to define the subject of revolutionary action, but also – in opposition to the big institutions and privileged classes – became the promise and the guarantor of a more just and true collective

---

1   Pouget, *Direct Action*, 23 (trans.: modifications my own).

2   Translator's note: this translation comes from Charles H. Kerr's long-popular translation of Eugène Pottier's "L'Internationale" (in *Songs of the Workers: On the Road, In the Jungles, and In the Shops* [Chicago: Industrial Workers of the World, 1919]). In the original French, the line reads "*Du passé faisons table rase*," which could be more faithfully rendered as "Let us wipe the slate of the past clean."

3   Deleuze, *Spinoza: Practical Philosophy*, 128.

life. Like other socialist currents, anarchism has long been linked to "the people," but without ever being duped by the mythic dimension of this concept. Proudhon is undoubtedly the most explicit on this point. For Proudhon, the "people," in the context of the 19th century, is first of all a "reality," a reality as complex and various as any other: diverse in its functions, sexes, ages, trades, positions, histories; diverse in *points of view* (see this term); in short, all that a society needs (and much is needed) in the present and the past in order to really exist. Therefore, the people constitutes a *force* and a *power* (see these terms) because of the richness and plurality of its components, and its consequently crucial and predominant role in the reproduction of society. But this real power, like any other power, is ambiguous. From its richness and its complexity, the diversity of the relations and elements that compose it, the contradictions that traverse and constitute it, the power of the people can produce equally diverse kinds of effects, transforming itself into an emancipatory force, passively accepting injustice and domination, or even becoming the object of other metamorphoses (Fascism, Nazism, Stalinism, xenophobia, and nationalisms of all kinds). For Proudhon (unlike Marx, for example), nothing is truly inscribed in history: neither what the future will be, nor the nature and quality of the forces that will combine to produce this future.

To this uncertainty resulting from the composite character of its reality must be added another ambiguity of the people (from an emancipatory point of view), this time pertaining to its size as a collective force and to the number of the forces that compose it. Because it is the *resultant* (see this term) of a *superabundance* of immediate, mutually entangled forces, the power of the people infinitely exceeds any consciousness that each of the elements, individuals, and groups comprising it can have of the role that it plays in this power. This power, then, tends to escape them and to mystify its own origin. Two dramatic consequences follow, from the perspective of emancipation:

- The power of the people changes from a material reality into a representation in which "everything becomes a fiction, a symbol, a mystery, an idol."[1] Separated from the material and immediate conditions that make it possible, the power of the people is transformed into a mysterious and transcendent power that comes from elsewhere, which the imagination of the people attributes at once to God and his representatives on Earth and to the State and all the bosses and tyrants who claim to incarnate this collective power, who claim to be its source.
- Incapable of perceiving that its power comes from its multiplicity and its internal differences, the people comes to believe, on the contrary,

---

1   Pierre-Joseph Proudhon, *The Principle of Federation*, trans. Richard Vernon (Toronto: U. of Toronto Press, 1979), 57.

that this power imperatively requires the unity and the uniformity that its character as a *resultant* confers on it: the "one nation, indivisible" of the republican State, the collective conformism that leads the people to refuse, with an extreme violence, any separation and any pluralism, any difference. A people is then transformed into "the People" – a *mass*, a plebs, a *multitude*, and a nation, a blind and limited, oppressive and totalitarian power, acting like a single man, at the service of all possible despots and despotisms, bosses, States, tyrants, Churches and religions.

Person (personalism) (see *bodies* and *indiscernibles*). In its most common usage, the "person" (and the apparent respect to which it is supposed to have a right) claims to embrace the totality of the human being, its body and its soul, the body as seat of the soul (the "body" of the poor, which one looks after, which one clothes and feeds, the "body" whose integrity and sacred character is guaranteed by law and religion). Sociologists like Pierre Bourdieu aptly demonstrate how this "person" rests on a double illusion: the scholastic and scientific illusion of the "self-conscious perceiving subject" that posits the world before it as an object, "as a spectacle or representation," but also the naive and immediate illusion of a human reality founded on "the self-evidence of the isolated, distinguished body," the self-evidence of the "biological individual" that is "situated" in a place, in physical space as well as in social space (see *localism*).[1] It is this last, most commonplace illusion of the biological individual to which one owes the division of labor between science and morality. The responsibility for measuring, weighing, counting, analyzing, preserving, and treating this individual like a thing falls to science. On the other hand, morality, on the basis of the self-evidence of the biological individual, leads us back to the "personalist" belief in "the uniqueness of the person." Against this double illusion, Bourdieu opposes *practical sense* (see this term) as a way to approach the "relation of immanence" that constitutes beings (the fact that their inside is only a singular fold of the outside, Deleuze would say). Bourdieu summarizes this by saying that any individual is "inhabited by the world it inhabits, *pre-occupied* by the world in which it actively intervenes, in an immediate relation of involvement, tension and attention, which constructs the world and gives it meaning [emphasis in original]."[2] With Proudhon, libertarian thought considers that "[t]

---

1   On all of this, cf. Pierre Bourdieu, *Pascalian Meditations*, trans. Richard Nice (Stanford, CA: Stanford University Press, 2000), 131-133, 142.

2   Ibid. 142. A way of being inhabited by the world in which one lives that takes place via the body, allowing Merleau-Ponty to affirm: "I inhabit my body, and by means of it I inhabit things" (Maurice Merleau-Ponty, *Nature: Course Notes From the Collège de France*, trans. Robert Vallier [Evanston, IL: Northwestern University Press, 2003], 74 [trans.:

he living human being is a group, like the plant or the crystal, but to a higher degree than those others."[1] Indeed, the person is only the *resultant* of a long labor of domestication and selection – both physical and spiritual – which, contrary to what it claims, attempts to deny the power and reality of the body, of that which the human being is capable. Through education (this "education for death" of which Bernard Edelman[2] speaks), the human being acquires a very particular *consciousness* of itself, dictated by the totality of the moral and behavioral rules, identities, and regulations that society requires of it, which it imposes in its turn on its body, by disciplining it into the docility, permanence, and unity that the social order requires. Whereas the *human body* (see this term) and particularly its brain, mobilize "our most immediate forces as well as those which, in terms of their origin, are *the most distant*,"[3] whereas they "are mechanisms for the transmission of psychic impulses that come from afar and are intended to travel afar,"[4] and which they seek to render comprehensible by a great number of symptoms and signs, the consciousness inculcated by the existing order is blind to these signs – or rather translates them into a "*code*...that inverts, falsifies, and filters what is expressed through the body."[5] "Grasped by consciousness," the body "*dissociates itself* from the impulses that flow through it...Its 'cerebral' activity therefore selects only those forces that preserve this activity, or, rather, those that can be *assimilated* to it. And the body adopts only those *reflexes* that allow it to *maintain* itself *for* this cerebral activity, just as the latter henceforth *adopts the body as its own product*."[6] As the "*instrument* of consciousness," the body "is no longer synonymous with itself." Separated from its own capacities, it ultimately becomes "the homonym of the 'person,'" its sacred seat: a transcendent and mysterious "person,"[7] identical to itself, whatever its age, its desires, or the situations its duration forces it to endure (even if it sometimes loses an arm, a leg, or its illusions thereby); a "person" guaranteed by its social security number and the identity card that accompanies it for life; a "person" having all the considerations necessary to its status as person, as long as it manages to narrowly circumscribe within the narrow circle of law and morality the *anarchy* of the forces and possibilities that its body contains.

---

modifications my own]).

1   Proudhon, *Philosophy of Progress*, 23 (trans.: modifications my own).

2   Edelman, *Nietzsche, un continent perdu.*

3   Klossowski, *Nietzsche and the Vicious Circle*, 23 (trans.: modifications my own).

4   Milet, *Gabriel Tarde et la philosophie de l'histoire*, 172.

5   Klossowski, *Nietzsche and the Vicious Circle*, 26.

6   Ibid. 27.

7   Ibid.

Perspectivism (perspective). The theory of knowledge based on the *point of view* as *resultant* of a given *collective force*. Philosophically, libertarian perspectivism can be linked to two philosophical traditions: that of Nietzsche, on the side of *force*, and that of Leibniz (an explicit point of reference in Proudhon's work), on the side of the *autonomy* of beings.

Perversion (see *sexuality*).

Pity (see *implication* and *suffering*).

Place/site (see *localism*).

Plane of immanence (plane of consistency, plane of composition) (see *nature, composition*, and *indeterminate*). The multitude of *planes of reality* on which our lives depend, within which we act, and which we must continually invent, define the spaces within which emancipatory forces can emerge. These forces tend to transform the *situations* within which they unfold and, by joining other emancipatory forces acting on other planes of reality, may constitute more extensive, powerful, and free beings or arrangements of forces.

This possibility for an association or composition of emancipatory collective forces operates within a totality that libertarian thought generally calls *Nature* (see this term). As Bakunin writes, "Nature is the sum of actual transformations of things that are and will ceaselessly be produced within its womb... the universal, natural, necessary, and real, but in no way predetermined, preconceived, or foreknown combination of the infinity of particular actions and reactions which all things having real existence incessantly exercise upon one another."[1]

What the libertarian vocabulary calls "nature," one can also call, following Deleuze's reading of Spinoza, the *plane of immanence* or the *plane of consistency* – or even the *plane of composition*: "one Nature for all bodies, one Nature for all individuals, a Nature that is itself an individual varying in an infinite number of ways. What is involved is no longer the affirmation of a single substance, but rather the laying out of a *common plane of immanence* on which all bodies, all minds, and all individuals are situated [emphasis in original]."[2] "Nature, the plane of immanence or consistency, which is always variable and is constantly being altered, composed and recomposed, by individuals and collectivities."[3]

Within this Nature, on this common plane of immanence, there exist an infinity of possible worlds. There is, for example, the world of the tick, as

---

1 Bakunin, *The Political Philosophy of Bakunin*, 53.
2 Deleuze, *Spinoza: Practical Philosophy*, 53.
3 Ibid. 128.

Deleuze describes it, "a world with only three affects, in the midst of all that goes on in the immense forest":[1] an affect of light (to climb up a branch), an olfactive affect (to drop on the mammal passing under the branch), and a thermal affect (to seek the area with the least hair and the most body heat). Many of these worlds – from the tick to the great ancient civilizations – can coexist within Nature[2] without too much interference, indifferent to whatever exists outside of themselves. But because they all operate by selecting (positively and negatively) what suits them within nature, by decomposing the relations that do not suit them and recomposing them into relations that do suit them, these worlds are all, more or less and in multiple ways – potentially or actually, voluntarily or involuntarily, and according to the number and the nature of the affects of which they are capable – in a situation of predation and competition. They struggle to affirm their own reality to the detriment of the worlds that are foreign to them, which they try to decompose or to appropriate, to subject to their own relations, in order to avoid themselves being decomposed and recomposed within the framework of other existing or possible worlds. This is why collective beings, as the combined modalities of a particular world, which may or may not have been captured (in a more or less limiting or damaging way) by wider beings and worlds, are marked, in their existence and coexistence, by struggle, *revolt*, and *domination*: struggling to affirm their own existence and their own reasons for being; revolting to escape the damaging or lethal effects of a more powerful being; dominating in order to subject other beings and other worlds to their own particular world, their own reason for being. There is an infinity of worlds, and each one can thus be evaluated from the perspective of emancipation according to its capacity to include the greatest possible number of relations, to liberate the maximum of the *possibilities* (see this term) that Nature contains, while avoiding reducing this to the sterile and limiting struggle of all against all, to avoid exhausting its own power in the domination, mutilation, and destruction of other collective beings.[3] It is in this sense, too, that libertarian emancipatory struggle can be characterized as a necessary *destruction* of the existing orders, since they are themselves founded on the destruction or repression and rejection of what is outside of themselves, on the domination or exploitation of others. It is then a matter of a subversive struggle (see *subversion*) on the part of all the forces that have been dominated and damaged to emancipate themselves from the narrow, hegemonic regimes that separate them from what they are capable of, to affirm a general and emancipatory recomposition of Nature as the totality of that which exists.

---

1   Ibid. 124-125.

2   By means of spatial separation, differences in scale, and a great number of other reasons to ignore one another even when they have occasion to meet.

3   As demonstrated by the relation to the world defined by *labor* (see this term).

For libertarian struggle deserving of the name, then, it is not only a matter of selecting a particular world (even what one takes to be the best of all possible worlds) and imposing it on others; it is a matter of undertaking – starting with the *affirmation* of the dominated forces – the construction of an emancipated world that would coincide with the plane of immanence itself, with nature as a whole, in a movement perpetually to be resumed.[1]

Planes of reality (planes of composition, worlds) (see *common, exterior/interior,* and *plane of immanence*). *Collective beings* (see this term) are manifold and changing. This multiplicity and this ceaseless becoming of that which constitutes both ourselves and others depend partly on the diversity of the worlds within which our existence unfolds. We are not the same at our various workplaces, in our experiences of love, at the wheel of a car, or within the framework of the family, a security crew, an armed militia, etc. These situations, ordinary or exceptional, belong to so many distinct planes of reality – actual or potential, enduring or fleeting, prolonged or temporary – which, each time, select and reveal the *possibilities* (see this term) that we and others contain, that of which we are capable, both for *good* and for *bad* (see these terms). These planes of reality or existence simultaneously arise 1) from the subjective *affirmation* of the beings that the planes constitute and that give the planes their being in turn; 2) from the more general, dominant, and external *order* or *orders* that (via the State, Law, Capital, etc.) render them compatible and impose their own demands upon them; but also 3) from a profusion of forces and possibilities foreign to and independent of these orders, which these orders capture or repel, but which generally escape them and, even in their most fleeting expressions, allow us to glimpse the possibility of other *orders,* or even the possibility of an order that would consist in the absence of any particular order, a general arrangement of forces that would express the greater power of the totality of that which exists (see *stoppage* and *plane of immanence*).

In this fettered and distorted world, the reproduction of *order* always entails restricting the power of the beings that this order coopts, subjecting them to its own logic and expelling from itself or repressing within itself the infinite

---

1   "It is no longer a matter of utilizations or captures, but of sociabilities and communities…
     Now we are concerned, not with a relation of point to counterpoint, nor with the selection
     of a world, but with a symphony of Nature, the composition of a world that is increasingly
     wide and intense" (Deleuze, *Spinoza: Practical Philosophy,* 126). We can find an enigmatic
     formulation of this "emancipated world" in Pierre Dupont's "Chant des ouvriers [Song of
     the Workers]" (1846): "Let us love and, when we can,/Let us meet to drink a round,/Let the
     cannon fall silent or erupt –/We drink, we drink, we drink/To the *independence of the world!"*
     (qtd. in Walter Benjamin, *The Arcades Project,* ed. Rolf Tiedemann, trans. Howard Eiland
     and Kevin McLaughlin [Cambridge, MA: Belknap Press, 1999], 710; emphasis my own).

remainder that constantly returns to threaten it by revealing the possibilities that it excludes. Within this framework, the relation and coordination of the various planes of reality that comprise our life (as sexual beings, workers, motorists, militants, philatelists, etc.) is not only managed externally – i.e., via the imposition of standardized procedures, representations, or restrictive codes and uniform models of action – nor only via the objective requirements of the law, the marketplace, and morality – procedures and demands that secure the State, Capital, and all manner of Churches and religious institutions. This coordination and coherence of the various planes of reality – which are so heterogeneous, so open to this infinite remainder that the dominant order neither manages to enclose or repel nor to separate from its capacities – also makes use of qualities shared by all the forces that these various *planes of reality* mobilize at a given moment, qualities *internal* to these forces (see *exterior/interior*), to that which produces them as desire and as imperative. These foundational qualities, carefully selected and perpetuated by the dominant order, ensure a relation of *analogy* (see this term) between the forces, binding them tightly together and guaranteeing the "correspondence" of all.

Thus, libertarian action is not primarily an *extrinsic* attack on all forms of domination (see *revolt*), nor, above all, does it take the equally extrinsic form of a broad "resistance front" that would comprise all dominated forces, on whatever plane of reality they occupy, on the sole shared basis of this domination and this single struggle, according to the absurd general principle that the enemies of our enemies are inevitably our friends. From a multitude of revolts, minuscule or general, intrinsic to all that exists, through "a passional struggle, an inexpiable affective combat in which one risks death,"[1] libertarian action attempts first of all to select and liberate new forces within situations and beings and in the interstices of the existing order. It attempts to create an emancipatory plane of existence in common that can traverse the totality of present worlds and realities, one that would someday perhaps be capable of recomposing the totality of that which exists, thus coinciding with what Deleuze calls the *plane of immanence* (see this term).

Plastic force (see *direct action, anarchy, apeiron*, and *limitlessness of the limited*). In *De la Création de l'ordre*, Proudhon explains how "labor is the plastic force [*force plastique*] of society,"[2] a definition to which he returns in a more explicit way in *De la Justice*, where he explains that "labor, one and identical in its domain [*plan*], is infinite in its applications, like creation itself."[3] However, it would be rather short-sighted to apply the concept of an *indeterminate* and plastic power

---

1   Deleuze, *Essays Critical and Clinical,* 145; see *common notions.*

2   Proudhon, *De la Création de l'ordre dans l'humanité,* 421.

3   Proudhon, *De la Justice,* 3:89.

solely to the *plane* of *labor* (see these terms) when it actually pertains to all forms of "creation" and is located by Proudhon equally at the source of, for example, artistic creation, love, or warlike activities (see *war/warlike*).[1] Present in all of the realities within which human activity unfolds itself, the concept of plastic force makes it possible to indicate that "stranger unity" of which Deleuze speaks, "that can only characterize the multiple."[2] This is a unity that Bakunin sometimes calls a *composed unity* or, more frequently, *nature* ("Nature is the sum of actual transformations of things that are and will ceaselessly be produced within its womb"[3]), but also *life, solidarity,* or *universal causality*. It is a reality that is singular and unfinalized, without beginning or end, yet always in motion, which exists only through an infinity of particular realities, each of which expresses the whole, each of which depends on the others, through an infinity of possible relations.[4] It is in this sense – the most *indeterminate* sense possible (see this term) – that Émile Pouget employs the concept of plasticity to specify what he means by direct action, another important concept of libertarian thought that cannot be reduced to a mere technique or identified solely with trade unionism. Since "force is the origin of every movement and every action," it follows that "Direct Action has no specific form." Through direct action, the future, the present, and the diversity of emancipatory forces find themselves united: "The tactical superiority of Direct Action consists precisely in its unparalleled plasticity: organizations actively engaged in the practice are not required to confine themselves to beatific waiting for the advent of social changes. They live in the present with all possible combativity, sacrificing neither the present to the future, nor the future to the present."[5] It is also in this sense that the plastic force of libertarian discourse can be related:

- on the one hand, to Nietzsche's *will to power* or *species activity*, this activity in the place of which "history presents us with races, peoples, classes, Churches," this species activity onto which "are grafted social organizations, associations, communities of a reactive character, parasites which cover it over and absorb it";[6]

---

1   See Proudhon, *La Guerre et la paix*, 31-32. On the relations between artistic activities, love, and work as manifestations of the same "creation" in Proudhon, cf. Rubin, *Realism and Social Vision in Courbet and Proudhon*.

2   Deleuze and Guattari, *A Thousand Plateaus*, 158 (trans.: modifications my own).

3   Bakunin, *The Political Philosophy of Bakunin*, 53.

4   "The world, in spite of the infinite diversity of beings which compose it, is one and the same" (Mikhail Bakunin, "On Science and Authority," trans. Steven Cox, in *Selected Writings*, ed. Arthur Lehning [London: Jonathan Cape, 1973], 159).

5   Pouget, *Direct Action*, 23 and 13. (trans.: modifications my own)

6   Deleuze, *Nietzsche and Philosophy*, 138.

- on the other hand, to the concept of the *potential*, which Simondon uses to account for processes of *individuation*, or to the *univocal being* of Deleuze, this "power" irreducible to the social forms and individuals that it helps to produce by acting within them "as a transcendental principle: as a plastic, anarchic and nomadic principle, contemporaneous with the process of *individuation*, no less capable of dissolving and destroying individuals than of constituting them temporarily."[1]

Platform, platformism (see *synthesis*).

Plenitude (see *generosity*, *power*, and *monad*).

Pluralism (libertarian pluralism) (see *monism*). A synonym for *multiplicity*. However, on the plane of the libertarian movement, it can be considered in terms of an ensemble of federated forces that Proudhon defines as a "cluster of *autonomies*."

Plurality (see *anarchy*, *multiplicity*, and *one*).

Point of view. Contrary to the common usage of the word, a point of view is not an opinion (be it vague or well-defined, broad or restrictive; see *synthesis* and *platform*) formulated within a language and its range of available meanings. As the origin of the word itself indicates (one must always return to the origin), points of view are always related to the positions in the world and in reality from which they emanate (the "point" from which one departs, from which one has a "view"). Even when it presents itself as the most ideal or abstract, an idea is, first of all, the product of a material arrangement of forces occupying a particular position at a *given moment* within the totality of material forces that constitute reality. Its quality and import closely depend on the arrangement that produces it. Every "point of view" is partial and partisan – from whence the need to multiply "points of view" and to constantly experiment with the ways in which they are associated. This is necessary not in terms of their ideological *resultant*, which is merely a field for games of logic, bad faith, and quibbles. Instead, it must be done "from *below* [à la base]," as has been said elsewhere (see *base*) – i.e., on the level of the collective arrangements of forces that produce these points of view – and, further, on the level of the forces that constitute these arrangements – forces themselves made up of other forces, etc. It is in its infinite capacity to decompose order and reality that *anarchy* finds the reason and the force needed for an attempt to reconstruct an order and a reality that would be entirely different (see *genealogy* and *evaluation*).

---

1   Deleuze, *Difference and Repetition*, 38.

Political commissar (see *chaplain*).

Political vitalism (see *vital* and *vitalism*).

Positive anarchy (see *negation, more than oneself, balancing of forces, tension,* and *power of the outside*). A Proudhonian concept that is also used to dissociate the libertarian project from the negativity and *ressentiment* that the struggle against relations of domination is always likely to evoke when it is not transformed at once by *refusal, rupture,* and revolt into an affirmative force able to recompose the world differently and in an emancipatory fashion. Positive anarchy is the affirmation of a new dynamic and a new arrangement capable of liberating collective forces from their confinement and enabling them *to do all that they are capable of.*

Possession (property) (see *body*). Proudhon, in his youth the author the famous slogan, "Property is theft!" has often been accused of having become, in the twilight of his life, a defender of this very property, which was, in his eyes, a necessary protection against the demands of the State, but also (in the form of "small property"), under the ossified gaze of dogmatic Marxism, proof of the bourgeois character of one of anarchism's principal theorists. This accusation, which is (from certain points of view) not completely unfounded, nonetheless masks and ignores a much more radical direction. In his *Solution du problème social*, written in 1848, Proudhon exclaims, "between property and communi-ty, I will build a world."[1] It is this world that the concept of possession makes it possible to glimpse. Possession and property are not lesser or greater degrees of a homogeneous right to the ownership and enjoyment of that which exists. Each of these two terms is a point of departure for a different construction of the world. And each, in imposing itself, changes the meaning of the other.

Taken as a point of departure, property (and its weak juridical variant, possession) tends to carve reality into fixed entities external to one another, *pars extra partes*, which draw their identity from this proprietary faculty of occupying the same place for a determinate length of time, a place from which anything else is excluded. On the contrary, the perspective of possession at-tempts to define an entirely new mode of "property," one that "does not yet exist," Proudhon tells us, and that holds implications for our very conception of existence as such.[2]

In this sense, libertarian thought converges with the recently rediscovered theories of Gabriel Tarde. In place of a conception of the world founded on

---

1   Pierre-Joseph Proudhon, *Solution du problème social* in **Œuvres completes**, vol. 6 (Paris: Lacroix, 1868), 131.

2   Pierre-Joseph Proudhon, *Théorie de la propriété* (Paris: Lacroix, 1871), 231.

"being," libertarian thought posits a conception founded on "having." In place of the "I am" of Descartes, which separates human beings from a reality that is external to them (a reality that can then be denied), it posits a having, so that "I am" what I have, in the sense that what I possess defines what I am. The world ceases to be comprised of self-contained beings appropriating one another in an extrinsic way in the manner of the Cartesian "subject," "master and possessor of nature," a "subject" that possesses various "objects" (including other subjects) or nothing. On the contrary, "reality," as it is conceived by libertarian thought, refers to an infinity of *collective forces* (see this term) or, in the vocabulary of Tarde, "impulses" that strive to manifest themselves, "wills" that seek to express themselves, to do all that they are capable of (see *will*). Possession can then be transformed into "properties," but properties without "proprietors," properties in the physical sense of the word, as when one speaks of the "properties of a body," that which a body is capable of by virtue of the forces that it composes and its manner of composing them. This conception forms part of a general line of thinking in which, as Jean-Clet Martin and Jean Milet put it, the crude representations of the existing order, "walled in by rigid categories of being, find themsel[ves]…overthrown in favor of the singular, the individual, the multiplicity of individuals that populates each individuality," giving way to a world made up of "nodes of forces" or "latent desires" able to compose an infinity of *possible* worlds (see this term).[1]

Possibilities (see *chaos* and *power of the outside*). "In the middle of the night/he asked for the sun/he wanted the sun/he demanded the sun/In the middle, in the very middle of the night…"[2] Without the idea of possibilities, the libertarian *will* (see this term) to a radical transformation of the current world is unthinkable. In the libertarian conception, however, a possibility is not at all a utopia, a mere "idea," not a thing that should be made real by some unspecified miracle of violence or leap into the unknown. For libertarian thought, the possible is already there, as real as the order that prohibits it from expressing what it is capable of. This libertarian sense of possibility can be related, via Proudhon, to Leibniz's theory of *monads* (see this term) and of the frequently mocked "best of all possible worlds." For Leibniz, there is an infinity of possible worlds among which God has chosen "the best" – the world in which we live – that is thus a necessarily harmonious world (since it is the best) in which everything has its *raison d'être* in relation to other things. Voltaire had

1   Milet, *Gabriel Tarde et la philosophie de l'histoire* and Jean-Clet Martin, preface to *L'Opposition universelle: Essai d'un théorie des contraires,* Gabriel Tarde (Le Plessis-Robinson, France: Institut Synthélabo pour le progrès de la connaissance, 1999).

2   Jean Tardieu, "Complainte de l'homme exigeant," in *Monsieur, monsieur* (Paris: Gallimard, 1951), 74.

no difficulty mocking the naïve (and thus odious) character of this conception, in light of the absurdity and injustice of this supposedly "best of all possible worlds." But as a cynical and self-serving Deist, Voltaire did not perceive the way in which Leibniz's theory might take on a very different sense if the divine mortgage were to be lifted. With the death of God, the plurality of possible worlds ceases to be subjected to a transcendent will that had chosen, from the *exterior* (see this term), the "best" from among them.[1] If the existing world is the "best," it is said to be so in three ways: 1) because it exists; 2) because other worlds do not exist elsewhere (neither in the divine will nor in the radiant future of socialism); 3) because this existing world, as odious as its current order may be, contains the totality of possible worlds. All these possible worlds coexist, generally in the form of *chaos* and *violence*, and thus in the *sadness*, *death*, and *oppression* (see these terms) denounced by Voltaire. Amid this chaos, from the *interior* of this superabundance of possible worlds (thus in a strictly immanent manner, without "God, nor Caesar nor Tribune!"),[2] and by experimentation, the libertarian movement attempts to make "the best" of these worlds emerge, one that would express in its plenitude the totality of that which exists, the power of being.

Potential (see *plastic force* and *possibilities*). A concept that Simondon uses to characterize the power of being that is at the origin of all possible collective beings, a being that is never at rest, that is "metastable," always in a state of becoming and transformation.

Power [pouvoir, puissance] (collective power) (see *anti-authoritarian, collective force, freedom, entelechy, virility*, and *plastic force*). As libertarian thought affirms – from Déjacque, Stirner, Proudhon, and Bakunin to Malatesta – power and freedom are two sides of the same reality. Every power is a freedom, every freedom is a power. The power of a being lies in its potential to go to the limits of its capacities, i.e., to go beyond its current *limits* (see this term), to compose a greater power and thus a greater freedom in association with others. To better understand the significance of the concept of power in libertarian thought, it is necessary to dismiss two uses of this word: one erudite, the other mundane or everyday.

---

1   On the rereading of Leibniz opened up by the death of God, in which the monad ceases to presuppose "the substance and identity of being [God] to found its activity," but, on the contrary, makes it possible "to explain the diversity and metamorphosis of being" on the basis of its own multiplicity and heterogeneity, cf. Maurizio Lazzarato, postscript to *Monadologie et sociologie*, 106.

2   Translator's note: this is another reference to Eugène Pottier's anthem for the International Workingmen's Association.

To begin with, the erudite usage. In libertarian thought, any collective arrangement or being has a specific and effective power: a physical power corresponding to the particular extent and mass of this being within the "universal movement" of all that exists.[1] However, it also has a subjective power, in the form of a specific interiority, a *spontaneity*, as Proudhon says, that corresponds to the quality and complexity of the relations internal to each of these arrangements, to the greater or lesser harmony of the functions associated with their being. This subjective power is expressed in a being's "activity" and in the "end" that it contains.[2] In this respect, libertarian thought contests a whole traditional and philosophical conception of power. For Proudhon – as for Spinoza, Leibniz and, later, Nietzsche – any power is an "active power," equipped with a "specific will" and thus with an equally specific "end."[3] As the "objective" of a force that attempts to do all that it is capable of, this "end" proper to each collective being, "actively pursued," is not really an "extrinsic" goal existing in itself or a final cause (see *entelechy*). For Proudhon, the end is not a cause but an effect (see *resultant*), a creation of the arrangement that produces it. And the "will" that pursues it (in a sense very close to Nietzsche) is nothing but a "will" to "power," the will of such-and-such a power as the twofold resultant or effect of a given arrangement, endowed with a particular quality. The end is not extrinsic to the activity that brings this end into being by pursuing it, to the power that makes this activity possible, or to the collective being that defines and produces this power. It is immanent to the process that seems to pursue it and to have arisen for its sake.[4] In this sense, any being, human or nonhuman – by definition, a collective being – has, to various "degrees," a "power of its own," a conception that Proudhon formulates as follows: "[P]ower exists in each being…it is specific to this being, inherent in its nature,… it belongs to its substratum or subject, which is individual, existing by itself and independent of all else."[5]

The libertarian conception of power is also radically distinguished from the common or ordinary sense of this word. Indeed, power [*puissance*] become concrete or effective is sometimes identified, wrongly, with power [*pouvoir*] and *domination*, a way of seeing often attributed to the beings that suffer the constraints of an external power stronger than their own, in the face of which they either do not *revolt* or they surrender to *ressentiment* (see these terms).

---

1   Proudhon, *Philosophy of Progress*, 12.

2   On this point, cf. Pierre Ansart, *Marx et l'anarchisme* (Paris: PUF, 1969), 313.

3   Ibid. 156 and 161-162. Conceived in opposition to the scholastic tradition, "active power" is a Leibnizian concept (see *New Essays Concerning Human Understanding*, trans. Alfred Gideon Langley [London: Macmillan & Co., 1896], 174).

4   Ibid.

5   Proudhon, *De la Justice*, 3:403.

However, one also finds this way of seeing among the dominators, in particular priests, *experts*, and *servants of the people* (see these terms), anxious to mask the bases of their own domination, to prohibit any revolt and any affirmation of a power foreign to theirs. For libertarian thought, domination is only a very particular and negative form of power (*pouvoir*), both damaging and damaged, that separates other forces from what they are capable of in order to subject them, in a partial and external manner, to the limitations of the dominators' own development, of their own *point of view*. The power that dominates is doubly damaged and limited: on the one hand, in terms of what it prohibits to the other forces, on the other hand, in what it is itself prevented from producing by this prohibition. Conversely, the emancipatory power of a being is that which, in managing to break the yoke of the constraints that are imposed on it and freely associating with other free forces, is able to exceed its own limits and to allow the development of an ever greater power and freedom (see *hierarchy* and *balancing of forces*). It should thus be clear that, in libertarian thought, the extent of a being's power (and thus its freedom) does not depend on the extent or limits of its *possessions* (see this term), in the restricted legalistic sense that the current order gives to this concept, a possession that would be measurable by a third party or on an external scale (in terms of surface, number of inhabitants or members, number of tanks, or gross domestic product, for example). Nor does power depend on the intensity of the *violence* (see this term) that it is able to impose on the beings that comprise it and that it associates or subjugates to its existence. Rather, power depends entirely on the more or less *internal* or *external* character of the relations that constitute it at a *given moment*. In this sense, (see *hierarchy*) the smallest can not only be equal to the greatest, but can command a power infinitely greater than the latter if it liberates the totality of the forces that constitute it, allowing them to *do all that they can* or to *go beyond their limits* (see this term). Because it is external to the beings that it subjugates and thus subjects them to *raisons d'être* (see this term) not their own, the dominating power not only distorts these beings' capabilities – thus limiting its own power by this distortion, in terms of what it is prevented from producing – but also transforms this power into a purely *negative* force, into a loss or waste of power in an external confrontation that opposes it to other comparable powers (States, Churches, Parties, Individuals, etc.) as well as in the equally external constraints that it imposes on its own constitutive forces. It is also in this practical and immediate sense that libertarian thought can be linked with that of Leibniz and Nietzsche. It can be linked to the Leibnizian concept of a *repugnance* to shocks and violence (see this term), to the polemical transformation of one's positive positions into negative positions fought over by others, to the fragmentation and opposition of forces (see *friend/enemy*, *putting to death*, and *locking horns*).[1] But it can also be linked to the Nietzschean conception of the *will to power* as a double opening onto the other and onto the new, at the limits as well as in the midst of the beings that it constitutes at a *given moment*.[2]

Power of the outside (see *anarchy* and *plastic force*). Among contemporary philosophers, Gilbert Simondon undoubtedly makes the most concerted and positive effort – in particular with the concepts of the *apeiron*, the *preindividual*, or the *indeterminate* (see these terms) – to leave the circle of the existing order (both a magic and a vicious circle) and the prison of humanism by refusing the opposition between culture and nature, between human and nonhuman. Thus, he has been reproached with some vehemence, and not without reason, for his refusal of "anthropology."[3] One might well be disturbed to see how his analyses lead to "the absolute *anarchy* of singularities and ruptures that thought…can no longer seriously bind," to the promotion of a "meaning shattered into *monads* and instants," "a shattered, marvelous, and terrible universe, without principle or truth, or with an infinity of principles and truths," "a universe of infinite possibilities – in which nothing is impossible."[4] As opposed to the dominant humanism, for Simondon and for libertarian thought, it is very much a question of affirming the specificity of human existence, which resides precisely in its capacity to open itself up to the other, to what is not itself and thus to what is not human, to open itself up to the outside that is within itself, to the polymorphic power of nature or of being, thus being able to continually create new forms of *individuation* or *subjectivity* (see these terms). This is why Simondon rejects traditional anthropology, in which, on the contrary, it is a question of locking humanity up within the "unalterable limits" of a fortress

---

1   On this dimension of Leibniz's philosophy, cf. Christiane Frémont, *L'Être et la relation, avec trente-sept lettres de Leibniz à Des Bosses* (Paris: Vrin, 1981), 20 et passim. Just such a position is to be found in Deleuze: "Every time someone puts an objection to me, I want to say: 'OK, OK, let's go on to something else.' Objections have never contributed anything." (Gilles Deleuze and Claire Parnet, *Dialogues II*, trans. Hugh Tomlinson and Barbara Habberjam [New York: Columbia University Press, 2002], 1). (Translator's note: although there are four cross-references to an entry for the term *friend/enemy*, this entry does not appear in the *Petit lexique*.)

2   On this point, cf. Müller-Lauter, *Nietzsche, physiologie de la volonté de puissance*, 105 et passim.

3   Simondon, *Individuation psychique et collective*, 205-206 and 181 et passim. On the virulence of the reception of Simondon's theses among French philosophers, cf. "Débat," *Bulletin de la société française de philosophie* 54 no. 5 (1960): 751-65, particularly the exchanges with Paul Ricœur and Jean Hyppolite (758-65).

4   Gilbert Hottois, *Simondon et la philosophie de la "culture technique,"* 116 and 110.

or an "island," to adopt Kant's expression,[1] and basing the specificity of the human being on the struggle against the nature that surrounds it and that it carries in itself – the nonhuman (or the primitive) – for mastery. For Simondon, "Nature is not the contrary of humanity,"[2] since the specificity of the human being lies precisely in the possibility of returning to nature, to being in its totality, and remobilizing the totality of the forces of the outside, the forces of being ("terrible" forces, Gilbert Hottois would say[3]), as the *reserve of being*, as the *limitlessness of the limited* (see these terms).

Simondon's philosophical project thus directly answers the charge that Nietzsche had given himself some 70 years earlier: "My task: the dehumanization of nature and thereafter the naturalization of man, once the pure concept of 'nature' has been won."[4] This "nature" is thought to be external to us, but we actually carry it in ourselves.[5] Simondon echoes Nietzsche's will to release humanity from its own prison, in which humanity also attempts to lock up the

---

1 "We have now not merely explored the territory of pure understanding, and carefully surveyed every part of it, but have also measured its extent, and assigned to everything in it its rightful place. This domain is an island, enclosed by nature itself within unalterable limits. It is the land of truth – enchanting name! – surrounded by a wide and stormy ocean, the native home of illusion, where many a fog bank and many a swiftly melting iceberg give the deceptive appearance of farther shores, deluding the adventurous seafarer ever anew with empty hopes, and engaging him in enterprises which he can never abandon and yet is unable to carry to completion..." (Immanuel Kant, *Critique of Pure Reason*, qtd. in Jean-Clet Martin, *Variations: The Philosophy of Gilles Deleuze*, trans. Constantin V. Boundas and Susan Dyrkton [Edinburgh: Edinburgh University Press, 2010], 3-4).

2 Simondon, *L'Individuation psychique et collective*, 196.

3 He also summarizes the anarchic dimension of Simondon's thought: "The entire history of life, up to and including the emergence of humanity and the totality of its achievements as a species, is nothing but an individuation of being, a complex and fragmented ontogenesis that has no other future but to return to being, the center from which it emanates, which it rejoins in death" (Ibid. 111).

4 Nietzsche, *Nachgelassene Fragmente*, 1881, 11 [211], qtd. in Franck, *Nietzsche and the Shadow of God*, 184.

5 Nietzsche, *Nachgelassene Fragmente*, 1881, 11 [238]: "Men and philosophers have, imaginarily, situated man *within nature* – let us dehumanize nature! Later they will *imagine* more within themselves; instead of philosophies and works of art there will be ideal men, who every five years will form a new ideal from themselves" [*Die M‹enschen› und die Philosophen haben früher in die Natur hinein den Menschen gedichtet – entmenschlichen wir die Natur! Später werden sie mehr in sich selber hineindichten, an Stelle von Philosophieen und Kunstwerken wird es Ideal-menschen geben, welche alle 5 Jahre aus sich ein neues Ideal formen*] (emphasis in original) (*Nachgelassene Fragmente: 1880-1882*, ed. Giorgio Colli and Mazzino Montinari [München: Dt. Taschenbuch-Verlag, 1988], 532).

world without the least "remainder,"[1] by capturing it, too, in the crude snares of its codes. Like Simondon, Nietzsche attempts to invent other perspectives, no longer the perspectives of a "well determined species of man" and "more specifically, a well determined instinct, the *gregarious instinct* [emphasis in original]" through which humanity "attempts to come to domination."[2] Instead, these are "the perspectives of a being…*greater* than ourselves,"[3] the perspectives of a being finding in itself the power of the *indeterminate*, the power of *chaos*: "I say to you: one must still have chaos in oneself in order to give birth to a dancing star. I say to you: you still have chaos in you. Beware! The time approaches when human beings will no longer give birth to a dancing star."[4]

"Rise up, all you great hunters of stars," cried Louise Michel, immediately adding, "the sea of revolutions will carry us in its rising."[5] Whether it is called *chaos*, the *indeterminate*, the *apeiron*, *anarchy*, or some altogether different name,[6] the power of the outside is certainly at the heart of libertarian thought and desire, of its will to give birth to another world, to give birth to new stars. However, it is also a wager or a challenge that, without fail, provokes many doubts and much *anguish*. Indeed, contrary to the picturesque images in which it is too often costumed – for example, the noble savage, the "naturally" good human being, corrupted by the artifices of society, Rousseauvian optimism, the will to surrender oneself naively or blissfully to the desires and other imperatives of Nature – anarchism is not a naturalism (see *vital/vitalism*). Neither is it a matter of indifference that anarchism's call to the forces of the "outside" is so often connected to despair and destruction, to the "remote and terrible horizons" of which Cœurderoy speaks,[7] to the chaos and death that the color of its flag explicitly symbolizes (see *war/warlike*). The "outside" to which

---

1   "[T]he existing world in its entirety is also a product of our evaluations – in addition to those that have remained equal to themselves" (*Nachgelassene Fragmente*, 1884, 25 [434], qtd. in Franck, *op. cit.*, 184).

2   *Nachgelassene Fragmente* 1886-1887, 7 [16], qtd. in Franck, *Nietzsche and the Shadow of God*, 185.

3   *Nachgelassene Fragmente* 1882-1883, 4 [172], qtd. in Löwith, *Nietzsche's Philosophy of the Eternal Recurrence of the Same*, 99.

4   Nietzsche, *Thus Spoke Zarathustra*, 2. For an example even closer to Simondon, see Nietzsche, *Nachgelassene Fragmente: 1882-1884*, 5 [1] 128: "Preserve within yourself a share of chaos: those who are to come must have material from which to form themselves" [*Ihr sollt Chaos in euch bewahren: alle Kommenden müssen Stoff haben, um sich daraus zu formen*] (Nietzsche, *Nachgelassene Fragmente: 1882-1884*, 201).

5   Qtd. in Xavière Gauthier, introduction to *Louise Michel: Je vous écris de ma nuit, correspondance générale (1850-1904)*, 11.

6   After Bakunin's expression (see *nature*).

7   Cœurderoy, "Hourra!!! ou la révolution par les cosaques," 337.

anarchism appeals, in its eyes, contains an infinity of other possibilities, liber-atory collective arrangements and emancipatory subjectivities, but also just as many oppressive and deadly forces and identities, as well as, as Guy Hottois is alarmed to find in Simondon, blind and destructive, "marvelous and terrible" forces, "without principle or truth," indifferent to the effects of their power.[1] As this entire lexicon permits us to understand, in no way does anarchism appeal to a "naturally" beneficial originary power, an élan vital, a direction of history (even dialectical), a creative or determining power (reduced, in Marx, to productive forces). For libertarian thought, on the contrary, originary power is inevitably identified, in all of these forms, with the false old myth of divine providence, with the oppressive illusions of a divine first principle (see *anar-chy* and *resultant*). Before it can correspond (someday, perhaps) to the *positive anarchy* that the libertarian movements declare to be *possible* (see this term), to the emancipatory expression and arrangement of the totality of the forces that reality contains (see *plane of immanence*), the "outside" to which anarchism appeals must first refer to *chaos*, the *indeterminate*, "anarchy" in the primary or original sense of the term, an anarchic power that is indeed terrifying, as each of us can testify. Gilbert Simondon emphasizes this terror in a very beautiful text on *anguish*, this experience in which each of us discovers deep within our-selves this *more-than-oneself* that we contain (see this term):

> The subject dilates painfully, losing its interiority; it is here and elsewhere, detached from here by a universal elsewhere; it takes up all space and all time, becomes coextensive with being; it is spatialized, temporalized; it becomes an uncoordinated world. This immense inflation of the being, this limitless dilation that denies it any refuge or interiority, represents the fusion, with-in the being, of the *charge of nature* [see this term] associated with the individual being and its individuality: the structures and functions of the individuated being mix with one another and dilate, because they take this capacity for limitlessness from the charge of nature: the already-individuated is invaded by the *preindividual*; all of its structures are attacked, all of its func-tions animated by a new force that renders them incoherent. If this experience of anguish can be sufficiently sustained and endured, it may even lead to a new *individuation* [see this term] within the being, to a veritable metamorphosis; anguish already

---

1   On the supposed celebration of this indifference in what is commonly called "French Nietzscheanism," this time in the name of Simondon and in a completely traditional mor-al sense, cf. the critique formulated by Nicolas Dodier in *Les Hommes et les machines: La Conscience collective dans les sociétés technicisées* (Paris: Métailié, 1995), 33 et passim.

bears a presentiment of this new birth of the individuated being from the proliferating *chaos*; perhaps the anguished being feels that it will be able to reconcentrate itself in an ontological beyond presupposing a change in all its dimensions; but to make this new birth possible, the old structures must be completely dissolved, the old functions reduced to mere potentiality, entailing the *destruction* of the individuated being [emphasis my own]…The present is hollowed out, losing its actuality; the plunge into past and future dissolves the screen of the present and strips it of its experiential density. The individual being flees itself, abandons itself. And yet, in this abandonment, there is an indwelling of a kind of instinct for recomposing oneself on a different basis elsewhere and reincorporating the world into oneself *so that everything can be lived. The anguished being founds itself in the universe in order to find another subjectivity* [emphasis my own]."[1]

This danger and anguish concerning the outside in anarchist thought and action is also to be found, albeit in a rather different form, in Gilles Deleuze's book on Foucault, in which the notion of *the power of the outside* becomes a major concept.[2] In the final chapter, Deleuze, quoting from a famous text of Foucault, wonders (unlike Simondon) about the inability of human beings to escape the prison of their humanity, to break through the magical and illusory walls of their dungeon, as if it were a kind of impossibility: "always with the same *incapacity to cross the line*, to pass over to the other side…it is always the same choice, for the side of power, for what power says or of what it causes to be said."[3] Undoubtedly Foucault, as Deleuze emphasizes, could at least tell himself "that power does not take life as its objective without revealing or giving rise to a life that resists power" or that "the force of the outside continues to

---

1   Simondon, *L'Individuation psychique et collective*, 112-113. This text should be read along-side that of Déjacque, who, alone in his attic, having just written of "utopia" – "that cyclops with the fiery eye who drags the satanic procession of humanity into the full heat of hell" – throws himself onto his bed: "Am I going to lose my life or my senses?…It seemed to me that my head was going to burst and that my breast was caught in a vise. I was strangling: iron muscles tightened my throat…I suffocated in sobs. Blood beat in my temples and raised torrential waves in my brain, boiling floods continually pouring through all the locks of my arteries" (Joseph Déjacque, "L'Humanisphère: utopie anarchique" (1857), in *À bas les chefs!*, 133-134).

2   Deleuze, *Foucault*.

3   Michel Foucault, "La vie des hommes infâmes," *Les Cahiers du Chemin* 29 (1977), qtd. in Deleuze, *Foucault*, 94.

disrupt the diagrams and turn them upside down." "But what happens, on the other hand" – and as is so often demonstrated by any experiences with emancipatory will – "if the transversal relations of resistance continue to become restratified, and to encounter or even construct knots of power?" "If power is constitutive of truth" through its categories, orderings, and definitions, through language itself, "how can we conceive of a 'power of truth' which would no longer be the truth of power, a truth that would release transversal lines of resistance and not integral lines of power"?[1] How do we "cross the line"? Such is the first question that anarchism raises.

But this first question immediately leads to a second, and its impotence or despair provokes a countervailing and even more intense anguish, the very anguish Simondon so forcefully expresses. Isn't the violence of breaking through the limits of the familiar and reassuring roles and functions that presently constitute us (as a mother, a data processor, a proprietor, or a citizen whose citizenship is guaranteed by the law, by the bureaucracy, by the social order) worse than the prison that we want to get out of, however much we have a presentiment of all that it prevents us from experiencing? "If we must attain a life that is the power of the outside, what tells us that this outside is not a terrifying void and that this life, which seems to put up a resistance, is not just the simple distribution within the void of 'slow, partial and progressive' deaths?"[2] How do we cross the line without dying? How do we escape from the human-all-too-human that confines and oppresses us without irrecoverably losing ourselves? How do we embody a power of the outside that is not a power of death, but, on the contrary, a power of life? Such are the questions that, each in his own way, Simondon, Nietzsche, Foucault – and, through them, Deleuze – attempted to answer. Such is the challenge that libertarian movements and thought have always faced in their moments of greatest intensity, from the insurrectionary events of 1848 to the May Days of 1968, from the Commune of Paris to the Commune of Shanghai, from the tragic passages to the act of the German and Hungarian insurrections to the fatal horizons of the Russian and Spanish revolutions, in Ukraine, in Munich, in Kronstadt, in Budapest, and in Barcelona.

From Déjacque to Bakunin, to count only some of the first anarchist references, one encounters many texts that – beginning shortly after the events of 1848 – call upon the power of the outside, in particular the pamphlet published by Cœurderoy in 1852 titled *Hourra!!! ou la révolution par les cosaques*:[3]

---

1   Deleuze, *Foucault*, 94-95.

2   Ibid. 95.

3   Cœurderoy, "Hourra!!! ou la révolution par les cosaques." A text undoubtedly written and diffused in an abridged form on the heels of the tragic events of June 1848 (on this point, cf. Max Nettlau's introduction to *Œuvres*, vol. 1, Ernest Cœurderoy [Paris: Stock, 1910], xxii).

"Oh! Great is Humanity, eternal the Future, immense the Worlds rocked in infinite Space!...And quite small are we, short-lived Civilized men who purport to impose laws on the Universe and boundaries on Time!...But who then are you, illustrious monarchs and profound legislators of the West, that you believe you are the first and last creatures to live under the sun? Misery and pity! But don't you hear the roaring of the abyss of fire that vomits up revolutions among men, the ever-gaping abyss, always famished, always vengeful? It will swallow you and your lying systems and your schoolmasters' vanities. For every system is false and every system oppressive! We will not suffer any more Governments, Austerities, Masteries. Whoever you are – Caesars, Jesuits, Communists, Traditionalists, or Phalansterians – aspire to lead us no longer. Man has finally left the school of Slavery!...The Revolution sweeps me towards remote and terrible horizons: it centuplicates the potentiality of my being; it passes over me like the breath of a hurricane...This world is my dungeon..."[1]

"As revolutionary anarchists, let us proclaim it in the highest: we place our hopes upon the human flood alone; we have no future but in *chaos*; there is no course for us to take but that of a general war that, mixing all races and breaking all established relations, will tear from the hands of the dominant classes the instruments of oppression with which they violate the liberties we have purchased with our own blood [emphasis my own]."[2]

"...When each fights for his own cause, nobody will need to be represented any longer; amid the confusion of tongues, the lawyers, the journalists, the dictators of opinion will fall silent...The same will go for language...The increasingly intimate relationship between nations will lead to the interchanging of the various idioms. We will converse in imperfect, incomplete terms; pronunciation, orthography, and grammar will be subjected to innumerable distortions. Thus the current languages will find themselves invaded in the very sanctuary of their absolute rules; thus the confusion of peoples will bring about the confusion of tongues, anarchy in speech as well as in thought."[3]

---

1   Cœurderoy, "Hourra!!! ou la révolution par les cosaques," 325, 332-333.

2   Ibid. 257.

3   Ibid. 257 and 305-306.

Of course, we might oppose Cœurderoy's dark appeal, penned shortly after the June 1848 insurrection was crushed, to the euphoric intoxication of Bakunin's remembrance of the revolutionary weeks preceding the massacre of the Parisian workers, while noting that same perception of the abolition of space and time, of an existing order, a perception no longer imaginary and prospective but positive and real:

> "And in the midst of this unlimited freedom, this mad rapture, all were so forgiving, sympathetic, loving of their fellow man – upright, modest, courteous, amiable, witty…it was a month of spiritual intoxication. Not only I but everyone was intoxicated: some from reckless fear, others from reckless rapture, from reckless hopes. I imbibed with all my senses, through all my pores, the ecstatic atmosphere of revolution. It was a feast without beginning and without end. Here I saw everyone and saw no one because all were lost in one infinite, aimless crowd. I spoke with everyone, but I do not remember either what I said to them or what they said to me because at every step there were new topics, new adventures, new information…It seemed that the whole world had been turned upside down. The inconceivable had become the usual, the impossible possible, and the possible and the usual unthinkable."[1]

However, it is Proudhon, in connection with the same events, who – by virtue of his personal propensity for order, his taste for grammar, and his refusal of any confusion in word or thought – most clearly highlights the challenge of the anarchist project and its thought. As Pierre Ansart demonstrates, if Proudhon spoke of *anarchy*[2] very early on, this word long remained vague and imprecise for him: a mere will to denounce, on moral and logical grounds, an existing order or "system" to which Proudhon dedicates the bulk of his reflections; the affirmation of another order to come, the antinomy of the existing order, because it is founded on freedom, subjectivity, and "spontaneity of action," but which Proudhon proclaims at first (in the manner of Marx) to be born and deduced from this existing order, from its *contradictions* (see this term and *stoppage*) and from their capacity to produce an entirely new society of a different nature in resolving themselves.[3] A dead end, as Pierre

---

1 Mikhail Bakunin, *The Confession of Mikhail Bakunin: With the Marginal Comments of Tsar Nicholas I*, trans. Lawrence D. Orton (Ithaca, NY: Cornell University Press, 1977), 55-57.

2 As of his first *Mémoire* of 1840, *What Is Property?*

3 Cf. primarily *System of Economical Contradictions* (1846). On the manner in which Proudhon reconsiders this initial line of thinking, see *balancing of forces*.

Ansart shows. Indeed, by what miracle or in the name of what providence should spontaneity, freedom, subjectivity, and anarchy be born, even dialectically, from a "necessary movement, escaping the will and action of men"? How could "a fully active society, free from all constraint" emerge "from an objective and restrictive process"?[1]

For Proudhon, as for many others, the necessity and possibility of developing the first intuitions of such a free society will emerge from the *outside* of the system and its contradictions. It was the *outside* of the revolutionary events of 1848 that led him to accept the full measure of the heterogeneity that opposes system to anarchy, to stop imagining the latter as the necessary consequence of the former, in a relation in which the system is everything, since, to paraphrase Marx, it is at once the problem and its solution. Violently denounced by the Proudhon of 1848[2] under its threefold identity as State, Capital, and Church, the existing order then ceases to define the framework or the limits within which the future of society's radical transformation would play out; it is no longer taken to express and constitute the whole of social reality. In the narrowness of its limits and the finalized character of its determinations, the existing order is nothing more than a particular dimension of things, eminently questionable in its pretensions, an "artificial society" that, far from "exhausting the real life of society" (and even farther from *producing* this real life), is content to "superimpose" itself on society by exploiting and subjecting this real life to its own requirements.[3] In the heat of the events of 1848, reality proves to be infinitely richer and more vibrant than the social formations of which it is the object. In the writings of the anarchist Proudhon, these economic, political, and religious formations are nothing more than extrinsic artifices, and their appearance of imperative necessity (even in the eyes of their most convinced detractors) vanishes in the face of a higher necessity: the manifest reality of society that events have so abruptly brought to light. Within the initial antinomy between system and anarchy, which he had attempted at first to resolve on the side of the system, Proudhon leans – not without some misgivings, as we can see – toward the side of anarchy.[4] Shaken by events and facts, it is not

---

1   Ansart, *Marx et l'anarchisme,*148-149.

2   Cf. Pierre-Joseph Proudhon, *Mélanges-Articles de journaux, 1848-1852,* 3 vols. (Paris: Marpon et Flammarion, 1868-1870).

3   On this point, see Ansart, *Marx et l'anarchisme,* 159.

4   As Pierre Haubtmann is sorry to report: "Let us trace the path taken since the *Contradictions économiques.* Now, the 'truth' no longer consists, as it did in 1846, in the 'reconciliation' of two opposed tendencies, that of property and that of anarchy and atheism, but in the exclusion of the former and the ascent of the latter" (*Pierre-Joseph Proudhon: Sa vie et sa pensée (1849-1865)* [Paris: Desclée de Brouwer, 1988], 196). On the difficulties this rupture creates for an overall interpretation of Proudhon's writings, cf. Pierre Ansart, *Marx et*

only the supposedly beneficial outcomes of the system's contradictions that he rejects, but the very idea that there can be a dialectic between anarchy and system.[1] After 1848, the coming anarchy not only ceases to be the possible consequence of the system and its contradictions, but also it no longer stands for a future reality, inevitably in sketchy outline, which occupies only a negative place in the present: an interstice, a vacuum created by the contradictions of the social order. By identifying it with the "real society" that he opposes to the artifices of State, Capital, and Church, Proudhon establishes spontaneity and anarchy as the originary condition of any possible life. Anarchy is thus transformed from a vague and dubious idea, added after the fact of (*a posteriori* to) human development, into a reality that is superabundant in its diversity and power, which would be better conceived as the source of (*a priori* to) this development, the disguised and walled-off source of the existing order and of any possible order, the limitless foundation out of which any institution takes form. Consequently, anarchy and social spontaneity are transformed into a preliminary condition.

As those who know the man of order and reason that was Proudhon might suspect, this reevaluation of the anarchist project in the heat of the events of 1848 did not come easily – testified to by the article he published in *Le Peuple* a year later, in which, with his usual frankness and meticulousness, he lengthily reconsiders those events and his feelings at the time:

> As a republican of the association, the workshop, the study, I shivered in terror at what I saw approaching the Republic…I fled before the democratic and social monster, the enigma of which I could not explain, and an inexpressible terror froze my heart, jarring me into thought….This revolution which was going to burst upon the public order was the zero hour of a social revolution that none could name. Contrary to all experience, contrary to the order hitherto invariably followed by historical development, the fact would arrive before the idea [see *propaganda by the deed*]…Thus, everything seemed to me to be alarming, amazing, paradoxical in this contemplation of a future that at every minute rose in my mind to the height of a reality. In this devouring anxiety, I rebelled against the drift of events, I dared to condemn destiny…My soul was in agony…On February 21st, in the evening, I still exhorted my

---

l'anarchisme, 311.

1   On this point, cf. Pierre Ansart, "Proudhon, des pouvoirs et des libertés," in *P.-J. Proudhon, pouvoirs et libertés: actes du colloque tenu à Paris et Besançon les 22, 23 et 24 octobre 1987*, ed. Pierre Ansart et al (Paris: Atelier Proudhon, 1989), 13-14.

friends not to fight. On the 22nd, I breathed a sigh of relief when I heard that the opposition had retreated; I believed myself at the end of my martyrdom. The day of the 23rd arrived, shattering my illusions. But this time, the die was cast, *jacta est alea*, as M. de Lamartine says. The shooting in the Rue des Capucines changed my dispositions in an instant. I was no longer the same man.[1]

How can we conceive of the events that inspired Cœurderoy and Bakunin, which seem to immediately outstrip not only words but concepts as such? How can we penetrate the enigma of a reality that was just as confusing for those who experienced it? How can one effectively become another human being, this more-than-human that Nietzsche would affirm 40 years later, capable of liberating the powers and the wills that it contains, so that the "*intoxication*" – this "exalted feeling of *power*" elicited by lived situations, this "*explosive* condition" – intensifies our bodies and our senses, alters our "sensations of space and time," and allows us to perceive "much that is extremely small and fleeting"?[2] How, with Tarde and Simondon this time, can we conceive of and "embrace," as a "manifestation of life," "every explosion," "all forms of dissidence, all rebellions, every insurrection, wherever they may come from and whenever they may occur"?[3] How can we conceive of these "pre-revolutionary state[s]," these "state[s] of supersaturation…where an event is very ready to occur, where a structure is very ready to emerge"?[4] Or, with Cœurderoy, how can we conceive of "the vastness of the worlds," the "infinite space," and the "remote and terrible horizons" of Revolutions? How can we conceive of the irruption and combination of "forces" issuing from a "universe" without "laws" and from a "time without boundaries"? In short (so to speak), as Proudhon already put it in his *Contradictions économiques*, how can we conceive of this "anarchy" and these "powers" of the "nature" that is to be found within the human being? How can we "penetrate the inaccessible…to set before the gaze of mortal man, in a word, the infinite"?[5]

---

1   *Le Peuple* (Feb. 19, 1849), in Pierre-Joseph Proudhon, *Pierre-Joseph Proudhon: Mémoires sur ma vie*, ed. Bernard Voyenne (Paris: Maspero, 1983), 75 et passim.

2   Nietzsche, *The Will to Power*, trans. Walter Kaufmann and R.J. Hollingdale, ed. Walter Kaufmann (New York: Vintage Books, 1968), 420-21, 428-29. Cf. Franck, *Nietzsche and the Shadow of God*, 141. (See entry for *life* for Bakunin's conception.)

3   Milet, *Gabriel Tarde et la philosophie de l'histoire*, 153.

4   Gilbert Simondon, qtd. in Alberto Toscano, "The Disparate: Ontology and Politics in Simondon," *Pli: The Warwick Journal of Philosophy* (Jan. 2012): 113.

5   Pierre-Joseph Proudhon, *Contradictions économiques*, vol. 2 (Paris: Rivière, 1939), 253 and 249.

Such are the questions that anarchism has constantly addressed: in theory (albeit not without difficulties), particularly through what Proudhon will call *positive anarchy*; and, above all (on a grand scale and over the course of half a century), in practice, through the various experiments in working-class emancipation that are conventionally grouped together under the terms revolutionary syndicalism and anarcho-syndicalism, in which new forms of *subjectivity* (see this term) strove to express the power of reality.

Practical sense (see *experience, intuition*, and *the midst of things*). The capacity to perceive what gives us life and thus to evaluate the things and relationships (with human or nonhuman beings) that we encounter within the *situations* that constitute these things and relationships (see this term), according to their capacity (or incapacity) to promote a stronger and freer life. The evaluation with which we are concerned here is thus, above all, a value judgment concerning the emancipatory quality inhering in each situation and in that which composes it. It has nothing to do with utility or the utilitarian (see *utilitarianism*). Or, rather, from the libertarian point of view, any utilitarian evaluation of a situation will sooner or later entail relations of domination.

Practice (see *action* and *theory/practice*).

Preindividual. Concept used by Simondon, synonymous with *anarchy, apeiron, reserve of being, indeterminate, the limitlessness of the limited* (see these terms).

Private/public (see *government* and *particular*). Along with Elisée Reclus, anarchism radically refuses the distinction between private and public.[1] For libertarian thought, everything is private in the primary sense of "particular" (*privatus*), of that which is "proper" or "individual." The public is a private that is unaware of itself, which only draws its "public" identity from the *violence, constraint*, and *domination* (see these terms) that it imposes on other forces, other collective beings, whether these are led to call themselves "public" or "private." In 1853, the painter and Proudhonian Gustave Courbet best expressed this refusal of the distinction between private and public, when he recalled his conversation with an arts minister who attempted to commission a painting from him in the name of the "Government": "I replied at once that I did not understand a word he had said, since he claimed to represent a Government and I did not consider myself in any way a part of that Government, that I was a Government too and that I challenged his to do anything whatever for mine

---

1   On this point, cf. Elisée Reclus *Anarchy, Geography, Modernity: The Radical Social Thought of Elisée Reclus*, ed. and trans. John P. Clark and Camille Martin (Lanham, MD: Lexington Books, 2004), 92.

that I could accept. I went on to say that to me his Government seemed just like any private citizen [*particulier*]…To this he replied: 'M. Courbet, you are very haughty!'"[1]

Prodigality (see *superabundance, generosity, war/warlike, power,* and *affirmation*). Against the prodigal son of the Gospel who submits to his father's law and sees his prodigality transformed into perdition and sin, which requires him, by the time the story ends, to seek forgiveness and a return to the narrow limits of the family economy, anarchism opposes a positive *prodigality,* infinite in scope because it draws on the sources of being and because it alone is capable of liberating this power.

Pro-feminist (see *pro-something*).

Project (see *action, ends/means, collective reason,* and *entelechy*). The libertarian project is not separate from the libertarian *movement* (for example, in the form of a distant end or an unattainable ideal). Project and movement are indissociable insofar as any movement – like any reality we take the time to investigate thoroughly, any reality existing at a given moment (i.e., in all cases) – contains in itself its project, its *raison d'être*, that toward which it tends and that which animates it. This is because the project is simultaneously the end and the beginning of the action, its past and its future, its motive and its goal, its internal logic (see *entelechy*). A libertarian perception of the forces or movements engaged in a struggle for emancipation always requires us to look behind the ostensible ends that these forces or movements set for themselves, to examine what really motivates them, the character of the desire (or *will*) that constitutes them as a collective arrangement at a given moment (see *a priori/a posteriori*).

Propaganda by the deed (see *practices, direct action, anarchist chemistry, terrorism, passage to the act,* and *transduction*). A concept invented at the end of the 1870s by the militant circles issuing from Bakuninism (Reclus, Malatesta, Cafiero, Brousse, Kropotkin, etc.) that attempts – both through *insurrection* via the explosive properties of chemistry and through all forms of revolt, as well as any other immediate and transformative action, however minuscule and insignificant it might appear – to substitute "acts" for "words," "action" for "discourse."[2] Associated with the individual *attentats* of the 1890s, "propaganda by the deed" generally has a bad reputation, but it is one of the primary concepts of the anarchist movement. With this concept, an emergent anarchism broke

---

1   Letter to Alfred Bruyas, October 1853, in Mack, *Gustave Courbet*, 109-10.

2   On propaganda by the deed, cf. Colson, "La science anarchiste."

radically with any idealist or ideological political concept. Militant action ceased to be identified with "propaganda" in the usual sense of the term, for which it is above all a matter of acting upon "opinion," of convincing others by ideas and reasoning (so that they will vote for you or join the organization that bears this message). With the concept of propaganda by the deed, anarchism refused to separate and establish a hierarchy between the *idea* (as a logical and cognitive preliminary, situated outside of time) and its consequent diffusion by militant action. The anarchist idea passes from *propaganda*, which must be propagated in the form of a discursive message, to a direct *propagation*, propagating itself by acts. By the imitation of these acts and in their direct effect, this fosters a revolutionary and transformative power of which anarchism is no more than, so to speak, the echo, the amplifier, or the detonator. In this development, the anarchist Idea ceases to be identified with a program or a utopia. It ceases to speak the truth of things and thus to attempt to act on them or shape them from the outside. Instead, the "things" (the "facts" [*faits*]), the "situations," the "events" are made to immediately and concretely express the Idea by their very movement, by the particular *selection* and *composition* of that which constitutes them, showing everyone the way in which another world is possible (see *action*). Under the name of *direct action* (see this term), propaganda by the deed is at the heart of the project and the development of revolutionary syndicalism and, subsequently, anarcho-syndicalism.

Property (see *possession*).

Pro-something (see *anti-something* and *servants of the people*). In the '70s, there was an ultra-left-wing political tendency, the "pro-Chinese," who declared themselves to be "at the service of the people." Currently, other militants, men, declare themselves to be "pro-feminist" and claim, if not to "serve" women, at least to place themselves under their leadership (see *rendering of accounts*). "Blacks," "women," "animals," "oppressed nations," "*sans-papiers* [undocumented immigrants]," "the environment," "the Third World," "nature," "the disabled," and other "causes" may fill the same function. The monstrosity of such a list should be enough to disqualify these militant practices that could perhaps only be justified by a fully assumed masochism. Anarchism rejects, violently and with *repugnance* (see this term), this hypocritical propensity to put oneself in the place of others, at the service of others, in a relation in which submission and domination, *guilt* and *ressentiment* (see these terms) stand in opposition to any real desire for emancipation. For libertarian thought, each collective being is, as Cœurderoy writes, its own cause.[1] It is only by start-

---

1 Cœurderoy, "Hourra!!! ou la révolution par les cosaques," 257: "When each fights for his own cause, nobody will need to be represented any longer."

ing with themselves and from themselves (see *monad*), fighting for their own emancipation, that they find reasons to associate with other beings. It is in this sense and this sense alone that, from a libertarian point of view, every force needs other forces to express that which it is capable of. Here, for anarchists, is where reciprocity and *equality* are to be found (see this term): in the absolute autonomy of beings, the equally absolute equality that this autonomy alone guarantees, and experimentation as the sole measure of the emancipatory (or dominatory) character of the multiple associations and disassociations that this autonomy and equality make possible.

Psychopathic (see *fractiousness, temperament*). This concept names a both positive and negative predisposition of a certain number of libertarians to negotiate their relations with others poorly. Psychopathic tendencies guarantee the *autonomy* of forces but are too often opposed to the *balance* or *hierarchy* (see these terms) of forces. Very often *reactive*, they are always likely to lead to *ressentiment* and to provide one of the important components of the *anarchism of the right* (see these terms).

Public confession (see also *rendering of accounts*). An old Christian practice of submission and humility, reintroduced by Marxist-Leninist movements under the title of *self-criticism*. It is generally staged within the framework of courtroom trials, where the culprits, by confessing their individual errors and sins to the community and its representatives, voluntarily subject what they are and what they are capable of to an external law, an external order, and external forces.

Putting to death (see *violence, war/warlike, guilty party* and *friend/enemy*[1]). A strange expression, the idea or enactment of which is always, for libertarian thought, the symptom of an oppressive order. Anarchist action does not shrink from the possibility of the death of its *project*, one's own death, and the deaths of others, according to the circumstances and the nature of the relations existing between beings. But anarchist death is always (and rightly so) a death in a situation, at a given moment, and in given relations of *violence*, when the affirmation of life and the constitution of a more powerful life require one to revolt and recompose these relations in another way. Death, always negative, then accompanies life as the condition of its affirmation. It is entailed in this affirmation and subject to its requirements, even, sometimes, when it is a matter of murder or assassination.[2] In no case, however, can death transform itself into

---

1   Translator's note: although there are four cross-references to an entry for the term *friend/enemy*, this entry does not appear in the *Petit lexique*.

2   On this point, see Spinoza, letter to Blyenbergh (XXIII), quoted in Deleuze, *Spinoza:*

an autonomous, privileged, or foundational reality, able to reorganize relations between beings around itself.[1] In this sense, anarchism is a stranger to any idea of putting to death, in which death becomes an "arrested" act, political in itself, producing its own ritual (in the form of tribunals, for example, even the most improvisational or supposedly "revolutionary" kinds).

Practical Philosophy, 35.

1   In a political logic that an author like Carl Schmitt could theorize and of which fascism and Marxism-Leninism are undoubtedly the best expressions. On this logic, see Carl Schmitt, *Political Theology: Four Chapters on the Concept of Sovereignty*, trans. George Schwab (Chicago: University of Chicago Press, 2005) and *friend/enemy*. (Translator's note: although there are four cross-references to an entry for the term *friend/enemy*, this entry does not appear in the *Petit lexique*.)

R

Raison d'être (see *collective reason*).

Rational (see *irrational*).

Reaction (see *action*). A political concept that, in the political discourse of Western societies, has traditionally indicated political forces attached to the past, whose action is limited to "reacting" to new forces, defining themselves negatively in relation to these forces. In libertarian thought, the concept of "reaction" becomes a criterion for evaluating the emancipatory quality of *collective forces* (see this term) attempting to fight for another world. In contrast to active forces, which are determined only in relation to themselves and by the types of association in which they are engaged, reactive forces exist only in relation to other forces, suffering the effects of these forces, then re-acting to these effects, generally in the form of *ressentiment* or *guilt* (see these terms). The trap of oppression and domination lies in the fact that they always tend to transform dominated and oppressed forces into reactive forces, into reactionary forces (in the first sense of this word). The originality of the libertarian project resides, on the contrary, in its capacity to transform dominated forces into active forces – forces that rely only on themselves, that are able to escape the traps of negation, to base their existence on the limitless resources that escape the grasp of the order from which they seek to liberate themselves (see *analogy*).

Refusal (see *revolt, rupture, insurrection*, and *anti-something*).

Relation of forces (see *balancing of forces*).

Relativism (see *evaluation*).

Rendering of accounts (see *utilitarianism*, *guilt*, and *domination*). A concept of Christian and Marxist-Leninist origin (see *public confession*, *direction of the conscience*, and *self-criticism*), revived by certain currents emerging from North America that, for reasons difficult to understand, call themselves anarchist. In the thought and the practices of these currents, situations of oppression do not furnish the starting point of *autonomous* emancipatory forces capable of breaking away from the frameworks of domination through *revolt* (see these terms) and recomposing reality in a new way through their association. Reproducing the divisions and classifications of the existing order in their own practice, the partisans of a rendering of accounts make these classifications into their own dominatory hierarchy-in-reverse, thereby taking on board all the potentiality for *guilt* and *ressentiment* that this order can contain (see these terms). In the interminable hierarchical series of dominations and discriminations – all the more durable and pregnant to the extent that the current order frequently inscribes them in the body (sex, skin color, shape of nose or cranium, etc.) – every dominated person is always dominant in relation to somebody else who is more dominated: a man with respect to a woman, a white person with respect to a black person, a city-dweller with respect to a rural villager, a graduate with respect to a non-graduate, a woman in good health with respect to a disabled woman, a cyclist with respect to a pedestrian, etc. Parallel to the Christian will to perpetually celebrate the poorest and the weakest, while making themselves guilty of that for which they reproach others (in order to better prevent them from revolting and giving rise to emancipatory forces), the partisans of a rendering of accounts require each rebellious force to immediately subordinate itself to one that is more dominated than itself, to "render account" to this other, to act and think "under its supervision." Affirmation and emancipation are then transformed into negation and submission. Separated from what they are capable of – since they must subject themselves to other forces – the emancipatory powers lose not only any capacity to subvert an order that thus imposes its hierarchies and classifications on them for a second time. Additionally, corrupted by guilt, they also lose any capacity to define for themselves, from the interior of what constitutes them, the modes of association, even the hierarchical modes (see *hierarchy*), that they are called on to establish among themselves. How, indeed, does one establish with any precision the long chain of mutual submissions that leads, at the end of the "accounts," to the ultimate dominated, the paschal lamb, pure of all sin, to whom all should render account?[1] Undoubtedly, white heterosexual men will have to subject their most

---

1　In Christian representations, this is God himself and, closer to us, the priests who claim the right, in spite of their sins and their unworthiness, to speak on his behalf and to constantly

intimate thoughts, acts, and movements (see *public confession*) to the white heterosexual feminists, who will be able, for their part, to do the same to white lesbian feminists, themselves placed under the "supervision" of black lesbians, dependent for their part on black lesbians of small stature, who would in turn render account to the black lesbians of small stature who are also obese, then struck with strabismus, illiteracy, or some other corporeal (or social) trait that marks them for discrimination or stigmatization. But how does one define precisely which – strabismus or obesity – is the more stigmatized, the greater source of oppression and domination? Where does one locate Asian lesbians in this chain of dominations? How, in the manner of the Brazilian racial hierarchies, does one classify the various "mixed-race" types? Before which court must one plead the preeminence of this group over that group in degree of misfortune? What scientific or revolutionary authority can define the coefficients of domination, measure the intensity of suffering and oppression, classify and rank the statuses and situations of the oppressed and the oppressors?[1] If a black man can doubtlessly demand a rendering of accounts from a white man, in this inverted hierarchy of the most visible of dominations, does he himself have to accept the supervision of a white heterosexual woman? Is skin color more discriminatory (from the perspective of degrees of oppression) than sex or species? Indeed, are not the animals (through the self-serving voices of their advocates and *representatives*) within their rights to demand to be regarded as the ultimate victims of a world so long dominated by humankind? Is it necessary to turn to natural classifications (in an ethological manner) and to distinguish, among the animals, between the innumerable classes of predator and prey, to establish with precision the modalities of the various food chains (see *anti-speciesism*)? To the pleasure, as old as Christianity, of suffering and wallowing in guilt then atoning and confessing one's guilt before others, the supporters of a "rendering of accounts" can thus add the equally intense pleasures of casuistry, bargaining (see *utilitarianism*), and quibbling (in the legal sense of the term), of the blind, brutal, and endless struggle for the recognition of the "rights" of victims and the oppressed. This struggle is *repugnant* because it is entirely founded on the order that it attempts to fight, on the advantages, compensations, and profits that can be drawn from the effects of inequality, discrimination, humiliation, frustration, guilt, and *ressentiment* that this order never ceases to produce, all the better to perpetuate it.

Repetition (see *eternal return*). One could reproach revolutionary syndicalism and anarcho-syndicalism with conceiving of strikes as a kind of revolutionary

---

point out to us our status as sinners and culprits.

1 On the way in which defenders of animals solve this problem on the terrain of "interests" and of quantities of happiness and suffering, see *anti-speciesism* and *utilitarianism*.

"gymnastics"[1] or "rehearsal [*répétition*]," in the theatrical sense of the term, in expectation of and preparation for the *Great Evening*, the *insurrectionary* and *general strike* (see these terms). This reproach expresses a real misunderstanding of the way that the libertarian movement thinks and of the continuous temporality and character of emancipatory movements. The libertarian repetition of struggles and revolts, this perpetually resumed irruption of another possibility within the framework of the existing order (see *stoppage* and *event*), has nothing to do with the mechanical and deterministic vision of a Trotsky or a Lenin, retrospectively transforming the Russian revolution of 1905 into a "dress rehearsal" [*répétition générale*] for 1917, an exercise during which the Party and its technicians-in-chief took the opportunity to polish their tools, their formulas, and their slogans. In libertarian thought, the repetitive character of revolts or insurrections, however tiny and imperceptible they may be, radically escapes both this linear conception of time – in which it is the past that rehearses [*répéterait*] and prepares for the future – and any instrumentalization and classification of the surface of facts and events.[2] As in the common sense of the word or the manner in which children play, libertarian repetition always repeats the past and its possibilities. It is always related to an anteriority and an accumulated power (see *Great Evening*). Each conflict, each moment of revolt, repeats all the others from a new point of view, through new circumstances, and with a new intensity. Every single time, despite their apparent discontinuity, these conflicts and revolts affirm once more, by return, variation, and selection, the power intrinsic to that which exists, without exception, without any external force being able to exploit what constitutes them. As Deleuze (like Nietzsche) demonstrates with regard to nature, repetition, in the libertarian sense of the word, is "a will willing itself through all change, a power opposed to law, an interior of the earth opposed to the laws of its surface."[3] In this sense, again with Deleuze, emancipatory repetition is opposed to *representation* (see this term), "just as movement is opposed to the concept and to representation which refers it back to the concept. In the theatre of repetition, we experience pure forces, dynamic lines in space which act without intermediary upon the spirit, and link it directly with nature and history, with a language which speaks before words, with gestures which develop before organized bodies" (see *direct action*).[4]

---

1   "The partial strike is a training, a salutary gymnastics, that toughens the proletariat for the supreme struggle that will be the revolutionary general strike" (Yvetot, *A.B.C. syndicaliste*, 40).

2   On this point, see Daniel Colson, "Reconnaissance collective et montée en singularité: L'accord d'entreprise de la Compagnie des Aciéries et Forges de la Loire (CAFL), 1956-1959," in *Les noms que l'on se donne: Processus identitaire, expérience commune, inscription publique*, ed. Étienne Savoie (Paris: L'Harmattan, 2001), 55-77.

3   Deleuze, *Difference and Repetition*, 6.

4   Ibid. 10.

Representation (representative democracy) (see *symbols*, *signs*, and *dialectics*). "When each fights for his own cause, nobody will need to be represented any longer."[1] By opposing direct democracy to "representative" democracy, by refusing all "representatives" (deputies or trade-union bureaucrats) who claim to speak in the name of others, to act in their place or (worse) on their behalf, anarchism expresses a much more radical critique of representation on the terrain of politics and institutions, and this critique forms the basis of a central institution of its revolutionary project. In the libertarian vocabulary, the word representation must be understood in all its various senses: political, religious, scientific, and *symbolic* (see this term) – each time persons, signs, or institutions claim to stand in for *things* or to say what these things are. Indeed, for anarchism, it is a matter of refusing not only political representation but any form of representation, which is perceived as inevitably external and manipulative, standing apart from the real forces that it appropriates and separates from what they are capable of. In this sense, the libertarian critique of representation can be linked to Nietzsche's thought, to his critique of science, of the State ("the state is a hypocrite hound...it likes to speak with smoke and bellowing – to make believe...that it speaks from the belly of things") and the Church ("a kind of State, and the most lying kind").[2] Science, Church, State – it is always a matter of subjugating reality to the lies of signs and representation, subjugating "*movement*" (see this term) to "substance," *active* forces to *reactive* forces (see these terms).

Repugnance (see *affinity* and *analogy*). "And the mother, shutting the school exercise book,/went away contented and very proud, without seeing,/in his blue eyes below his forehead full of protuberances,/her child's soul a prey to repugnance."[3] In spite of what its immediate, physical dimension might lead one to believe, repugnance involves the very nature of beings at a *given moment*. Each arrangement of a collective force in its associations with others defines the quality of the resulting *desire*. And from this quality and this *resultant*, tastes and distastes arise as invaluable indicators of the nature of the worlds within which these beings take on their force and signification. In this sense, repugnance is the repulsive side (see *repulsion*) of *affinity*. In its subjective intensity and violence, in the intuitive and apparently unreasoning character of its manifestations, it always indicates with exactitude a judgment on the world in which one wants to live and on the quality and nature of the associations that correspond to it, the associations that render it possible.

---

1   Cœurderoy, "Hourra!!! ou la révolution par les cosaques," 257.

2   Nietzsche, *Thus Spoke Zarathustra*, 34, 104.

3   Arthur Rimbaud, "The Seven Year Old Poet," trans. Stanley Appelbaum, in *A Season in Hell and Other Works* (Mineola, NY: Dover Publications, 2003), 146-149.

Repulsion (see *repugnance, affinity,* and *association*). In place of a frontal and brutal opposition in which conflicting beings are tightly and fixedly dependent on damaging relations that destroy power (see *power* and *dialectics*), the libertarian strategy is to substitute repulsion: the expulsion from ourselves, our desires, and our appetites of forces that do not suit us because they belong to another world, a damaged and damaging world, which is alien to that which we are attempting to construct.[1]

Reserve of being (see *indeterminacy* and *power of the outside*).

Respect (see *equality* and *autonomy*). The mutual recognition of the *autonomy* and thus the *equality* of beings. The respect that is central to methods of association and disassociation implies paying close attention to others, to what constitutes them, and to what this constitution enables in the way of new relations. As a source of *revolt* and the very particular *violence* pertaining to it, respect excludes any attempt at domination and any intrusive or destructive violence. In this sense, it is at the center of libertarian relations.

Responsibility [*responsabilité*] (see *guilt* and *eternal return*). An internal umbrella or prosthesis meant to stabilize human beings and to subject them to an order that is extrinsic to what constitutes them as living beings. If the eye of God was fixed on Cain all the way to his tomb,[2] then responsibility is the eye that God and the State implants within each of us in order to guarantee the perpetuity of the order upon which their power is founded.

Ressentiment. The lingering reaction of the dominated who have not managed to transform the relations of domination to which they are subject into *revolt* and into an *emancipatory* and *affirmative* force (see these terms). *Ressentiment* (which does not spare the anarchist movement itself[3]) is always characterized by negativity, sourness, complaint, and denunciation. The men and women of

---

1   On the importance of the concept of "repulsion" in astrophysics ("dark energy"), see the report on the 13th Rencontres Internationales at Blois in *Le Monde* (June 29, 2001). (Translator's note: see also *Frontiers of the Universe: Proceedings of the XIIIrd Rencontres De Blois, Château De Blois, France, June 17-23, 2001*, ed. Ludwik M. Celnikier and Jean T. V. Trân [S.l., Vietnam: Thê Giói, 2004].)

2   Translator's note: This is a reference to Victor Hugo's famous poem, "La Conscience," which narrates Cain's wanderings through the world, pursued by "the Eye of God"; even in the end, "the Eye was in the tomb and fixed on Cain" (Hugo, *The Works of Victor Hugo* [Boston: Little, Brown, 1887] 439).

3   As John Clark rightly notes, following Nietzsche (see Clark, *Anarchy, Geography, Modernity,* 33).

ressentiment always claim to fight against the oppression that they suffer from, to fight against those who dominate or exploit them, to put an end to this domination or exploitation, but they cannot do without this domination or exploitation. It has become their reason for living. They need it, need to find it everywhere and to continue to be able to feel the injustice of which they are the object, this injustice that also indefinitely authorizes them to issue perpetual denunciations of others.

Resultant (see *collective force, association/disassociation, individuation*, and *one*). Bergson explains, in connection with William James, how "one can be a spiritualist, a materialist, a pantheist, just as one can be indifferent to philosophy and satisfied with common sense: the fact remains that one always conceives of one or several simple principles by which the whole of material and moral things might be explained."[1] The concept of the resultant was created by Proudhon, following Leibniz,[2] in order to think the primacy of the collective force, but also the anarchist refusal of any originary principle and thus the priority of the multiple over the one. Any collective force (i.e., any collective being, any individual) is a resultant of the multiple forces that, in associating and composing their relations, give it life. In the reality that constitutes us, there is no principle, no beginning, no primary being, only resultants. Capital, State, Idea, theory, nation, class, and sex are resultants. God is a resultant. The human being itself, Proudhon tells us – along with the illusions of its ego, its consciousness, and its freedom – is a resultant, a "composite of powers."[3] In other words, in the human being, as in everything, what seems to exist in principle, from the beginning – freedom as much as the soul, faculties as much as the totality of the elements or the essences apparently at the origin of the human composite, the unity of creation as much as the unity of the ego – only comes afterwards, is only an effect of composition. Bakunin demonstrates this way of seeing when he explains that "each person" is "nothing other than the resultant of an innumerable quantity of actions, circumstances, and innumerable physical and social conditions that continue to produce this life for as long as it lasts."[4] This is also true for the totality of that which exists: "Universal Solidarity cannot have the character of an absolute first cause; on the contrary, it is merely the *resultant* [emphasis in the original] produced by the simultaneous action of *particular* causes, the totality of which constitutes *universal*

---

1   Bergson, *The Creative Mind*, 249.

2   On the concept of the resultant (and its relation to the concept of the *vinculum subtantiale*) in the theory of Leibniz, cf. Yvon Belaval, *Leibniz: initiation à sa philosophie* (Paris: Vrin, 1962), 245 et passim and, more generally, Frémont, *L'Être et la relation*.

3   Proudhon, *La Guerre et la paix*, 128.

4   Bakunin, "Considérations philosophiques," *Œuvres*, 3:245.

causality. It creates and will always be created anew; it is the *composed unity*, everlastingly created by the infinite totality of the ceaseless transformations of all existing things... [emphasis my own]."[1] It is in this sense that anarchism can recognize itself in the thought of Whitehead, for whom "actual *entities*" (see this term) "are not substances, but processes; not static realities, but results."[2]

Revocability (see *direct democracy*). As a procedure of direct democracy, the revocability of delegates expresses a more general attitude of the libertarian movement: the *determination*, in the moment and in a given situation, of the validity of a collective *action* or *arrangement* (see these terms). Libertarians may prefer to wait before deciding on such-and-such a position or such-and-such a rupture in order to be sure not to compromise an action in progress in the name of some other imperative. However, from a libertarian point of view, it is always possible by right (i.e., in terms of the specific conception of *rights* that they recognize) for them to call into question any stance or commitment the moment they judge that it falls under an oppressive logic or bears too strong a trace of the general dominatory order. Accepting responsibility for the consequences of this breaking-off from a *common* action or project (see this term), they are always able to separate, provisionally or permanently, from the collectivity engaged in this action or this project.

Revolt (see *indignation* and *insurrection*). An essential and foundational moment of emancipation, when dominated forces brutally and radically escape from the traps of dominatory relations, refuse any solution within these relations, affirm another possibility, and create the conditions for a radical recomposition of reality. As René Furth explains, revolt is always affirmative: "[t]hereby, in opposition, people posit themselves. At the most spontaneous level, this means an explosion of force, an irruption of a vital dynamism that has been dammed up by the established order...The negation that bursts forth in a revolt discloses a deeper affirmation, the affirmation of a freedom that is constitutive of human reality."[3] And this is why anarchism can endorse Jean Genet's words: "I do not love the oppressed. I love those whom I love, who are always handsome and sometimes oppressed but who stand up and rebel" (see *master/slave*).[4]

---

1   Bakunin, *The Political Philosophy of Bakunin*, 53-54 (trans.: modifications my own).

2   Domenica Janicaud, "Traduire la métaphysique en procès," *L'Effet Whitehead*, 71.

3   René Furth, "L'anarchisme ou la révolution intégrale," in *Dictionnaire du mouvement ouvrier*, ed. André Nataf (Paris: Éditions universitaires, 1970), 52.

4   Jean Genet, *Miracle of the Rose*, trans. Bernard Frechtman (New York: Grove Press, 1988), 246.

Revolution. An old conception of the 19th century, issuing from the French Revolution. In this conception, the transformation of the world is imagined in the form of a coup d'état or a popular uprising, as a result of which a change of Constitution or regime affects the head of state (Republic, Empire, absolute monarchy, constitutional monarchy). Supplanted for a moment in the mid-19th century by the idea of the *Social Revolution* (see this term) – a very different way of conceiving the transformation of society – the old political revolution regained its currency a century later within the framework of Marxism and Marxism-Leninism. Once again, the question of the State became the key to change, and the dictatorship of the proletariat came to join fascism and Nazism in the long procession of travesties that States have invented to perpetuate their domination. The idea of revolution should not be confused with those of the *Great Evening* and the *insurrectionary general strike* (see these terms) invented by the libertarian workers' movements at the turn of the 19th and 20th centuries.

Revolutionary syndicalism (see *direct action*, *movement*, and *general strike*).

Right wing (left wing) (see *classification*). A vague political distinction, resulting from the seating arrangements of the popular representatives in the five hundred square meters of the French Revolution's first representative assemblies. Inscribed within the narrow limits of the existing social and economic order, this distinction serves primarily to subject the "citizens" to this order by giving them the illusion that they freely decide its direction, generally every five years, at the time of the processing and counting of ballots.

Rupture (see *revolt*, *insurrection*, *hierarchy*, and *direct action*). The free association of collective beings (in love as in politics) imperatively requires that they always be able to break this association whenever they consider it necessary. If *revolt* is the form assumed by a rupture within a relation of domination and oppression, a rupture between collective forces in an association can simply correspond to an unproductive contradiction that carries *sadness* and thus a reduction of the association's *power* (see these terms). Any rupture necessarily accentuates this feeling of sadness, at least temporarily, but, unless it transforms itself into a lasting *ressentiment* (see this term), it gives rise to the conditions for new associations and, thereby, for an emancipatory recomposition of the relations that link us.

S

Sadness/joy (see *good/bad*).

Science (see *manual/intellectual, symbols/signs, movement, becoming*, and *life*). Bergson, and Deleuze after him, demonstrated the reductivist and domina- tory character of science. In order to dominate and instrumentalize beings, by means of a simple and manipulative "practical utility," science substitutes signs for things, arrests them in their movement or becoming, and thus claims to express the truth of what they are while it separates them from their own capacities.[1] As Deleuze writes, "[t]he taste for replacing real relations between forces by an abstract relation which is supposed to express them all, as a mea- sure, seems to be an integral part of science and also of philosophy."[2] "[A] lthough it is a simple means subordinated to life, knowledge sets itself up as end, judge, supreme instance."[3] But it was undoubtedly Bakunin who most forcefully set forth the anarchist critique of science as the field had been con- stituted since the 17th century. It is he who most clearly denounces its re- ductive and oppressive role.[4] For Bakunin, if "the government of science and of men of science…cannot fail to be impotent, ridiculous, inhuman, cruel, oppressive, exploitative, maleficent," it is because science, in depending on

---

1   "[I]t is of the essence of science to handle signs, which it substitutes for the objects them-
    selves. These signs undoubtedly differ from those of language by their greater precision and
    their higher efficacy; they are none the less tied down to the general condition of the sign,
    which is to denote a fixed aspect of the reality under an arrested form" (Henri Bergson,
    Creative Evolution, trans. Arthur Mitchell [London: Macmillan, 1911], 329.)
2   Deleuze, *Nietzsche and Philosophy*, 74.
3   Ibid. 100.
4   On the relationship between science and anarchism, cf. Colson, "La science anarchiste."

signs and claiming to speak the truth or the essence of things, fails to grasp the life and the movement – the simultaneously *intimate* and *fugitive* character – of that which exists, wherein the power of being unfolds itself. For Bakunin, as for Nietzsche later on, what is most intimate, what is most real, is at the same time that which is most fugitive, immediate, and apparent, that which the "senses" alone can apprehend because they involve a *direct* and *immediate* relation to the world: "[t]here really exists in all things a hidden aspect or, if you like, a kind of intimate being that is not inaccessible, but that eludes the grasp of science. It is not at all the intimate being of which M. Littré and all the metaphysicians speak, which constitutes, according to them, the in-itself of things and the why of phenomena. It is, on the contrary, the least essential, the least internal, the most external aspect and at once the most real and the most momentary, the most fugitive aspect of things and beings: it is their im-mediate materiality, their real individuality, such as it is presented to our senses alone, which no reflection of the mind could contain, nor any word express."[1] One finds this same conception in Nietzsche: "[t]he 'apparent' world is the only one: the 'real' world has only been *lyingly added*…We possess scientific knowledge today to precisely the extent that we have decided to accept the evidence of the senses…The rest is abortion and not-yet-science: which is to say metaphysics, theology, psychology, epistemology. Or science of formulae, sign-systems: such as logic and that applied logic, mathematics. In these reality does not appear at all…"[2] As Bakunin writes, while it believes itself capable of knowing the innermost depths of things, "science concerns itself with nothing but shadows…The living reality escapes it and gives itself only to life, which, being itself fugitive and momentary, can and indeed always does encompass all that lives, that is to say, all that is passing or fleeting."[3]

Scientific laws (causes) (see *law/right, science, matter,* and *determinism*). If sci-ence, according to Bakunin's phrase, "concerns itself only with shadows,"[4] its own theoretical and logical instruments are equally phantasmic. This is even more true of the "laws" and "causes" asserted by the natural sciences. As Bakunin maintains, for libertarian thought, the "natural laws that govern the world" are merely the transposition of legal and political representations (which themselves issue from theology) onto the terrain of science.[5] In their aspiration to generality, "laws" and "causes" have no real existence: "[t]hey are

---

1   Bakunin, "Considérations philosophiques," *Œuvres*, 3:393.

2   Friedrich Nietzsche, *The Twilight of the Idols and the Anti-Christ*, trans. R.J. Hollingdale (London: Penguin Books, 1990), 46.

3   Bakunin, "Considérations philosophiques," *Œuvres*, 3:395.

4   Ibid.

5   Ibid. 3:341-342.

nothing apart from the real things…*they are nothing but these things.*" Even "considered as a totality," "things do not obey these laws because, apart from them, there is neither anyone nor anything that could dictate laws to them and impose laws on them." "Each thing contains its *own* law, i.e., its particular mode of development, existence, and action, within itself [emphasis in original]" (see *monad, entelechy,* and *slavery/freedom*).[1]

Scientists (see *science* and *experts*).

Secession (see *rupture, revolt,* and *master/slave*).

Secrecy/transparency (see *direct action, intimacy, private/public, affinity,* and *symbols*). Anarchists have often been described as conspirators – hidden in the shadows and dressed in long black capes to conceal their bombs and daggers[2] – a representation accentuated by Bakunin's taste for secret societies (see *intimate*). Anarchism is indeed on the side of secrecy, as opposed to transparency and to the illusions of communication, on the side of the *private* (or the *particular*), as opposed to the *public* (or the general) (see these terms). But this anarchist secrecy does not have much to do with the way in which it is represented by the existing order. Most often informal, this secrecy arises from the *intimate*, the *affinitary,* and the *implicit*. If it refuses the traps of communication and of a transparency aimed primarily at depriving beings of all interiority (and thus of all autonomy), subjecting them to its own order, pinning them down on its tables of *classification,* and forcing them to confess what they are upon the priest's prayer-bench [*prie-dieu*] or the psychoanalyst's couch – anarchist secrecy is, at the same time, entirely on the surface (see *intimate being*), easily accessed or destroyed according to one's interest in or suspicion of it. Perpetually renewed, it is on the side of *intuition, immediacy,* and *direct action* (see these terms): action without intermediaries, without any interpretation required, without translators or translation, to the extent to which the relation it establishes between beings is actually an *internal* relation, a relation rendered possible by this preservation of intimacy. Seemingly paradoxical, it is in this sense, as Deleuze and Hawad demonstrate, that anarchist secrecy or intimacy can be identified with the open and "smooth spaces" of the nomadic war machine, where collective beings are no longer subordinated to "the monopoly of an organic power," but are carried away by "the power of a vortical body in a nomad space."[3]

---

1   Ibid. 3:352-354.

2   On these representations, in particular during the period of *attentats* in France between 1892 and 1894, cf. Uri Eisenzweig, *Fictions de l'anarchisme* (Paris: Christian Bourgois, 2001).

3   Deleuze and Guattari, *A Thousand Plateaus,* 364-366 (trans.: modifications my own).

Selection (see *eternal return*). Like many other concepts, selection has a wide variety of meanings from a libertarian point of view. In the hierarchical and external order that currently prevails, selection designates the procedures that authorize certain beings to graduate from one rank to another, to climb the rungs of a *hierarchy*. It also indicates the way in which, using the same procedures, this order can simultaneously reject and suppress the infinity of *possibilities* that reality contains while choosing from within that reality all the elements it needs so as to reproduce and expand its own dominance, as the very word "selection" indicates (see *exterior/interior*). In the libertarian usage of the term, selection is at once internal, horizontal, and perpetual. It designates the manner in which collective beings compose their relations, choosing some encounters while avoiding others (see *affinity*), thus composing, within themselves as well as in association with others, a world of greater *power* and *freedom*, an *arrangement* of collective forces capable of liberating the totality of the power of that which exists (see *plane of immanence*).

Self (see *body*).

Self-criticism (see *public confession*).

Self-discipline (see *discipline*).

Self-improvement (see *rendering of accounts*). An old, oppressive, prescriptive notion from morality and religion, which is reproduced by all the modern apparatuses of subjectification and culpabilization (psychological, political) and which aims to make each of us his or her own torturer (see *conscience* and *self-criticism*). While anarchism's denunciation of *work* (see *labor/work*) and of its relations of submission does not prevent it from observing the ways in which its conditions and effects might also allow for the affirmation of new relations, it refuses without the least reservation to submit to the framework constituted by self-improvement [*travail sur soi*], whereby the "self-improver," [*travailleur*] in taking himself or herself for raw material, inexorably traps himself or herself in an inexhaustible source of *guilt* and *ressentiment*.

Self-management (self-government) (see *autonomy, collective force, positive anarchy*, and *balancing of forces*). A recent notion in libertarian thought that was emphasized for some time within the French labor movement, dating from the beginning of the 1970s, before vanishing with the integration of the unions into the State apparatus, co-administration with employers, and the disappearance of the working classes that had comprised its motive force and condition of possibility. Appearing at the beginning of the second half of the 20th century, the idea of self-management can be placed squarely within a long emancipatory tradition. For this tradition, the *power* monopolized by the State, Capital, or God and his representatives must be reappropriated by the multitude of the collective beings that produce it, each in its own manner, however infinitesimal it may be. A century earlier, following Proudhon, the painter Gustave Courbet most forcefully expressed the immediacy of the relation to the world that underlies the idea of self-management in the account that he made of his 1853 interview with a member of the "government" intending to commission a painting from him in the name of the State. "I replied at once that I did not understand a word he had said, since he claimed to represent a Government and I did not consider myself in any way a part of that Government, that I was a Government too and that I challenged his to do anything whatever for mine that I could accept. I went on to say that to me his Government seemed just like any *private citizen [particulier]*."[1] This is a conception to which Courbet returns in a broader sense 18 years later, under the Commune, when the painter, in his declaration of principles for the election of the delegates of the district, invites artists to give themselves their own "government" and to create the "Federation of Artists": "I am happy to tell you that the painters, on my instigation, have just taken the initiative in this order of ideas [the principle of federation]. May all the trades of our society follow their example, so that in the future no government will be able to prevail on ours. All associations that are self-regulated and constituted according to their own interests will be our cantons, and the more they govern themselves, the more they will ease the task of the Commune."[2] Despite what this text might (wrongly) lead us to believe – in the manner whereby certain libertarian aspirations have been denatured in recent decades – in the management of enterprises, publicity, or political organization, libertarian self-management does not consist in decentralizing power, entrusting a little limited autonomy to the lower levels of the social organization in order to "interest" them in what they are to do so that they will more effectively carry out the task assigned to them as required, with more enthusiasm, initiative, and perhaps even job satisfaction (see *self-discipline* and *neoliberals*). Whatever the nature of the *collective being* under consideration, the *autonomy* (see this term) associated with libertarian self-management is an absolute autonomy. This is an autonomy founded on a true *subjectivity* (see this term) equipped, like any subjectivity, with all the prerogatives that usually pertain to the concept of subject – sovereignty, sensitivity, the right to existence, separateness, and respect, an overall point of view on the world, an equal right to speak – whatever the size of the *collective force*

---

1 Courbet, Letter to Alfred Bruyas, October 1853, in Mack, *Gustave Courbet*, 109-10.

2 Gustave Courbet qtd. in Gonzalo J Sánchez, *Organizing Independence: The Artists Federation of the Paris Commune and its Legacy, 1871-1889* (Lincoln, NE: University of Nebraska Press, 1997), 46-7 (trans.: modifications my own).

under consideration (see *equality*). Always in motion, made possible by an infinity of provisional or temporary collective beings, existing only through the modalities of association of the forces that compose them at a *given moment*, with each of these forces commanding its own right to autonomy and subjectivity, libertarian self-management is always placed under the sign of *tension* (see this term), of *conflict*, and of an unstable balance that must be constantly sought (see *balancing of forces*). In this sense, it is linked to the concept of *anarchy* (see this term) in its double aspect of chaos and voluntary construction.

Self-sufficiency (see *other* and *more than oneself*). In its ambiguity, this word makes it possible to grasp the originality of libertarian thought. In its proper sense, self-sufficiency (in the sense of autarky) appears to characterize the will to autonomy generally ascribed to anarchists. However, it is precisely the opposite. Reduced to the individualization of the roles and functions defined by the existing order, self-sufficiency prevents collective beings from opening up to the infinite power that they contain, which can only be liberated through association with others (see *balancing of forces*). It reduces this power to the sterile, negative, and external game of competition. It subjects this power to the limitations of an order that self-sufficient beings vainly believe that they can appropriate (see *totality/totalitarianism*).

Sensibility (see *sensitivity*). The ability of a collective being to perceive the diversity and the often minute delicacy of the relations that constitute it and that either unite it with or oppose it to other collective beings at a given moment. Sensibility contrasts with the reassuringly automatic facility of words, external to these relations, which too often stand in place of this judgment and appreciation. As Nietzsche writes: "Anger, hatred, love, pity, desire, knowledge, joy, pain – all are names for *extreme* states: the milder, middle degrees, not to speak of the lower degrees which are continually in play, elude us, and yet it is they which weave the web of our character and our destiny. These extreme outbursts – and even the most moderate conscious pleasure or displeasure, while eating food or hearing a note, is perhaps, rightly understood, an extreme outburst – very often rend the web apart, and then they constitute violent exceptions, no doubt usually consequent on built-up congestions: – and, as such, how easy it is for them to mislead the observer! No less easy than it is for them to mislead the person in whom they occur. *We are none of us* what we appear to be in accordance with the states for which alone we have consciousness and words…"[1]

---

1   "115: The so-called 'ego'," *Daybreak: Thoughts on the Prejudices of Morality*, trans. R. J. Hollingdale, ed. Maudemarie Clark and Brian Leiter (Cambridge: Cambridge University Press, 1997), 71. While it claims to capture the essence of things, science remains external to a determining interiority, which expresses itself only in that which is most immediate, most

Sensitivity (see *sensibility*). A prickliness that, within a collective being, ensures a vigilant attention to the diversity and the nuances of the relationships constitutive of this being, guaranteeing autonomy and respect to the forces that it associates.

Separatism [non-mixité] (see *anarchy*). "May '68 abolished the separation between girls' and boys' schools, and now the feminists want to reinstate them!" It is in just such terms that a great number of anarchists have long perceived feminists' demand to meet on their own, to constitute themselves as autonomous groupings. In the name of an abstract universalism, of an anarchism transformed into an idealistic ideology and structures blind to the reality of their own functioning, this rejection of separate association [*non-mixité*] testifies to a total ignorance of the libertarian project. The demand of the women's movement for separate associations is only the singular expression of a pluriform and foundational demand of the anarchist project: the autonomy of collective beings; the need to constitute an infinity of radically autonomous collective forces charged with proving concretely, through experimentation with the various methods of association and disassociation, their effectively emancipatory character. The autonomy of forces, a plurality of mutually entangled forces that multiply the modes of belonging and relation that associate and oppose them constitutes the primary, necessary, and permanent condition of a libertarian recomposition of that which exists, of a world able to liberate all the power that reality contains.

Serial dialectic (see *series [seriation]*, *balancing of forces*, and *tension*). Notion used by Proudhon (especially in *De la Création de l'ordre*) to think the manner in which collective forces can, by the mastery and the *selection* of their oppositions, compose an immanent order capable of liberating the most *power* and thus the most *freedom*. With the serial dialectic, during the brief interlude of his discovery of Hegel,[1] Proudhon engaged, some years before Gabriel Tarde, in the elaboration of a non-Hegelian dialectic for which, in order to think and to allow for life and movement, he had to affirm and construct "insoluble antinomies, simultaneous and fecund."[2]

---

apparent, most fugitive.

1 After Proudhon had assiduously frequented Marx over the course of the autumn of 1844. In a letter of 1865, Marx explained how "in long discussions, often lasting the whole night, I infected him with Hegelianism – to his great prejudice, since, not understanding German, he could not study the thing at base…" (Karl Marx, *The Poverty of Philosophy*, trans. H. Quelch [Chicago: Charles H. Kerr and Co., 1913], 186).

2 According to the formula that René Schérer employs with regard to Tarde ("*Homo ludens*: Des stratégies vitales," preface to *La Logique Sociale*, Gabriel Tarde [Le Plessis-Robinson,

Series (seriation) (see *serial dialectic, balancing of forces, analogy, planes of reality,* and *tension*). A concept suggested by Proudhon in the wake of his readings of Charles Fourier, mainly in *De la Création de l'ordre,* in order to think the nature of the relations and arrangements that make the infinite multitude of possible beings compatible. Seriation is not solely or primarily of the order of knowledge, and it has nothing to do with the fixed, arbitrary, damaging classifications (see *classification*) that every dominatory order establishes. It takes place within forces and their relations, as well as within the knowledge that we can have of them. Proudhon's seriation operates by *analogy, affinity,* and *contrariety* – in a transductive fashion, Simondon would say – across the most widely variegated domains of existence, making possible a multitude of different orders. This is why one can never tell in advance what a being may find itself capable of within the events in which it takes part and the situations it traverses, or alongside the beings it encounters and associates with. A member of the Assault Guard in Barcelona can be found at the sides of the militants of the FAI,[1] firing on the insurgent soldiers; a devout and scrupulous German accountant may turn out to be an effective concentration camp commandant; a model employee may become a famous painter; a signal of revolt can transform itself into an emblem or fetish of power; a hammer can become a weapon; swords metamorphose into plowshares; the wind can destroy forests and make the flight of birds possible; oceans can devastate the coasts and allow the discovery of new continents, "as if the ship were a folding of the sea."[2]

Servants of the people (of the State or any other cause or authority that is called "higher") (see *pro-something* and *experts*). Be wary of all those who claim to be "servants" or to place themselves at the service of any reality other than themselves. Be especially wary of the so-called servants of the people, inevitably among the most hypocritical. As the word should indicate, a "servant" always draws its power from oppression (see this term), generally making an effort, behind the appearance of service or common interest, to justify its own domination.

Sexuality (see *body, person* and *power*). Because "[t]he living human being is a group," a "composite of powers,"[3] we contain a multitude of *desires* and im-

---

France: Synthélabo, 1999]).

1   Iberian Anarchist Federation. (Translator's note: the Assault Guards [*Guardias de Asalto*], a special police force created by the government of Spain's Second Republic to reassert discipline over the cities, nonetheless fought against the fascist coup in Barcelona and Madrid [Helen Graham, *The Spanish Republic at War, 1936-1939* (Cambridge, UK: Cambridge University Press, 2002), 37-38, 92].)

2   Deleuze, *Foucault,* 97.

3   Proudhon, *Philosophy of Progress,* 23 (trans.: modifications my own); Proudhon, *La Guerre*

pulses that the existing order and its language classify and fix within a number of hierarchically arranged domains (alimentary, motor, sexual, spiritual, etc.). Sexuality is only one of these fields, provisional and *constrained*, that, in libertarian thought, can no more be made into a founding principle or a primary motor (Eros, libido) than any other or be considered as more or less dominant or primary for human activity. Like any *thing*, sexuality or sexual desire is only a *resultant* (see these terms): the resultant of a particular arrangement of forces, given its form by the order within which it operates. The social order consecrates a great deal of energy and care to the task of subjecting this resultant to norms and stigmatizing deviations (for example, under the name of *perversion*), the better to transform this resultant into a first principle, beneficial or dangerous, so that the effect becomes the cause, so that nature and culture, *good* and *bad* can at the same time be irremediably bound up with and opposed to one another. Because anarchism attempts to recompose the totality of that which exists, it also attempts to recompose the constitutive elements of sexuality into new arrangements. It attempts to give birth to new associations and new desires that correspond to other needs. Because it affirms, with Spinoza, that "nobody as yet has determined the limits of the body's capabilities: that is, nobody as yet has learned from experience what the body can and cannot do…solely from the laws of its nature,"[1] it attempts (against Christianity and a multitude of other forces imposing uniformity) to invent new bodies in which the forces constitutive of that which is conventionally called sexuality would change in meaning and quality and could finally do all that they are capable of, within other *arrangements* and other *associations*.

Signification (see *symbols/signs*, *subject*, and *collective reason*).

Singularity (see *differences* and *indiscernibles*). Each collective being is different from all the others. Bakunin formulates this position as follows: "all things are governed by inherent laws which properly constitute their own particular nature;…each thing has its own peculiar form of transformation and action…"[2]

Situation. Because it rejects *dualism* (see this term), anarchism rejects any distinction between noble beings (human beings) and other beings that they would appropriate as objects (tools, animals, etc.). But libertarian thought also refuses to distinguish between beings that are stable (capable of being isolated in a pure state, fixed in time and space), thus meriting study, and merely

---

et la paix, 128.

1   Spinoza, *Ethics*, Part III, Scholium to Proposition 2, trans. Samuel Shirley, in Spinoza, *Complete Works*, 280-81.

2   Bakunin, *The Political Philosophy of Bakunin*, 54.

fugitive beings (see this term), which are accidental or external to beings of the first category, even if beings of this second category may be decisive for what those of the first can become (storms, auto "accidents," chance events, etc.). On the contrary, with Bakunin, Gabriel Tarde, Leibniz, or Nietzsche, anarchism tries to suggest that stable and permanent beings are only conspicuous exceptions, "infinitely slowed movements" (Tarde) that mask the ceaseless becoming of that which exists, the infinity of "small perceptions" (Leibniz) that comprise the reality of beings. As Bakunin writes, "There really exists in all things an aspect...the least essential, the least internal, the most external aspect, and at once the most real and the most transitory, the most *fugitive* of things and beings: it is their immediate materiality, their real individuality, such as it is presented to our senses."[1] From this point of view, situations constitute a decisive element in the associative modalities of collective beings, not as the mere context or backdrop for these associations, but as the (non-hierarchical) accounting for the totality of forces that help define the emancipatory or oppressive quality of the collective being thus formed. Again from this point of view, a situation is itself always a collective being (a rioting district, a successful party, a sunset), an *event* that is decisive for the ebb and flow of emancipation. The Situationists[2] spoke of "constructed situations," neglecting the fact that, because it mobilizes the totality of that which exists in a singular way, in no case can a situation be subjected to the will, the mastery, or the desire of only one of the collective beings concerned, unless it is to be instantly transformed into external relations of domination.

Slavery/freedom (see *exterior/interior, nature, law/rights* and *freedom*). In a passage from *L'Empire knouto-germanique*, Bakunin asks, "What is freedom? What is slavery? Does man's freedom consist in the revolt against all laws? We say *No*, in so far as laws are natural, economic and social laws, not authoritatively imposed but inherent in things, in relations, in situations, the natural development of which is expressed by those laws. We say *Yes* if they are political and juridical laws, imposed by men upon men: whether violently by the right of force; whether by deceit and hypocrisy – in the name of religion or any doctrine whatever; or finally, by dint of the fiction, the democratic falsehood called *universal suffrage*. Against the laws of Nature no revolt is possible on the

---

1   Bakunin, *Œuvres* 3.393.

2   Translator's note: The Situationists: members of the Situationist International (1957-1972), an organization of radical theorists and artists that took its name from the concept and practice of the "constructed situation": "A moment of life concretely and deliberately constructed by the collective organization of a unitary ambience and a game of events" (*The Situationist International Anthology*, ed. and trans. Ken Knabb [Berkeley, CA: Bureau of Public Secrets, 1989], 45).

part of man, the simple reason being that he himself is a product of Nature and that he exists only by virtue of those laws…Nature envelops, penetrates, constitutes his whole existence. How can he ever escape this Nature? [emphasis in original]."[1]

One can easily be ironic about Bakunin's inconsistency. How can one distinguish between oppressive laws and emancipatory laws, those in which *freedom* and *necessity* coincide (see these terms)? How could the human being be entirely traversed by a nature that "envelops," "penetrates," and "constitutes his entire existence," which must be obeyed, yet at the same time produce oppressive laws that must be rebelled against, these being unnatural laws? How can *nature* (see this term) be all that exists and, at the same time, be subject to the violence and power of a reality other than itself? In other words, can anarchism really do without the belief in God, without a transcendence that would always justify its will to break free, its ceaseless swinging between "yes" and "no," this false dialectic that Marx denounced with such irony in the work of Proudhon?

Bakunin's apparent inconsistency is, however, beyond the rules of language – the "lying systems" and "schoolmaster vanities" denounced by Cœurderoy[2] – the clearest contradictory indication of the problem posed by anarchism, as well as of the solution that it proposes. It is because anarchism calls for a radical monism and immanentism (see *monism* and *immanence*) that a human being cannot in any case aspire to separate itself from a nature that "envelops, penetrates, constitutes his whole existence." But the arrangement of this nature corresponds to infinite modalities of internal composition. Within these modalities of composition, the human being is led to distinguish between two types of laws: oppressive laws and emancipatory laws (see *good/evil*).[3] This distinction does not pertain to the nature of the laws in question but to the relations that they form between beings and the relations that the beings maintain with one another. What we might call emancipatory, for a given being or *thing* at a *given moment*, is any law that is "inherent" to this being or thing and that "expresses [its] development." For this reason, Bakunin can explain that "[e]ach thing contains its *own* law, i.e., its particular mode of development, existence, and action, within itself [emphasis in original]."[4] What one calls "oppressive," for a given being or thing at a given moment, is any law that is external to it, that subjects or submits it to an order external to itself. To compose a world in which the freedom of some multiplies the freedom of others,

1   Bakunin, *The Political Philosophy of Bakunin*, 263.

2   Cœurderoy, "Hourra!!! ou la révolution par les cosaques," 325.

3   For a considerably different interpretation of Bakunin's texts, see Eduardo Colombo, "Anarchisme, obligation sociale et devoir d'obéissance," *Réfractions* 2 (Summer 1998): 83-117.

4   Bakunin, "Considérations philosophiques," *Œuvres*, 3:352-354.

in which the law of some becomes the law of others within a more powerful being, authorizing its components to *do all that they can* – such is the project of the anarchist movement (see *monad, equality,* and *plane of immanence*).

Social (see *collective*).

Social bond (see *direct action*). As the term indicates, the social bond is a form of binding or bondage that keeps collective forces subjugated to an order external to that which constitutes them. In the name of a *direct* encounter and *composition* of relations between beings (see these terms), libertarian association is opposed to any bond.

Social Explosion (see *anarchist chemistry, Great Evening, general strike,* and *revolt*). A phrase that has fallen out of use, the invention of which stemmed directly from *propaganda by the deed* and the era of the anarchist *attentats*. Jean Maitron was wrong to be astonished that, many years later, a revolutionary syndicalist journal as moderate as *La Révolution prolétarienne* could celebrate the decisive importance of the anarchist *attentats* for the renewal and development of the labor movement in France.[1] In 1907, Pierre Monatte had identified revolutionary syndicalism as the direct heir to propaganda by the deed, "since the great voice of anarchist dynamite [has] fallen silent."[2] If *direct action* took the place of *propaganda by the deed* in the thought and discourse of the syndicalist movement, and if calls for a "general and insurrectionary strike" came to relay the explosive power of chemistry, this was merely a new metamorphosis of the libertarian project, the elements of which had changed place and meaning without ceasing to compose a mixture (indeed, an explosive mixture) of signs and reality, forces and ideas, science and politics. As the word indicates, social explosion escapes the dialectical relation of class struggle. Extended to broad segments of the population, revolt breaks up class relations and creates an entirely new situation in which, for a period of time, as the expression goes, "everything is possible," until the play of social relations resumes, refastening the bonds that the social explosion had momentarily disrupted (see *stoppage* and *event*). In this sense, the conceptions of the social revolution and the general strike are directly dependent on *propaganda by the deed* and its *chemical* dimension (see these terms). With the revolutionary general strike (the *Great Evening* of the popular imaginary), the reality and the political and social meanings of anarchist chemistry were merely reversed. The revolutionary signification of the anarchist bomb is made material enough in the intense mobilization

---

1   *La Révolution prolétarienne*, November 1937 and October 1947; see Jean Maitron, *Le mouvement anarchiste en France*, vol. 1, *Des origines* à 1914 (Paris: F. Maspero, 1975), 259.

2   Pierre Monatte, "Syndicalisme et anarchisme," in *La Vie ouvrière* 94 (Aug. 1913): 235.

and concentration of working-class forces making ready for the general strike. Meanwhile, its chemical and explosive reality is charged with the responsibility for giving political meaning to a strategy and a project thought in the form of a social "explosion," "a revolution that comes from everywhere and nowhere," "bursting suddenly" like "lightning" (Pelloutier, Griffuelhes). Once again, as Fernand Pelloutier writes, the "dynamite" of collective action comes to replace the *attentats'* "individual recourse to dynamite."[1] As the anarchist bomb ceases to give voice to the social revolution, the social revolution takes its turn to speak, replacing the physical and chemical discourses of nitroglycerin and fulminate.

Social Revolution (see *Great Evening* and *general strike*). A vast project of social and economic transformation born in the mid-19th century that momentarily supplanted the idea of revolution bequeathed by the destruction of the absolute monarchy in France. In becoming *social* (parallel to "the social question," as it was called), the Revolution ceases to be thought from the celestial heights of the State, political power, and the grand apparatuses of power. On the contrary, it is staged within social relations – on the terrain of *classes* (see this term) and differences, property and justice, relations of authority and methods of association, i.e., in whatever fields the general order or balance of society operates – and takes place in a multitude of ways, through an overall (because multiform) transformation that cancels the great dominatory authorities: God, the State, and Capital. Synonymous with a polymorphous revolt against the existing order, a revolt that refuses to be instrumentalized in any way, that becomes the single subject of emancipatory history, the social revolution also ceases to be identified with mere crowd movement that takes place only on "insurrectionary days," at revolutionary conjunctures as rare as they are transitory. Developing in the very heart of things, toughened by perpetual struggle, strengthened by the overall rearrangement [*réagencement*] of emancipatory forces, the social revolution can finally lead to a more widespread conflagration completely armed with its power. This conflagration – the *Great Evening* of an earlier day's popular imaginary – is one in which all find themselves transformed, as all have contributed, without hierarchy, without tactical and strategic distinction, to this movement of transformation. The idea of Social Revolution is closely related to that of anarchy (see the series of articles published by Proudhon in 1849 in *La Voix du peuple*). The project of social revolution lasted all the way to the war of 1914-1918, in particular through the idea of the *Great Evening* and the *general strike* (see these terms), until it was

---

1   Fernand Pelloutier, "Anarchism and the Workers' Union," in *No Gods, No Masters: An Anthology of Anarchism*, ed. Daniel Guérin, trans. Paul Sharkey (Edinburgh: AK Press, 2005), 409.

supplanted by the new forms of coup d'état invented by Marxism-Leninism, fascism, Nazism, and the appetites of military leaders.

Solidarity (see *monad*). A notion important to libertarian vocabulary, used to express, from an internal point of view, the quality of the relations linking emancipatory collective forces to one another. But Bakunin also uses it in the neutral and general sense of *universal causality* or in the sense of *life* and *nature*. In this usage, solidarity expresses the totality of that which exists, the totality of the relationships that are possible between all the beings that reality contains, the "ten thousand things" of which the Daoist tradition speaks. The anarchy of beings is due to this limitless character of the relations that constitute the collective forces and thus the relations that they can establish among themselves. In this sense, the practical or subjective sense that this word takes on within libertarian discourse, solidarity serves to indicate a certain emancipatory quality of the relations that collective forces establish among themselves – relations that are constructed, through struggle and selection, out of a great number of other possible relations, often including ones that carry death and oppression.

Solitude (see *friends of our friends*). In his farewell to the Makhnovist insurrection crushed by the Red Army, and in a counterpoint to the call of the First International ("Workers of the world, unite!"), Peter Arshinov made the following appeal: "Proletarians of the world, look into the depths of your own beings, seek out the truth and realize it yourselves: you will find it nowhere else."[1] Indeed, much more frequently than one imagines, there are moments – tiny or historical, obvious or hardly perceptible – in which all communication, all connection, should be refused (see *stoppage*) in order to take refuge in the deepest of solitudes: the only place in which one can reconstitute the conditions of the call to others, of new associations that open onto other possibilities. As Simondon demonstrates, the forms of connection and communication established between groups and individuals are generally limited to dictating and maintaining the bonds of *submission* and *exteriority* that unite them within the framework of the dominant orders, making the roles and the functions necessary to these orders operative, as was so long the case within the Third International. In opposition to these functional relations, which he calls "interindividual," Simondon proposes relations that he calls *transindividual*. These relations traverse individuals and groups by calling upon that within them which is not reducible to what presently defines them as individuals and groups, upon that which they contain that is *more than themselves*, in the form of the *apeiron*, and thus in the form of novelty, of revolutionary possibilities. And it is in this sense, during this withdrawal into solitude – this flight from all the impoverished forms of communication that are

---

1   Peter Arshinov, *History of the Makhnovist Movement*, 261.

subject to the existing order, from the requirements imposed by this order's monopoly – that Pascal can understand, with the entirety of his being, that Christ is in anguish until the end of time, that Zarathustra can "have a presentiment of the enigma of the universe and…speak with the sun," discovering not "a God the creator" but the presence of "a world subject to the eternal return."[1] It is also in this sense that the desire to recompose a radically different world can reappear in the heart of vanquished and despairing beings, inviting them to revolt once more, to associate anew. As Simondon writes, "the true transindividual relation begins only on the other side of solitude."[2] "How can a politics of separation be founded?" asks Jacques Derrida.[3] This is the question that anarchism attempts to answer (see *one*).

Species activity. Nietzschean concept (see *plastic force*).

Spontaneism (see *spontaneity*). Spontaneism has one of two meanings, depending on whether one refers it to an *intrinsic* or *extrinsic* logic (see these terms). In its intrinsic and libertarian sense, spontaneism indicates the capacity of a being to act by and for itself, on the basis of its own resources, in a movement toward the outside that draws it to associate with other forces in order to constitute a more powerful being. In this sense, spontaneism is synonymous with freedom. Any emancipatory and insurrectionary situation in which factories, districts, or universities gradually self-organize, constituting coordinating bodies, unions, federations of councils, or other forms of collective expression, corresponds to this first meaning. This emancipatory *spontaneity* (see this term) should not be confused with the extrinsic and authoritarian "spontaneism" that refers to the manner in which collective beings can be subordinated to a generalized logic of history that is external to them. This second meaning was especially developed by Marxism under its twin aspects of spontaneism and *voluntarism* (see this term): the Party taking it upon itself, as depository of the science of the laws of history, to subject the totality of emancipatory forces to its dictatorship in the name of those laws, as the Church did in the name of God (see *determinism* and *determination*).

Spontaneity (spontaneity of action) (see *freedom*). An important Proudhonian concept, allowing us to think both the infinite diversity of collective beings and the shared dimension conferred on them by their composite character (see *composition*). Though initially thought only on the terrain of the social and the economic, in the form of a creative and anarchic power, in opposition

---

1 Simondon, *L'Individuation psychique et collective*, 154-156.
2 Ibid. 154.
3 Derrida, *The Politics of Friendship*, 55.

to order or "system,"[1] the concept of spontaneity would then make it possible for Proudhon to conceive of human action within the context of the totality of that which exists: "[t]he living human being is a group, like the plant or the crystal, but to a higher degree than those others."[2] For this reason, spontaneity – as the *resultant* of any composition of forces – makes it possible to extend the concept of freedom to the totality of beings: "spontaneity, at the lowest degree in unorganized beings, higher in the plants and animals, attains, under the name of freedom, its plenitude in humanity, which alone attempts to liberate itself from all fatality, objective or subjective, and which indeed liberates itself."[3] In this sense, Proudhon comes close to Nietzsche and his wish to extend "feeling," "thought," and "will" to the inorganic world,[4] but he also invites comparisons with Charles Peirce, William James, A.N. Whitehead, and all of those for whom, in the words of David R. Griffin, "a degree of real freedom (self-determination) is to be attributed to all individuals, including nonhumans, each type of individual having a different degree of freedom."[5]

State. It is Nietzsche who gives the two best anarchist definitions of the State. The first is widely known: "State is the name of the coldest of all cold monsters. It even lies coldly, and this lie crawls out of its mouth: 'I, the state, am the *people* [see this term].'" The second, however, is undoubtedly even more precise: "the State is a hypocrite hound;…it likes to speak with smoke and bellowing – to make believe…that it speaks from the belly of things."[6]

Statistics (mathematics) (see *gesture, anarchist chemistry,* and *symbols/signs*). With wits darkened by the pretentions and the sarcasms of Marxism, certain historians have gratuitously mocked the naive and obstinate passion of the emancipatory workers' movements for figures and statistics.[7] This is due to their complete ignorance of the libertarian critique of language and its effects of domination, as well as of the great wealth of symbolic and expressive models, both practical and theoretical, by means of which this critique expresses the

---

1   On this point, cf. Ansart, *Marx et l'anarchisme*, 141 et passim.

2   Proudhon, *Philosophy of Progress*, 23 (trans.: modifications my own).

3   Proudhon, *De la Justice*, 3:403.

4   On this point, cf. especially Montebello, *Nietzsche, la volonté de puissance*, 97 et passim.

5   David R. Griffin, "Whitehead et la philosophie constructiviste postmoderne," in *L'Effet Whitehead*, 174.

6   Nietzsche, *Thus Spoke Zarathustra*, 34, 104 (trans.: modifications my own).

7   For the First International, see Ladislas Mysyrowicz, "Karl Marx, la Première Internationale et la Statistique," *Le Mouvement Social* 6 (1969): 51-84. For the French Bourses du Travail, see Peter Schöttler, *Naissance des Bourses du travail: un appareil idéologique d'État à la fin du XIXe siècle* (Paris: PUF, 1985).

power and complexity of that which exists. Following Nietzsche and Michel de Certeau, and with the oppressed of every time and place, libertarian thought distrusts words and discourses – discourses that lie and words that try to fix and trap reality in their nets, enclosing it in relations of domination that they both justify and render possible (see *capture* and *propaganda by the deed*). Faced with the multiplicity of languages, the complexity of working-class realities, the attempts of theorists to impose their views, and the rhetorical power of language, labor statistics constituted both an alternative and a polemical instrument for an egalitarian and communal affirmation of the totality of working-class forces, particularly as they associated within the First International. And it is in this sense, faced with the twisted arguments of a nascent Marxism, that these forces could demand that the coordinating authorities of their movement limit themselves to a mere "mailbox for correspondence and statistics" and could believe, as Ladislas Mysyrowicz perceptively notes, that statistics were to "deliver the coming society from the intellectual tyranny of all the Karl Marxes, present and future" by making possible "a planning without a planner, a free exchange without the blind mechanism of the market," by making possible relationships in which the contradiction between "particular interests and the general interest [would be] resolved through spontaneity and freedom."[1]

One would be wrong, however, to reduce the emancipatory thought of the libertarian workers' movements to a crude fetishization of numbers and statistics (see *utilitarianism*). Along with the concepts of *force, balancing, instinct, desire, composition, justice, possibility, collective reason*, etc., libertarian thought historically appealed to a great number of other expressive models: electrochemical, biological, ethical, philosophical, religious, chemical (see *anarchist chemistry*). Furthermore, it is not in the least unaware of the limitations and dangers of numbers and statistics, as is demonstrated by the comment made in 1840 by Proudhon, that enthusiast of mathematical models, on a work by the philosopher and mathematician Antoine-Augustin Cournot:[2] "M. Cournot's work serves just one purpose...which is to demonstrate that inequalities of fortune, distribution, possession, and poverty operate on mathematical bases. This is not very interesting for me; I know that any kind of error, any aberration of judgment or equity, can only take place under the terms of the laws of reason, the very reason from which it conceals itself, but what I want to know is whether mathematics can serve to demonstrate the morality or immorality, the possibility or impossibility of the inequality of conditions. Undoubtedly, a calculation always answers what one asks of it: if I must have 99 shares, when others divide the 100th, calculation will serve to regulate my interests in the

---

1   Mysyrowicz, "Karl Marx, la Première Internationale et la Statistique," 73-74.

2   Antoine-Augustin Cournot, *Recherches sur les principes mathématiques de la théorie des richesses* (Paris: L. Hachette, 1838).

matter. But *whether or not I have the right* to 99, that is something else [emphasis in original]."[1]

Stoppage (see *general strike, event, repetition, indeterminacy,* and *power of the outside*). "We've stopped everything, we have time for thinking, and it's not a sad thing [*On arrête tout, on réfléchit et c'est pas triste*]!"[2] This May 1968 slogan (even if its overvaluation of "thinking [*réflexion*]" could be questioned) aptly expresses an important aspect of the libertarian movement. The stoppage [*l'arrêt*] should not be confused with the decree [*l'arrêté*], in the sense, for example, in which one speaks of a death sentence [*arrêt de mort*] (see *putting to death*). As Deleuze and Guattari demonstrate, our reality can be conceived of in terms of "machines": couplings of machines in which everything is mutually bound up and interconnected, in which each machine "produc[ing] a flow" connects to another machine that, in a more or less chaotic way, "interrupts" it to produce a new flow, which is itself interrupted in its turn, etc.[3] Social or desiring, the machinic production of our actual being thus makes for us an organism, the *organization* of our life (see this term) (of eating, sleeping, producing, consuming, moving, procreating, militating, loving). But in this continually renewed sequence of our existence, we thus "[suffer] from being organized in this way, from not having some other sort of organization, or no organization at all."[4] As Proudhon writes, "Man does not want to be *organized*, to be *mechanized*. His tendency is toward disorganization, which is to say to *defatalization* – if one will allow me the word – everywhere he feels the weight of a fatalism or a mechanization. Such is the work, the function of freedom [emphasis in original]."[5] From where can this freedom emerge? In the interstices and pauses, when one dreams for a moment or when a cigarette is rolled. It is in the passage from one machine to another, from a machine flow to a machine interruption, that the social machinery marks a multitude of stoppages or hesitations – even imperceptible ones – which give place to the desire for another organization or the absence of any organization. In the linear series of human production, there is a "third term," when "everything stops dead for a moment, everything freezes in place" before "the whole process will begin all over again."[6] It is in this stoppage that another *possibility* appears (see this term): in the stoppage of

---

1   Qtd. in Pierre Haubtmann, *Proudhon: sa vie et sa pensée, 1809-1849*, 243.

2   Gébé, *L'An 01* (Paris: L'Association, 2014).

3   Gilles Deleuze and Félix Guattari, *Anti-Oedipus: Capitalism and Schizophrenia*, trans. Helen Lane, Mark Seem, and Robert Hurley (Minneapolis, MN: U. of Minnesota Press, 1983), 1 et passim.

4   Ibid. 8.

5   Proudhon, *De la Justice*, 3:422.

6   Deleuze and Guattari, *Anti-Oedipus*, 7.

the strike, for example,[1] limited to just one service or workshop, but also in the strike that is extended to a whole society; or, in a much more general way, in these multiple stoppages, generally tiny, barely perceptible, when one suspends a gesture, a glance, a sequence of actions or when one stops – always – to buy cigarettes. But these stoppages, which precede all *revolts*, have nothing of the negative in them. And therefore the libertarian stoppage is distinguished from the way in which Claude Lefort uses the concept of *indeterminacy* (see this term). The libertarian stoppage cannot be compared to a mere "contingency," an "interstice" into which could be inserted the "choice" and the "invention" of another thing. It cannot be compared to an "empty" place, but refers, on the contrary, to a plenitude, to the infinite power of that which exists (see *power of the outside*) – a power that, following Tarde, Proudhon, or Simondon, falls within a rather different tradition of thought and action than that on which Lefort (or, in another manner, Castoriadis) draws.[2] On the contrary, because they express the infinite power of being, of what it is "capable" of doing, libertarian stoppages contain all *possibilities* (see this term). Historically, the libertarian movement has considered these in the broadest manner, through the singular working-class slogan of the *general strike* (see this term), when indeed "everything" stops; when, having stopped, the social actors perceive for one moment the manifestation and the source of their collective power and, thereby, engage in a total recomposition of that which exists.

Subject (revolutionary subject) (see *subjectivity, choice, individuation, body, force,* and *power of the outside*). "What is a subject? What is a being? It is a force."[3] The anarchist subject has nothing in common with what this concept indicates in the representations of the modern Western tradition. This is because of its diversity (see *subjectivity*), its differences in scale, and its constant metamorphoses (according to events and modes of association among collective forces), but also because of the ontological difference between what this libertarian concept indicates as force and *possibility* and the reality of the collective beings that this force and this possibility happen to produce at a given moment. Gilbert Simondon, in particular, allows us to think this libertarian conception of the subject as an emancipatory force with the greatest precision.[4] For Simondon, the "subject is more than individual."[5] In other words, it is not

---

1 On the nature of the "stoppage" of even the tiniest strike, cf. Colson, "Reconnaissance collective et montée en singularité," 55-77.

2 On the "enigmas" and "challenges" with which Lefort and Castoriadis astonish readers ignorant of libertarian thought, see Dewitte, "La mise en abyme du social."

3 Pierre-Joseph Proudhon, *Économie*, 2864 [184].

4 See Simondon, *L'Individuation psychique et collective*.

5 Ibid. 199.

identified with the functions, identities, or denominations and roles (family, professional, ethnic, religious, personal, etc.) that constitute individuals within a given framework and solely in terms of this framework. It contains the totality of the power of that which exists – this power that every social order aspires to reduce, fix in place, and dominate. It contains the other of this order (see *other* and *analogy*), its outside (see *power of the outside*), a conception that Gabriel Tarde summarizes as follows: "[t]o exist is to integrate the infinite into the finite."[1] From this perspective, with Deleuze, one can affirm that the subject is "stripped of interiority" because it is equipped with an inside that is only a fold of the outside – a fold "in the interior of the exterior and inversely."[2] As Simondon writes, "the subject is the ensemble formed by the *individuated* individual and the *apeiron* it contains" (see these terms).[3] In this sense, the libertarian subject is radically distinct from those grand theories that appeal to the concept of the subject and claim to ground this concept, for example theories of language and Freudianism.

Indeed, if the subject is thoroughly tied to *signification*,[4] in libertarian thought, this signification is not dependent on language, one of the principal instruments of domination (see *propaganda by the deed, action, collective reason,* and *symbols/signs*). Signification is born from the difference between the power of the possible, the *limitlessness of the limited*, and the forms of *individuation* existing at a given moment, in a given order, and according to this order. Signification, in art as in politics or love, is always prior to the language that claims to codify it, to enclose it, and, like God, to produce it and make us believe that it depends on this language.[5] Signification arises from the power of being, from anarchy, the "*apeiron* associated with the individuality defined in the subject" (see also *collective reason*).[6] For this reason, the painter Pierre

---

1   Gabriel Tarde qtd. in Milet, *Gabriel Tarde et la philosophie de l'histoire*, 157.

2   Muriel Combes, *Gilbert Simondon and the Philosophy of the Transindividual* 41; Gilles Deleuze qtd. in Combes, 42.

3   Simondon, *L'Individuation psychique et collective*, 199.

4   From the amoeba to the human being, to speak only of living things, each collective force has a perspective on the world that surrounds it, since not all environments are the same for it (each one is more or less *good* or *bad*). This perspective of collective beings renders a "meaning of things," a signification immanent to reality, while constituting them as subjects. On all of this, cf., with reference to Karl Popper, Isabelle Stengers, in *The Invention of Modern Science*, trans. Daniel W. Smith (Minneapolis, MN: U. of Minnesota Press, 2000), 44 et passim.

5   "If there were no signification to support language, there would be no language" (Simondon, *L'Individuation psychique et collective*, 200).

6   Ibid. On the importance of this question for Artaud's thought, see Norbert Bandier, *Sociologie du surréalisme (1924-1929)* (Paris: La Dispute, 1999), 207 et passim.

Soulages can explain that "painting is not a means of communication. I would rather say, not that it transmits a meaning, but that it only makes meaning. The meaning it makes for the viewer depends on who the viewer is."[1]

If, for his part, Freud perceives, through the concept of the unconscious, the power, the forces, and the invisible, hidden, or repressed desires that human beings harbor, he is wrong to reduce this power to an individual psyche, to enclose human beings within a loneliness that has sickened them, and to place them in the hands of priests who claim to treat them while making a living from their suffering. He is especially wrong to identify the "subject" of this course of treatment (inevitably of indefinite length) with the individual as defined and instrumentalized by society at a given moment. If mental pathology or "psychological" suffering is linked to the *preindividual*, to the *power of the outside* that any being contains, it is precisely because this *power of the outside* that forms the basis of the individual's subjectivity, unable to express itself outside of the individual prison (psychic and social) within which the existing order confines it, fails to form other subjectivities alien to the order that confines their power. As Gilbert Simondon writes, "mental pathology…appears when the discovery of the *transindividual* is lacking, i.e., when the *charge of nature* that inheres in the subject with the individual cannot encounter other charges of nature in other subjects with which it could form an individual world of significations."[2]

Subjectivity (see *intimate, collective force, collective beings, individuation,* and *subject*). Anarchism can be defined as, among other things, a radical subjectivism.[3] Anarchist subjectivity has nothing to do with the modern "subject" quite content to carry an identification card and to play the roles, think the thoughts, and be all the things that society requires of those subjected to its law. Contrary to what is often believed even within the libertarian movement, neither does this anarchist subjectivity have much to do with "the individual" – the other face of the modern subject. Anarchist subjectivity refers to a greater characteristic: it is plural in the diversity of the elements, human and nonhuman, that comprise it at a given moment and plural in the ceaseless variation of its forms and extent. Traditionally or historically, anarchism distinguishes between three broad types of subjectivity, which are nonetheless not mutually exclusive and do not foreclose the possibility of other types:

- an individualistic subjectivity, of which Stirner is the first and principal theorist. This individualism is often confused, wrongly, with modern

---

1   *Le Monde* (September 8, 1991).

2   Simondon, *L'Individuation psychique et collective*, 203.

3   On this point cf. Daniel Colson, "Subjectivités anarchistes et subjectivité moderne," in *La Culture libertaire: Actes du colloque de Grenoble, mars 1996* (Lyon: ACL, 1997), 149-162.

individualism. However, in the anarchist sense of the term, each individual – far from having its existence defined within a single, generalized model alongside other individuals exactly like it – violently affirms its absolute singularity, thus expanding the irreducibility of libertarian subjectivity to the scale of all human possibilities;[1]

- an *affinitary* subjectivity (see this term) called libertarian-communist, in which, at a given moment, individualities link their singular powers (their temperaments, tastes, sensitivities, predispositions, appetites). They thus constitute, through "relations ever more *intimate* [see this term] and complex" (Malatesta), a new and stronger subjectivity, an equally singular *resultant* (Proudhon and Malatesta; see this term), able in turn to join other similar or different subjectivities "to the point where the association extends to all mankind and all aspects of life" (Malatesta);[2]

- a collective subjectivity that is even more diverse from the perspective of its scale and, especially, its components, historically related to the labor and syndicalist movements. Trade unions, industrial unions, local associations of unions, federations (by trade or industry), confederations, internationals each compose so many subjectivities, each different from the others and differing from itself, both over time and at any given moment. These differences arise not only from human singularities but also from materially singular nonhuman beings (wood, coal, iron, paper, trowels, power hammers, brushes, bows, velocities, seasons, etc.). Federated and embedded in one another, combined with affinitary and individualist subjectivities (Pelloutier, one of the founders of the Bourses du Travail, was an individualist), these collective individualities or subjectivities can be combined with an infinity of other subjectivities arising from any other plane of reality (sexes, family relations, shared history and culture, arts, classes, ages, "masses" in the revolutionary periods, revolutionary situations themselves, etc.).

In this sense, libertarian subjectivities, in all their diversity, express the *anarchy* called for by the libertarian movements.

Subversion (see *stoppage*). An old criminological term that aptly expresses how a power accustomed to locating its enemies and rivals on the terrain of power

---

1   This is the "absolute singularity of the anarchist" of which Rene Schérer speaks, which implies, even in Stirner, all the "others" as forming an "integral part of the sphere, the sphere of the singular, of his own" (Rene Schérer, *Regards sur Deleuze* [Paris: Kimé, 1998], 124).

2   Errico Malatesta, *Anarchy*, trans. Vernon Richards (London: Freedom Press, 1994), 28.

itself, when faced with a polymorphous and disconcerting threat, becomes obsessed with localizing them (see *place/site* and *localism*) within an institution, a party, a territory, a uniform – anything that can be definitely circumscribed and marked, something against which it can fight, but also something with which it can make compromises, treaties, and *alliances* (military, economic, matrimonial, etc.). Contrary to the fantasies of authority, but also contrary to the many myths that assure its longevity as well as to the etymology of the word, subversion is neither the flip side of order – its hidden and demoniacal aspect – nor its mere inversion. If subversion often seems invisible to the gaze of power and if it can appear so menacing, this is, first of all, because it operates within a radically different world and on a radically different scale from that of power. It operates on the margins of its codes and its laws, within the totality of the smallest relations constitutive of its order, deep inside the bodies and souls of those in power, and within the institutions of power that it always threatens to blow up and to recompose into another possibility.

Suffering (see *implication*). Anarchists are not insensitive to suffering, their own or that of others (in particular through the feeling of *pity*), insofar as this feeling is freed from the subterfuges and falsifications of morality and religion. But for libertarian thought, suffering can in no case serve as an *extrinsic* justification (see this term) for emancipatory action, which would then instantly be transformed into an oppressive force (see *utilitarianism*). Because it is entirely negative and a symptom of disempowerment, suffering – even when it is directly experienced by those who revolt and refuse it – can never be a source of emancipation if it does not manage (and this is generally the case) to transform itself at once into *revolt* and creative affirmation.

Superabundance (see *power*). A concept employed by Bergson and William James to characterize the power of *nature*: "[w]hile our intelligence with its habits of economy imagines effects as strictly proportioned to their causes, nature, in its extravagance, puts into the cause much more than is required to produce the effect. While our motto is *Exactly what is necessary*, nature's motto is *More than is necessary* – too much of this, too much of that, too much of everything. Reality, as James sees it, is redundant and superabundant [emphasis in original]."[1]

Symbols (signs) (see *expression, representation, passage to the act, object*, and *collective reason*). It is Proudhon who most clearly expresses the ambiguity of signs and symbols.

---

1   Bergson, *The Creative Mind*, 249.

- On the one hand, in a sense very close to that which Plato gives to this word, symbols play an essential role in the relations of "reciprocity" that the various collective beings can maintain among themselves.[1] Through these relations of reciprocity and exchange (economic, romantic, intellectual, etc.) and by means of the signs that they share for this purpose (money, language, theory, reasoning, art, and mimicry), collective beings have the possibility not only to increase their own power but also, by associating, to give rise to much vaster collective beings, equipped with a *collective reason* (see this term) and able to "translate," in the field of signs and language, the "modalities of action" that these collective beings contain.[2] But this positive power of signs imperatively requires that they never cease to be the *expression* (see this term) of the forces and combinations of forces that they help to make possible. Thus, emancipatory and libertarian action achieve "embodiment and signification at the same time," in a relation in which "collective reason" is "inherent in the collective being" in the form of a "logic of the concrete."[3]
- On the other hand, the force and the danger of symbols and signs is precisely their ability to substitute themselves for the reality that they should *express*, to take its place and to turn themselves into *representation* (see these terms), thereby elevating themselves above the collective forces as a transcendent force in the hands of priests, leaders, and proprietors. Signs and symbols are then transformed into a "trap,"[4] into "apparatuses of capture."[5] As a "third power" alongside Capital and the State, according to the formula of Proudhon, symbolic power then comes to complete the work of oppression and to legitimate a dispossession by conferring absoluteness upon what is created by human beings.[6]

Synthesis, synthesism (platform, platformism). An old, useless organizational and polemical distinction born at the beginning of the interwar period within certain specifically anarchist circles. This was a moment in which, with the

---

1   Ansart, *Marx et l'anarchisme*, 156. Also see, in a very similar manner, Simondon, *L'Individu et sa genèse physico-biologique*, especially 62.

2   Ansart, *Marx et l'anarchisme*, 293.

3   Ibid. 290, 275, 271.

4   See Louis Marin, *Le récit est un piège* (Paris: Les Éditions de Minuit, 1978). (Translator's note: an excerpt from this is translated as "Writing History with the Sun King: The Traps of Narrative," trans. Richard Miller and Edward Schneider, in *On Signs*, ed. Marshall Blonsky [Baltimore, MD: Johns Hopkins University Press, 1985], 267-288.)

5   See Deleuze and Guattari, *A Thousand Plateaus*.

6   Ansart, "Proudhon, des pouvoirs et des libertés."

notable exception of Spain, the libertarian movement was lastingly eliminated from the social and revolutionary scene (Italian fascism, the crushing of the Bulgarian libertarian movement, the victory of Bolshevism in Russia, the general collapse of the libertarian labor-union movement in France, in Argentina, in the USA... and the enduring hegemony of Marxist communism). In isolation from all practice, "platformists" and "synthesists" argued over who knew better what organization was appropriate to anarchism (whatever remained of it after all had been lost): whether it should be unified around a strict and imperative theoretical and tactical program (the "platform," built approximately on the Leninist model of democratic centralism that had just triumphed in Russia) or around a consensual and eclectic theoretical "synthesis." Because it calls for federalism and the multiplicity of collective beings and points of view, anarchism refuses both platform and synthesis. It does so for the same reasons in both cases, in the sense that, contrary to these two ideological references, anarchism never refers back to programmatic and organizational "opinions" or "ideas" that would be unified within a "synthesis" of broad ideas or within a narrow and exclusionary "platform." Federalism and the diversity of points of view are grounded in real, practical, concrete forces and movements (women fighting and organizing themselves against male oppression, employees fighting and organizing themselves against economic exploitation, neighborhood or student groups fighting against fascist ideas and practices, cultural minorities' resistance to domination or colonization, experiments in self-management, in artistic creation, etc.). Because they are inevitably multiple and singular, these real forces and movements are also inevitably irreducible (by definition) to any "synthesis" or "platform" that purports to glue together their differences, to define or rank their roles and their political meanings, to reduce them to a lowest common denominator, or to subject them to organizational, tactical, and strategic imperatives. Because they are ideological, the platform and the synthesis are both opposed to the reality of practice and thus tend to undermine federalist principles as conceived by Proudhon and Bakunin and as practiced in Spain or wherever the libertarian movement saw itself as only the beginning of a real development. Indeed, only insofar as they are real forces and real movements can the components of the libertarian movement simultaneously 1) be radically different from one another, even contradictory (as is reality and as should delight anyone who identifies with *anarchy*), and 2) let these differences and contradictions play out, associating and disassociating them, evaluating all of their consequences. This evaluation takes place not in the heaven of ideas, programs, and flags – where the object of struggle is nothing more than power, the power to be in the right, to exclude and excommunicate others – but in the context of the reality and the real problems that each of us witnesses every day in his or her own way and from his or her own perspective and can experience, analyze, and evaluate every day, both alone and with others.

T

Temperament (idiosyncrasy) (see *sensibility, composition,* and *affinity*). An ancient chemical notion from Greek medicine, frequently employed in libertarian milieus to indicate the *singularity* of each being and to emphasize the need to account for this singularity within the various methods of association. Each collective being is singular (idiosyncratic) because it is an original composition of particular forces and aptitudes for being affected by other collective beings and for affecting them through the relations that it establishes with them. With the concept of temperament as the always singular constitution of a collective being, which is subject to a balance all of its own (and is thus relatively durable), anarchism introduces a certain stability into the ceaseless play of association and disassociation through which it conceives reality. But because it is a mixture, a combination, a properly individual alchemy, temperament should not be thought of (as is sometimes the case) as a determinism or a predestined and intangible fate, with which it would be necessary to act [*faire*] but which could neither be demolished nor recomposed [*refaire*]. Temperament is not located outside of the ceaseless movement of composition, decomposition, and recomposition that, for anarchism, affects all beings without exception. In this sense, it is itself only a *resultant* (see this term).[1] Proudhon and Bakunin themselves can serve as examples of different temperaments, as demonstrated by their different ways of experiencing the revolutionary events of 1848 (see *power of the outside*).

Tension (see *balancing of forces* and *one*). An important concept, borrowed from electrochemistry to characterize the nature of libertarian methods of

---

1   On the concept of temperament in Spinoza, cf. François Zourabichvili, "L'identité individuelle chez Spinoza" in *Spinoza: puissance et ontologie*, ed. Myrian Revault d'Allonnes and Hadi Rizk (Paris: Kimé, 1994).

association. If *positive anarchy* is the capacity of an order based on the multiple to express the *power of the outside* without dying, Proudhon did not found this capacity solely on the collective beings that happen to exist at a given moment: "individuals," families, workshops, industrial companies, unions, cooperatives, trades, communes, "societies" that vary in size, in *raison d'être*, etc. He did not found this capacity solely on the basis of their autonomy, the associations that this autonomy enables and on which these beings depend, the objectives that they set for themselves. He also conceived of it in a form seemingly more abstract or detached from these beings and subjectivities: on the basis of reciprocal relations of forces that mark the existence and power of these beings in an equally singular manner by traversing them all, polarizing their capacities. He theorized it on the model of the poles of an electric battery,[1] in the form of autonomous and contradictory or antithetical forces, struggling only to recognize their mutual polarity, to join with one another, to find a balance, and thus to produce maximum *energy* and meaning. This conception of contradiction and thus of tension, of the multiple and the "different" as the condition of being and its capacities, can also be related to the way in which Simondon critiques and completely rethinks the concepts of information and "good form."[2] This Proudhonian "tension" between forces that are radically autonomous and contradictory, radically different from one another yet paradoxically rich in affinities, that draw power from their effects and from their capacity not to resolve what opposes them but to select and seriate "good" contradictions, corresponds, by way of a similar choice of models (electrochemistry), to the "tension of information" of which Simondon speaks. In this conception, since "the qualitative refers to potential difference," the possible quantity of energy depends both on the proximity of the "antithetical terms" that confront one another and on their "good" isolation from one another.[3] In a schema that Proudhon could have endorsed, it would thus be possible, with Simondon, to conceive of a "good form" (i.e., the best arrangement of that which exists; see *possible*) not as a probabilistic encounter of like with like, in which "the best form would be…that which requires the smallest quantity of information,"[4] but as the ordered tension of the different with the different. This would not be the stable and well-defined ordering of beings in terms of their commonality and compatibility, but a tension of information capable of "structuring a field, propagating through it, ordering it," "animating and structuring…increasingly

---

1   A model that Proudhon never ceased to try to apprehend and infuse into his whole body of work.

2   Simondon, *L'individuation psychique et collective*.

3   Ibid. 52.

4   Ibid. 51.

varied and heterogeneous fields."[1] Good form, according to Simondon (or *positive anarchy*, according to Proudhon), would thus be "that which contains a certain field, i.e., a separation of two antithetical, contradictory terms that are nonetheless, at the same time, held in a reciprocal relation with one another," or better yet "a plurality of dyads coordinated with one another, i.e., already a network, a schema, something of the one and the multiple at the same time": "a joining of opposites in unity."[2] In this sense, very close to Proudhon and 150 years of libertarian thought, Simondon would help give meaning and content to Deleuze's proposed definition of anarchy and its bond with unity: "anarchy and unity are one and the same thing, not the unity of the One, but a much stranger unity that can only characterize the multiple."[3]

Terrorism (see *anarchist chemistry, propaganda by the deed*, and *passage to the act*). Terrorism is wrongly identified with the *attentats* of anarchist *propaganda by the deed*. The anarchist assassinations and bombings of the turn of the century differ from terrorism in six ways:

1. As the word indicates, a "terrorist" action aims primarily at producing an effect of fear upon public opinion and thus at blackmailing political leaders in order to obtain political benefit. In opposition to this, the anarchist *attentats* (even if they did not recoil from the pleasure of "making the leaders tremble" by threatening them directly), present a will to contagion in which the *attentat* aims at no goal other than itself, in which the act is its own desired effect. It is an invitation and incitement to *revolt*, a trigger for a general explosion *analogous* to its own material and symbolic reality, and it does so by means of a simple effect of imitation, extension, and contagion, in the manner of the future *active minorities* of revolutionary syndicalism, according to the proclamation made in 1888 by the Le Havre newspaper *L'Idée ouvrière*: "You who are exploited and robbed every day; you who produce all social wealth; you who are tired of this life of misery and degradation, revolt! Prisoner of work, burn down the industrial prison! Strangle the slave-driver! Knock down the cop who arrests you! Spit in the face of the magistrate who condemns you! Hang the landlord who tosses you into the street when you're hard up! Prisoner of the barracks, run your bayonet through the body of your superior!...LONG LIVE REVOLT!"[4]

---

1   Ibid. 54 and 53.

2   Ibid. 53.

3   Deleuze and Guattari, *A Thousand Plateaus*, 158 (trans.: modifications my own).

4   *L'Idée ouvrière* 23 (Feb. 11-18, 1888), qtd. in Maitron, *Histoire du mouvement anarchiste en France*, 191.

2. A terrorist action is enacted by an *organization*, a clandestine apparatus, a mini-State apparatus with its own leaders, propaganda ministries, hierarchies and structures of command, commandos and henchmen, spies and fellow travelers, traitors and informers. The *attentats* were strictly individual acts that emerged solely from a milieu "supersaturated" with the desire for revolt, as Gilbert Simondon would say, without leaders or strategists, without an organizational master plan, so that even if, *a posteriori*, the effects of the act are confounded with the act itself, its causes or its *determination* (see this term) are also entirely contained in its enactment.

3. A terrorist action is one planned in time, in which the timing, the date, and the degree of gravity of the attacks, as well as truces and negotiations to take advantage of or measure their effects, fall within a monotonous and foreseeable tactical and strategic scenario that is determined by the rigid rules of political relations of force. In contrast to this, propaganda by the deed constitutes a *passage to the act*, a spontaneous action, the sudden irruption of an immediate will to recompose the world, to which only the effects of imitation can give the appearance of a concerted plan programmed in time.

4. A terrorist action is undertaken in the shadows, the authors of which take care to escape the effects of their *attentat* and to eliminate any risk for themselves. In contrast to this, an *attentat* was an action undertaken in broad daylight in which the author directly exposed his life to the *attentat* itself or to the playing out of its judicial consequences and their inescapable effects.[5]

5. Terrorism implies a mechanical, instrumentalized causal chain – from clandestine leaders to the future heads of State they aspire to (and often do) become, passing through the various levels of the terrorist organization, the attacks themselves, their effects on public opinion, the response to these effects by the powers concerned, the negotiations inevitably entered into, and the territorial or legal redistributions or partitionings that these negotiations entail. The *attentats* were singular acts that concentrated in themselves, without division or exteriority, all

---

5   Only a certain number of current terrorist actions with strong religious connotations, in Palestine for example, appear to manifest this dimension – "disinterested," desperate, or fanatical, as one likes – of the anarchist *attentats* of propaganda by the deed, although there are infinitely many different ways to will and carry out a suicide bombing, as there are infinitely many ways of willing and living anything. And it is in this sense (which it would be necessary to explore further) that, while the *attentat* undertaken for religious reasons undoubtedly has every reason to radically differ from the anarchist *attentat*, at the same time, it seems to be closest to it.

the emancipatory virtues that their authors mobilized in one moment, at the cost of their own lives.

6. Terrorist actions tend to be discriminatory: almost all of them are tied to a distinct religious or national group (Corsican, Basque, Protestant, Irish, Tamil, Catholic, Islamist, Hindu, Palestinian, Breton, etc.) and take as their targets people from the enemy group whose sole misfortune is to be defined by other circumstantially dominant religious or national affiliations. In contrast to this, the *attentats* were attacks that refused any external division, that were addressed to the totality of that which exists (rightly or wrongly, with regard to the type of violence employed) in order to entirely recompose it, addressed to the interior of the infinity of relations and possibilities that constitute it.

Theory/practice (see *midst of things, manual/intellectual, collective reason,* and *common notions*). In libertarian thought, social reality contains an infinity of possible distinct *planes of reality* (see this term): provisional arrangements of forces joining together on a specific plane (e.g., that of war, labor, sex, gardening, syndicalism, etc.). These arrangements or planes of reality, like the beings and forces that compose them, all possess two dimensions or aspects. One side, in the vocabulary of Deleuze, is a discursive aspect – the side of form, expression, and signs – and the other side is a machinic aspect of contents, bodies, forces, and desires (see *collective reason*). But these arrangements or planes of reality also associate or combine, like any collective being, in vaster arrangements, so that, in certain instances, each one of them can occupy the discursive dimension or the machinic dimension with respect to another. This relation between these two realities has been called the question of theory and practice. Any practice has its discursive aspect and any theory its machinic aspect (see *gesture* and the role of this concept in mathematics). Byvirtue of what constitutes them, however, theories and practices can also function together (without losing their double symbolic and machinic dimension) as a specific being in which, through a process that Simondon would call "analogical" (see *analogy*), some particular theoretical arrangement becomes the discursive aspect for some particular practical arrangement with which it is associated, while this specific practical arrangement itself occupies the machinic dimension. Within that particular association and on the level where it is located (just as in any other association, however small it may be), the alignment in time between the discursive aspect and the machinic aspect is not at all automatic.[1] Placed in

---

1 This absence of an automatic accord between the discursive aspect and the machinic aspect does not conflict with the idea that any being or collective arrangement existing at a given moment always has these two dimensions and that they are indissociable from one

a relation of synchrony that is possible but not a given, subjected to constant slippages, this mutual alignment requires, on the one hand, a great number of voluntary efforts and experiments on the part of the forces thus associated – where it is a question, as Deleuze emphasizes, of directly composing "a new, more 'extensive' relation"[1] – and, on the other hand, continually being subject to the chances, favorable or not, for the conditions necessary to its realization. (On the uncertainty of this synchronization as well of its effects from the perspective of emancipation, see *common notions*.) This is demonstrated, for our present purposes, by the history of the libertarian movement. Indeed, the paradox of the short history of anarchy could be formulated thus: during the period when the theories of Proudhon and Bakunin found an explicit and important practical corollary in social and political reality, particularly in the development of the libertarian workers' movements, these movements and practices – for reasons that are not only or even primarily due to the chronological gap between them, but that are owing to a great number of factors (see, among others, *manual/intellectual*) – appeared in large part unable to make these theories their own, to fulfill their promise and to recognize themselves in them except in a *hagiographic* or *extrinsic* way (see these terms). Through this incapacity, these movements and practices were not only deprived of an important condition of their development. Through the image of their own reality that they established and transmitted, these movements and practices rendered themselves partially incomprehensible for the times to come, while they in turn changed into mere external representations of varying accuracy after their disappearance.[2] This slippage between theory and practice at the heart of the history of the libertarian movement must, of course, be understood in a nuanced way. As the whole of this lexicon demonstrates, the practices of the libertarian workers' movements managed to equip themselves, rather effectively, with their own theories and theorists, to cite only the French example (see *direct action, social explosion, master/slave, focal point, movement*, but also

---

another. This indissociability holds true only in the present moment of the continual and endless processes of *association* and *disassociation* (see *given moment, movement*, and *becoming*) through which the nature of the bond between forces and statements [énonciations], contents and forms, bodies and expressions, desires and signs is continually constructed, deconstructed, and reconstructed.

1   Deleuze, *Spinoza: Practical Philosophy*, 126.

2   On this historical shift between practice and theory, real movements and representations, cf. Daniel Colson, *Anarcho-syndicalisme et communisme: Saint-Étienne, 1920-1925* (Lyon: ACL, 1986). On the risks of a transformation of the libertarian movement's history into images (holy icons or nostalgic portraits; see *hagiography*) that radically mask the reality of this movement and produce practices with little relation to what it was and what it could be, cf. Michel Onfray's harsh critique in *L'Archipel des comètes* (Paris: Grasset, 2001).

the importance, in this lexicon, of theorists such as Pouget, Griffuelhes, or Pelloutier). While this theoretical expression was not unrelated to the texts and thought of Proudhon and Bakunin,[1] albeit diffusely and indirectly, it did not discover – particularly on the side of anarchism proper (with the exception of some great historical texts[2]) – the philosophical corollary, essential to its own development, that these two principal theorists of anarchism had so forcefully initiated in the 19th century.[3]

Thing (see also *object*). Concept frequently employed by Bakunin to indicate any collective being, whatever it may be, a position also found in the work of Gabriel Tarde, for whom "*everything* [from molecules to human realities, including plants, animals, and every other 'phenomenon'] *is a society*,"[4] but also in Whitehead, for whom "thing," "being," and "entity" are synonymous, for whom any "ordinary physical object…is a society," in which even a "stone" is "a society of separate molecules in violent agitation."[5]

Time (see *chaos, entelechy, end/means, plastic force, movement, implication, given moment, tradition,* and *eternal return*).

To be separated from oneself. Any collective being is *more than itself* (see *more than oneself* and *individuation*), since it contains in itself the totality of that which exists (see *monad*). In this sense, it possesses a subjectivity containing other possibilities (see *subject*). However, any dominant (and thus partial) order requires the collective beings that it subsumes to be only what they are within this order (a role, a function, a place, an identity). Thus, it separates them from what they are capable of, from the power that they contain (see *power of the outside*).

To do all that one is capable of/To go to the limits of one's capacity (see *limits* and *balancing of forces*).

---

1 For an evaluation of this diffusion, cf. all 120 issues of the revolutionary syndicalist review *La Vie ouvrière*.

2 Cf. especially Voline (V.M. Eichenbaum), *The Unknown Revolution* and Guillaume, *L'Internationale, documents et souvenirs (1864-1878)*.

3 On the contrary, however, and in contrast with this general lack, see the writings of Gaston Leval, one of the rare libertarian theorists of the first half of the 20th century to have really read Proudhon and Bakunin. Cf. especially Gaston Leval *La Pensée constructive de Bakounine* (Paris: Spartacus, 1976).

4 Tarde, *Monadology and Sociology*, 28.

5 Whitehead, *Process and Reality*, 21, 35, 78.

To risk one's life (see *war/warlike* and *power of the outside*). To go to the limits of one's capacities, i.e., beyond one's limits, to the end of the life that one contains within oneself, knowing that this life is also, according to Deleuze's expression,[1] a power of the outside in which one always risks losing the individuality that constitutes us at present (see *other, apeiron, anarchy*).

To the post! (see *guilty party*).

Tools/weapons (see *object, gesture, labor/work*, and *war*). Every object, behind its plain meaning and present use, has a power of its own that stems from its twofold nature as collective arrangement, as form and content, meaning and force (see *collective reason*), as well as from its genesis and its history, from the power that produced it and that it still contains.

From this originary power that gives rise to meaning and possibility (the source of "the ten thousand things" in Daoism), from this power of the *limitless*, below the level of signs and words, objects find the force that they contain, of which they are a manifestation and to which libertarian movements have always attempted to return in order to start all over again, in two ways:

- first of all, through struggle and practice: through *propaganda by the deed* and *direct action*, for example (see these terms); through a return to acts, to the extreme concentration of an action that attempts – for a given instant in time and point in space – to discover all the meaning and power that human beings are and are capable of; to do this through a constantly repeated movement that must, in returning to the originary power, simultaneously refuse the oppressive autonomization of signs (and the various "absolutisms" that this has permitted) and create a new world, redeploying the power that beings contain in different ways; to do this, generally, by means of a violent movement of rupture and destruction, the human dimension of which remains incomprehensible if we fail to perceive how this return to the originary force always carries with it the totality of the meaning and possibility to which it once gave birth and which it has never ceased to produce (see *eternal return*);
- secondly, through theory, when libertarian thought, from Proudhon to Deleuze, makes an effort, in a genealogical and analogical way (Simondon), to grasp the originary meaning and power of the relations between objects and signs, content and form, signification and force. Proudhon seeks this recovery of the origin, where signs and forces merge, first of all in *labor* and in the *tools* by virtue of which primitive human beings could finally exit the "state of nature," possessing the objective

---

1   Deleuze, *Foucault*, 95 et passim.

and external code capable of "initiating" them, "leading [them] step by step," "stopping [them]" at each "term" of the "relations" that their "acts" at first expressed so poorly, in an "intuitive" way, in the form of "images" without "reflection."[1] For Proudhon, "the inner vision that primitive man follows in his spontaneous acts," this "dream" dwelling within him, discovers in the "machines" and "instruments" of industry the objective corollary to human "intuition," the "series" able to "speak to the mind."[2] In this sense, for Proudhon, "all the instruments of work are analytical instruments":[3]

> Instrument of compression, clamping, support, damming, enclosure;
> Instrument of gripping;
> Instrument of percussion;
> Instruction [sic] of puncture;[4]
> Instrument of division or section;
> Instrument of locomotion;
> Instrument of steering, etc.[5]

As "coarse" and "primitive" as they may be at first, for Proudhon, these "instruments" of human industry are not only the crude, obsolete ancestors of the seeming abstraction of linguistic or mathematical signs.[6] Like the "acts" that they redouble by objectifying the relations they contain, tools are always at work in the deployment of human potentialities and capacities for accurately apprehending the laws of that which exists. Proudhon proposes to reinvigorate this inherent and essential role theoretically and thereby – in a movement parallel to the return to *action* of the anarchism to come – to justify the workers'

---

1   See Proudhon, *De la Justice*, 3:78, 72 and 74. "These are the first machines of industry, which we may call, as we like, either Elements of Knowledge or Elements of Labor" (73).

2   Ibid. 74 and 78.

3   Ibid. 85.

4   We preserve here the wording of the Rivière edition, certainly mistaken, but which, in the form of a typographical error, correctly translated Proudhon's thought, since the tool indeed was for him the "instructor" of the human intelligence, the "tutor from without" (Ibid. 78).

5   Ibid. 75.

6   On the "invention" of the "signs of the word and calculation," "pure mathematics" and "categories of the understanding," from the "decomposition" of the product of human industry, cf. Ibid. 77. On the symbolic dimension of tools, concomitant with that of language, cf. André Leroi-Gourhan, *Gesture and Speech*, trans. Anna Bostock Berger (Cambridge, MA: MIT Press, 1993) and *L'Homme et la matière: Évolution et techniques* (Paris: Albin Michel, 1971).

struggle and emancipatory will. He attempts to "overturn" a "spiritualist philosophy" from "bottom to top," to foster a "new form of philosophy" in which "the worker, degraded serf of civilization," would become again "the author and sovereign of thought, the referee of philosophy and theology."[1] As a meaningful expression of humanity's practical relations with nature and thus of the relations of "balance" and "imbalance" with the principles of all things, the "instruments of labor," like the "letters" of literature, the "numbers" of mathematics, or the "scales" of music, form a different and revolutionary "alphabet," an "industrial alphabet" of which Proudhon, with his usual boldness, immediately proposes one possible formulation: an "alphabet of the worker."[2]

Proudhon thus attempts to provide the working-class and libertarian struggles and practices of his time with a theory and a genealogy of signs internal to the sphere of labor, which could justify the affirmation of Labor against Capital and, gradually, by analogy, against all the absolute powers (State, Church, etc.) – the affirmation of an entirely emancipated world. But aren't this industrial theory and this genealogy of signs too narrow for the purposes of libertarian emancipation? Up to what point can the relation to the particular world and symbolic system entailed in work and its machines, tools, and products really account for the practices and aspirations essential to the workers' struggle? In what respect does the genealogy of signs arising from labor – as "vehicles and instruments of knowledge," "in the archives of the human mind," as Proudhon tells us[3] – make it possible to account for the return to facts and acts of *propaganda by the deed* and *direct action*, for example, to express a return to an originary power in which the libertarian project attempts to find its force and its novelty? (See *plastic force*.) Worse yet, isn't the "analytical" power of signs and labor, aside from the language that it is meant to displace, rather closely bound up with the servitude that workers' revolts aim to denounce and defeat? Can other objectified products of human activity, other objects, other *planes of reality* (see this term) express human beings' emancipatory power, as expressions of the relations that constitute it, better than tools and labor? These are the questions that Proudhon and then Deleuze and Guattari attempt to answer by

---

1   Proudhon, *De la Justice* 3:73 and 75.

2   "ALPHABET OF THE WORKER: A. BAR OR LEVER (*pile, stem, column, stake, picket*); B. CROOK, BENT BARS (*hook, staple, key, serger, gripper, anchor, tenon, harpoon*); C. GRIP (*clipper, vice*, combination of two hooks); D. BOND (originally consisting of a flexible stem, rolled around, object; - *wire, cord, chain*); E. HAMMER (*bludgeon, mallet, piton, flail, grinding stone*); F. POINT (*lance, pike, javelin, arrow, dart, needle*, etc.); G. ANGLE [etc.]" (Ibid. 75-76).

3   "I say now that there is in the archives of the human mind something anterior to all the signs that, from time immemorial, have served as the vehicles and instruments of knowledge" (Proudhon, *De la Justice*, 3:73).

bringing together work and war, tools and weapons as the expressions of two historically important *planes of reality* of human activity.

From the perspective of Proudhonian semiotics,[1] weapons and tools have one aim in common: to objectify themselves into external "instruments," fixed and isolable "objects," crystallizing significations in themselves, which can be arranged into classifications, nomenclatures, and retail racks. However, as Proudhon sees and as Deleuze and Guattari demonstrate, this objectification and the symbolic intelligence it enables are situated within radically different movements and relations to the world. This is true in four senses:

1. "Work is a motor cause that meets resistances" and "operates upon the exterior," that "instrumentalized" and objectified exterior, which, in Proudhonian terms, then comes to "guide" and "initiate" human intelligence. "Introceptive" and "introjective," the tool is determined by its relation to an external matter that human beings, through labor, seek to gather to themselves and to appropriate.[2] "Passive" and "inert," varying in consistency, this matter "resists." This "resistance-consistency" – specific to each occasion, "separated," "divided," "joined," "tied up," "meshed together," "cut down," "wrought into shapes," "reinforced" – determines the signification, form, and resistance belonging to the tools employed.[3] The weapon is involved in a rather different movement. *Warlike* activity is no longer concerned with gathering external materials in order to appropriate them, overcoming and selecting resistances or dividing, untying, and uncoupling them in order then to couple, bind, or link them differently by obtaining tools corresponding to this aim and this relation. In war as in hunting (as these two activities were traditionally practiced, at least) the exterior is not an inert and passive matter. The human or animal "other," on the *plane of reality* from which it takes its meaning, is an "other" in its own right, a composite similarly equipped with movements, wills, and desires. It is a "mobile," "active" other that may be overcome or tamed (when it is not killed), in the manner of Hercules with the Cretan bull or the Hind of Ceryneia, as Proudhon describes in *La Guerre et la paix*.[4] "Projective" in counter-attack and parry, solitary in its movement, the weapon does not depend on any external material anchor, on any matter that would fix and define the meaning of its action. Its anchor is purely internal or of the same nature, coterminous with the impulse that commands

---

1   Proudhon speaks of "*séméiologie*" (Proudhon, *De la Justice*, 2:362).

2   Deleuze and Guattari, *A Thousand Plateaus*, 395-397.

3   Proudhon, *De la Justice*, 3:77 and 79.

4   Proudhon, *La Guerre et la paix*, 16.

it and that it expresses, or with the parry and the threat that manifest themselves to it in movements and expressions of the same type.[1]

2. Because it operates on the exterior, on resistances that it takes for the object of its manipulation, "work is a motor cause that meets resistances, operates upon the exterior, is consumed and spent in its effect, and must be renewed from one moment to the next."[2] As Proudhon writes, just as a "steam engine needs to be fed, maintained, and repaired, until the moment when, due to natural wear and tear, it can no longer be serviced or repaired and must be thrown upon the scrap heap, so the force of man expended each day requires daily repairs, until the day when the worker, out of service, enters the hospital or the grave."[3] In this sense, work, "repugnant and arduous," can be regarded as a "principle of servitude and degradation."[4] As opposed to this wear and tear of labor, in which motor activity must always confront external pressures and be fed by external resources, there is the "free action" of war, which "is also a motor cause, but one that has no resistance to overcome, operates only upon the mobile body itself, is not consumed in its effect, and continues from one moment to the next."[5] The servitude and loss of energy entailed in work are opposed to the "game" of combat, "the superhuman force," "courage," and "skill" of Hercules described by Proudhon: "It was a game for him to stop a chariot pulled by two horses that had been spurred to a gallop, to seize a bull by the horns and turn it around by twisting its neck. His hands were pliers; his thighs, long and strong, untiring. He could run 45 miles in 18 hours and continue for seven days along the same path."[6]

3. A third difference between war and work, weapons and tools concerns the kind of subjectivity, intelligence, "desire," and "emotion" defined

---

1 On the importance of the differences that distinguish between work arrangements and warlike arrangements and on the difficulty in passing from the one to the other – indeed, from the latter to the former – cf., in connection with the possibility of creating scallops through breeding and thus of transforming the fishing-boat sailors from "hunter-gatherers" into "breeder-farmers," Michel Callon, "Some Elements of a Sociology of Translation: Domestication of the Scallops and the Fishermen of St. Brieuc Bay," *Power, Action and Belief: A New Sociology of Knowledge?* ed. John Law (London: Routledge & Kegan Paul, 1986), 196-233.

2 Deleuze and Guattari, *A Thousand Plateaus*, 397.

3 Proudhon, *De la Justice*, 3:15.

4 Ibid. 81.

5 Deleuze and Guattari, *A Thousand Plateaus*, 397.

6 Proudhon, *La Guerre et la paix*, 16.

by each.[1] As Proudhon demonstrates, the "intelligence" that work helps make possible is ultimately a "pupil's" subjectivity.[2] "Reflexive" and "analytical," it obliges one to "stop," to proceed "step by step," through "each term of the intuition that labor and its instruments break up into sequences and visible signs."[3] Deleuze and Guattari call the "desire" or "emotion" belonging to this laboring subjectivity "feeling [*sentiment*]." "Feeling implies an evaluation of matter and its resistances, a direction[4] to form and its developments, an entire gravity...Feeling is an always displaced, retarded, resisting emotion."[5] Here, once again, war mobilizes a desire and a subjectivity that are quite different. Going beyond labor and its role in the emergence of consciousness to reunite with the primary impetus of "acts" and "facts," war makes an "appeal" to human "spontaneity," to the "immediacy" of a "creative power," external or anterior to any spirit of "analysis," deconstruction, reflection.[6] Proudhon calls this "spontaneity" that belongs to warlike activity "divine." "War is a divine fact": "I call divine everything in nature that proceeds immediately from the creative power in man, from the spontaneity of the mind or consciousness. I call divine, in other words, all that, occurring apart from the series, or serving as the initial term of the series, admits neither question nor doubt on the part of the philosopher. The divine imposes itself with sharp force: it does not answer the questions one addresses to it, nor does it suffer demonstrations."[7] This "spontaneity of the mind or consciousness" that belongs to the warrior is what Deleuze and Guattari call "affect": "[a]ffect is the active discharge of emotion, the counterattack...Affects are projectiles just like weapons; feelings are introceptive like tools."[8]

4. A fourth and final difference between war and work, weapons and tools: in their closeness to the power of the human being and its capacity for action, war and its weapons are not bereft of the powers of symbolization as such. And therefore, they have historically offered human beings another possibility for achieving consciousness. As opposed to the semiology of work, objectified in the tools that link the

---

1   Deleuze and Guattari, *A Thousand Plateaus*, 399-400.

2   Proudhon, *De la Justice*, 3:73.

3   Ibid. 78.

4   Translator's note: in French, *sens* can mean "direction," but also "meaning."

5   Deleuze and Guattari, *A Thousand Plateaus* 399-400.

6   Proudhon, *De la Justice*, 3:72.

7   Proudhon, *La Guerre et la paix*, 29.

8   Deleuze and Guattari, *A Thousand Plateaus*, 400.

human being to matter, in which the autonomized sign "ceases to be inscribed on the body and is written on a motionless, objective matter,"[1] war offers another semiotics, expressive and mobile, inscribed on the bodies and weapons of primitive people, close to them, the direct display of their power. No doubt, "metalworking," "jewelry making," and the "ornamentation" of bodies and weapons "do not form a writing"; nonetheless, they have "a power of abstraction that is in every way equal to that of writing."[2] "These fibulas, these gold or silver plaques, these pieces of jewelry...constitute traits of expression of pure speed, carried on objects that are themselves mobile and moving...They are attached to the horse's harness, the sheath of the sword, the warrior's garments, the handle of the weapon; they even decorate things used only once, such as arrowheads."[3] And so it is, in Proudhon's words this time, that "the warrior walks with head held high, his helmet surmounted with a plume, his armor gleaming...All his desire is to be recognized far and wide and to measure himself against an adversary beloved of the gods,...and show himself worthy of this adversary, between two armies, under the gaze of the sun."[4]

Totality/totalitarianism (see *point of view, individual, anarchy,* and *monad*). As one may notice (with Nietzsche), even the human being most bereft of imagination cannot prevent itself from perceiving "to what extent the pulsation of life...is boundless, inexhaustible,"[5] but also how little of this life it can deploy from itself, how little of this life it can express to itself and to others. Anarchism conceives of this capacity (among others) of beings to grasp the totality of that which exists on the basis of their own resources – albeit from a limited *point of view,* through an *individuation* that is infinitely less than what it contains as *possibilities* – on the basis of its interpretation of Leibniz's *monads* (see this term). And anarchism conceives of and experiments with the capacity of beings to deploy this unlimited power of the possibilities that they perceive from a certain point of view and to make this potential power actual through *federalism* – through association with others, the recognition of the *other* within oneself (see also *affinity*) – as alone capable of revealing the powers that each being possesses. This is the collective composition of increasingly powerful

---

1   Ibid. 401.

2   Ibid.

3   Ibid.

4   Proudhon, *La Guerre et la paix,* 58.

5   Giorgio Colli, *Après Nietzsche,* trans. Pascal Gabellone (Paris: Éditions de l'Éclat, 1987), 42-43.

forces within a world in which "unity can only characterize the multiple" (see *multiplicity* and *balancing of forces*).[1]

But, even in its own development, this libertarian experimentation with an emancipated world runs up against the insane aspiration of beings to express the totality, of which they have a presentiment in themselves, by themselves alone – solely on the basis of their individuality, each on its own account – and to subject it to their point of view alone, to subordinate all the others to themselves. The aborted opening of beings onto the totality of reality is then transformed into power and domination, *ideomania* and totalitarianism, the will to possess and master the world. Instead of opening itself horizontally onto the perspectives and desires of others and giving birth, from the interior of reality, to a more powerful being, the point of view and desire specific to each being, at a given moment and in a given situation, is projected onto the others, subjecting others from the outside to their own movement and their own logic. The totalitarian conquest of the world by one sole point of view and one sole desire thus entails a model of hierarchy in which, from their position at the top of the pyramid, the dominant powers hope to interpret and instrumentalize the base from which they result, so as to appropriate the "totality of life," to ensnare it in nets of abstraction, in bonds of seduction and constraint.

Tradition (see *a priori/a posteriori*). "*We need tradition,*" Landauer exclaims. "Socialism cannot be established in the abstract, but only in a concrete multiplicity that is simultaneous with harmony among peoples." And it is in this sense that we cannot foresee all the paths that revolution might take. Unlike authoritarians, who are always in a hurry, anarchists often find that a straight line between two points is the longest. And as Landauer was already able to write in 1907, two years after the first revolutionary attempt in Russia, if this road "may lead through Russia, it may lead through India," as well as through any other tradition, any historical expression of human cultures.[2] Along these lines, the Berber poet Hawad disputes the idea held by certain Western anarchist theorists that anarchism is uniquely European, something radically new born at the end of the 19th century.[3] In this sense, one might indeed maintain that the libertarian idea existed anterior to the Western reaction to the birth of the centralized nation-State, as we can see, for example, with Hawad, in Berber civilization, or in Chinese *Daoism* (see this term), as well as in a great number of other human traditions.

Contrary to what a superficial interpretation might lead us to believe, anarchism is not opposed to tradition, since tradition is not only a past to which

---

1   Deleuze and Guattari, *A Thousand Plateaus*, 158 (trans.: modifications my own).

2   Gustav Landauer, qtd. in Martin Buber, *Paths in Utopia*, 48-49 (trans.: modifications my own).

3   Discussion at the La Gryffe bookshop, April 15, 2000.

one refers in an extrinsic way. History, in unfolding, accumulates a multitude of experiences that, like everything that constitutes the real, continue to act within the life that constitutes us at a given moment. These experiences can be both good and bad, emancipatory and dominatory – libertarian action selects from among these and reconsiders them in a different manner (see *eternal return*). In this sense, Elisée Reclus observes that "[p]resent-day society contains within itself all past societies."[1] Like the "natural" forces that constitute the reality of which they are just one dimension, traditions tied to institutions, language, myths, and representations continue to act in the present, the only time that exists. And it is on the basis of these, on the basis of what they make possible, as on the basis of all that exists, that libertarian action can attempt a radically different recomposition of the world. For this reason, anarchism is radically foreign to the unfortunate slogan of the International: "No more tradition's chains shall bind us [*Du passé faisons table rase*]!" For libertarian thought and the libertarian project, there is neither past nor future, but only a present in which all is given, in which everything constantly plays itself out, in which all forces are engaged, limited, and deployed in an infinity of possible arrangements.

Transcendence (see *immanence*). Libertarian thought is opposed to any transcendence, to any being or reality that claims to be external to others or of another nature. God is the fullest expression of a transcendence that always, in all that exists, justifies a domination.

Transduction (see *propaganda by the deed*, *direct action*, and *intimate being*). A concept forged by Gilbert Simondon that makes it possible to think both the *becoming* of a being and the way in which *action* (see these terms) can contribute, by propagation, to its constant recomposition: "[w]e understand by transduction an operation – physical, biological, mental, social – by which an activity gradually propagates through a field, founding this propagation on a structuring of the field that is effected from place to place."[2]

Transindividual (see *subject*, *subjectivity*, *solitude*, and *midst of things*). A concept invented by Gilbert Simondon that allows us to think the way in which emancipatory subjectivities are formed beyond the false opposition between society and the individual.

---

1   Elisée Reclus, *L'Homme et la Terre*, vol. 6, *Histoire contemporaine (suite)* (Paris: Librairie universelle, 1905), 504, qtd. in *Anarchy, Geography, Modernity: The Radical Social Thought of Elisée Reclus*, trans. John P. Clark and Camille Martin (Lanham, MD: Lexington Books, 2004), 225.

2   Simondon, *L'Individuation psychique et collective*, 24-25. (Translator's note: see also Scott, *Gilbert Simondon's* Psychic and Collective Individuation, esp. 77-80.)

Transparency (see *secret*).

Trust (see *commons*).

U

Unconscious (see *subject*).

Union (revolutionary) (see *direct action*, *power*, and *collective beings*). Along with affinity groups and individualities, the union historically constitutes one of the libertarian movement's principal forms of *grouping*. The union should thus be understood from the perspective of its emancipatory potentialities, which warrant its being called "revolutionary" in order to distinguish it from other varieties of trade union, the emancipatory powers of which are rather weak as they are concerned only with protecting or improving the lot of the employees they represent (see *representation*), generally within the nets and snares of the existing order, which they leave uncontested. The "revolutionary" or emancipatory character of the libertarian union, then, must not be sought in its program, in the partisan commitments of its leaders, nor in the constraints that bring it into existence (see *class*). Its emancipatory character is entirely founded in the rupture of this mode of grouping with the order within which it emerges (see *revolt* and *direct action*) and, at the same time, in the very nature of the collective being that is thus constituted under the title "union," in the emancipatory or affirmative quality and the intensity of the force and the revolt that results from its mode of composition. This is why the libertarian union so often opposed the Marxist organizations that denied the intrinsically revolutionary scope of the collective beings constituted by the unions (see *alienation*) while (at the same time and, very logically, for the same reasons) affirming their revolutionary utility in the class struggle – their sole justification when viewed externally. This was the rationale for the equally extrinsic attempt of these Marxist organizations to infiltrate the unions in order to use them and to lead them in the name of the transcendent character of the class struggle, as pathetic as these attempts might seem from the emancipatory point of view. In opposition to the extrinsic and utilitarian character of the usual conceptions of syndicalism (whether they arise from capitalism or from an allegedly revolutionary Marxism), libertarian thought sides with the emancipatory interiority of which any collective being is capable at one moment or another, an emancipatory interiority of which unions were historically one of the manifestations.

Unity (see *one*).

Universal (see *government* and *particular*).

Universal causality (see *plastic force*). A Bakuninian concept, synonymous in his vocabulary with *life*, *solidarity*, *nature*, and *composed unity*. Also synonymous in the vocabulary of Nietzsche or Deleuze with *species activity*, *univocal being*, and *will to power*.

Univocal being. Deleuzian concept (see *plastic force*).

Utilitarianism (see *anti-speciesism*, *liberalism*, *neoliberals*, and *rendering of accounts*). There would be no reason for utilitarianism to appear in this lexicon if it did not serve as a theoretical reference for certain currents – such as *anti-speciesism* – that sometimes claim to be close to the libertarian movement and its thought. In its various forms, utilitarianism is the philosophical double of liberalism and its generalization to the totality of that which exists, its justification, and its social and psychological condition. Like a course in applied morals (along the lines of the primary-school math exercises of yesteryear), utilitarianism aims at reducing our life to a kind of marketplace investment strategy for our acts and feelings, reduced to a few simple principles (pleasure, pain, interest) that it purports to measure,[1] in which the totality of what constitutes us must be instantly and constantly translated into a common, convertible, and universal currency: the laws of commerce extended to the totality of that which exists. Transformed into an economic calculation, utilitarian moral judgment is always extrinsic to beings and their practices.[2] Contrary to libertarian tendencies and analyses, it never treats the inevitably subjective, singular, and internal nature and quality of the desires, affects, and reasons (see *collective reason*) that produce such-and-such an act, such-and-such an effect. Rather, it prescribes an evaluation of these acts and effects that is merely

---

1   Jeremy Bentham employs seven criteria: intensity, duration, certainty, propinquity, purity, fecundity, and extent.

2   As a precondition, ethics takes the form of a judgment (mobilizing reasons, calculations, and arithmetic) that must then "guide practice." (See Peter Singer, *Practical Ethics* [New York: Cambridge University Press, 2011], 2.)

quantitative and general (because it is objective or external), converting them into costs and profits, so that, as Bentham writes, "the only common measure the nature of things affords is money."[1] "A quantified assessment can thus be established, which is, as in political economy, a balance of credit and debit, profit and loss."[2] In other words, the extension of the "principle of utility" to moral life and to the quality of acts and affects (particularly in Mill) modifies neither the nature of its principle, nor its reductivist and *extrinsic* character (see this term). The "justice of the peace" of money and purely economic sanctions is merely replaced (so to speak) by the tribunal of others, a differently demanding judge and inquisitor, before whom it is always a question of justifying one's acts and the effects of what one is (male, white, etc.) (see *rendering of accounts*).[3] Nevertheless, this moral-commercial court (to which the current extension of Anglo-Saxon legal practices provides a sinister horizon) never ceases to correspond to the contemptible calculations of economic benefit.

One example (among a multitude of other possibilities) will suffice to illustrate both the generality and externality of the utilitarian mode of reasoning, the equivalence between the morals resulting from it and the logic of liberal capitalism, and, finally, the deeply *repugnant* character (see this term) of the relation to the world that this kind of moral and legal expertise always induces (see *experts* and *law/rights*). In his book *Practical Ethics*, Peter Singer (the principal theorist of anti-speciesism) writes, "When the death of a disabled infant will lead to the birth of another infant with better prospects of a happy life, the total amount of happiness will be greater if the disabled infant is killed.[4] The loss of happy life for the first infant is outweighed by the *gain* of a happier life for the second. Therefore, if killing the haemophiliac infant has no adverse effect on others, it would, according to the total view, be right to kill him [emphasis my own]."[5]

---

1   Jeremy Bentham, *Bentham's Political Thought*, ed. Bhikhu Parekh (New York: Barnes & Noble, 1973), 122.

2   Michel Meyer, *La Philosophie anglo-saxonne* (Paris: PUF, 1994), 93.

3   "When...people cannot put forward any *justification* for what they do, we may reject their claim to be living according to ethical standards, even if what they do is in accordance with conventional moral principles [emphasis my own]" (Singer, *Practical Ethics*, 9).

4   Singer starts from the assumption that, if the disabled child is killed, the parents will probably want (here intervenes the theory of probability) to make another child who has a serious chance of not being ill.

5   Ibid. 163. In Singer's defense, let us stress the importance of this "if" ("*if* killing the haemophiliac infant does not have adverse effects on other people"), an "if" that certainly does not completely exclude a utilitarian calculation of the "harmful effects" (ad infinitum), but that, like the scientific "all things being equal" with which Singer's reasoning is aligned, also opens onto a rather different solution, this time of a genuinely ethical order, a solution

We do not hasten to cry scandal in the name of the Decalogue, social customs, or moral principles. As opposed to what one might believe, the scandal and shame of the preceding sentence does not primarily lie in the object of its utilitarian calculation: the quality of the life of a haemophiliac infant compared with the possible quality of other lives and the decision to kill or not to kill. They reside in the apparatus of legality or expertise that is able to posit this choice in the first place. They reside in the particular form of pleasure that this apparatus induces. They reside in the mode of calculation that this type of dilemma prompts (whom do you love better, your father or your mother? Tide or Gain brand detergent?) and thus in the relation to the world that this calculation entails. This relation is quite ancient, closely related to the casuistry of the great authoritarian religions. It can be found in any advertisement – whether for the local supermarket or a multinational – or in the practice of any expert or manager, whatever his or her field of *application* (see this term) – from the anti-tobacco campaign to the management of a trust or a State – as well as in questions of retirement, euthanasia, and social security, not to mention in the proliferation of "ethics committees." In this way, for example, under the terms of its commercial and universal principle of equivalence, Singer's statement can be neatly, instantly, and naturally converted into the following form (and thus into many others that you may freely deduce for yourself, whether this depresses you or makes you *indignant* [see this term]): "when the liquidation of a company in financial difficulties leads to the birth of another company whose chances of profit are better, the total quantity of profit is greater if the company in financial difficulty is liquidated. The liquidation of the first company is compensated by the gain of a greater possibility of profit for the second. This is why, according to the total economic perspective, if the liquidation of the ailing company does not result in more onerous effects on other companies, its liquidation will be justified."

Because it affirms the absolute singularity of beings, situations, and events, as well as the equally absolute right of these beings, situations, and events to experiment and define for themselves what they are capable of and what they want without ever referring to an external authority (not even the falsely objective product of reductivism and mathematical formulation [see *statistics*]), anarchism turns away in disgust from utilitarianism and utilitarians.

Utopia (see *ideal*).

---

that radically shatters utilitarianism and its shopkeeper's good sense. For a critique of the reductive reasoning of science, cf. Michel Serres, in particular, *The Five Senses : A Philosophy of Mingled Bodies,* trans. Margaret Sankey and Peter Cowley (London: Bloomsbury, 2016).

V

Vengeance (see *ressentiment*). A delayed response to suffering from aggression or domination. Anarchism is foreign to any notion of vengeance, to any "settling of scores," to any inevitably retrospective "trial." This is because, in a given situation, it always attempts to act immediately and directly on the basis of what that situation permits and what it prevents, because it maintains that everything is always possible, for better or worse (see *good/bad*), within this immediate situation. From the point of view of habitual morals and from the point of view of its (apparent) opposite, force, anarchism always starts over again from zero – as in the famous Edith Piaf song, "*Non rien de rien, je ne regrette rien!*"[1] – without scorekeeping and without accounts ledgers, on the basis of all that exists.

Violence (see *revolt, contradictions, responsibility, putting to death,* and *war/war-like*). As an indication of *external* relations of *constraint* and *domination* (see these terms), violence displays two aspects. While it is pure negativity in terms of its dominatory and restrictive aspect, violence can be transformed into a positive force in its aspect as *revolt* and *insurrection* (see these terms) – when a force affirms its *right* and its capability against that of the other forces that attempt to subordinate it to their own *raisons d'être* (see this term). In the very action that corresponds to it, violence then contains another *possibility* founded on the absence of *external constraints* (see these terms), but it also constantly runs the risk, as can often be attested, of changing immediately into domination, into an external constraint: when the Russian worker, an insurgent in 1918, changes in turn into a torturer and agent of the Cheka; when the CNT worker takes advantage of the black-and-red cap on his head in order to transform

---

1   Translator's note: The lyrics here translate directly, "No, absolutely nothing, I regret nothing!"

himself into a police officer, a judge, and a torturer.[1] How do we distinguish between an emancipatory violence and an oppressive violence? Like Spinoza, anarchism refuses to judge acts of violence categorically, following the model of the Ten Commandments ("Thou shalt not kill!"). There are as many ways (*good* or *bad*, to varying degrees) of taking lives as there are of saving them. Anarchism also refuses to judge these acts according to their intentions or their objectives (see *ends/means*, *friend/enemy*[2]), judging them instead on the basis of the *determination* specific to each act, the quality of the *will* and the *desire* that animate it (see these terms). Does the act of violence increase the power of the being that corresponds to it and the feeling of joy that accompanies this power, which is its only judge? What is the quality of this joy? Is it active and contagious, as in a revolt or insurrection, or is it reactive (see *reaction*), as when one is delighted by the sadness inflicted on one's enemies? Such are the criteria of an anarchist judgment of acts of violence, singular in each case. And it is in this sense that Proudhon can attempt to rehabilitate the meaning and value of war, celebrating the anger and violence of Hercules:

"Hercules, already an illustrious young man by virtue of his many exploits, but whose education had been extremely neglected, accepted from his father the order to attend the school of Thebes. But the son of Amphytrion applied all the power of his will and his understanding to these subtle studies in vain. His intelligence, all intuition, did not succeed in grasping anything analytically. Grammatical rules slipped through his brain without leaving the slightest trace. At the end of a year, Hercules knew absolutely nothing. On the other hand, his strength was superhuman; his courage and his skill in each exercise were the equals of his strength. Like all heroes, as soon as he faced the enemy, a kind of inspiration seized Hercules. Immediately, he knew what must be done – his intelligence at that moment exceeded that of the cleverest.

"At the end of the school year, the schoolmaster announced the awarding of prizes. On the appointed day, the entire city went to the ceremony. The parents, the children – everyone was happy. Hercules alone did not receive a prize. For all his prowess, for all his free services,[3] the schoolmaster had not even granted him an honorable mention.

---

1   Translator's note: the Cheka was the first secret police force established in Soviet Russia; the CNT (Confederación Nacional del Trabajo or National Confederation of Labor), a large anarcho-syndicalist union organization, was a major participant in the Spanish Civil War of 1936-1939.

2   Translator's note: although there are four cross-references to an entry for the term *friend/ enemy*, this entry does not appear in the *Petit lexique*.

3   He killed an enormous wild boar in Arcadia, pierced the Stymphalides (a flock of antediluvian vultures, able to carry off a two-year-old pig or a heifer) with arrows, crushed the head of the Nemean lion with a blow of his club, ate a cannibal tyrant alive, split the Hydra of Lerna

"And there was laughter.

"Furious, Hercules kicked over the podium, overturned the triumphal arch, toppled the benches, the seats, and the perfumed altar, broke the tripod, scattered the crowns, made a heap of them all, and called for fire. Then he seized the schoolmaster, forced him into the skin of a boa – the head of the man sticking out of the snake's mouth – crowned him with the head of a wild boar, and strung him up, thus accommodated, from the poplar tree under which the prizes were to be distributed. The women fled, terrified; the schoolboys vanished; the people kept away: nobody dared to face the anger of Hercules."[1]

Virility (see *affirmation* and *collective force*). The image and concept of virility play a great part in the discourse and imaginary of the revolutionary syndicalists and anarcho-syndicalists. The fact that the libertarian workers' movements were mainly composed of men should not as such lead us to reduce this concept solely to its connotation of sex or gender. In its discursive and iconographic form, virility, within the anarchist movement, is primarily synonymous with *affirmation* and *force* and thus with a power common to all collective beings without exception. The militant experience, like that of life and its various associations and disassociations, is enough to show that virility, in the libertarian sense of the term, is unrelated to categories of gender and sex. From the perspective of force and will, men cannot rule by virtue of any particular predisposition, whether anatomical or discursive.

Vital (vitalism, élan vital, political vitalism) (see *nature*, *life*, and *power of the outside*). Because anarchism very often identifies itself with "life" (particularly in Bakunin) and because its working-class expression could, for many reasons, be likened to Bergson and Nietzsche, one might be tempted, at first sight, to compare it to a particularly obvious form of political vitalism. However, anarchism has nothing to do with vitalism and with what is generally understood by this word. The life that it claims to express is in no way reducible to a biological or organic vision of reality. It primarily refers to the power of being of which the living, properly speaking, is only one particular manifestation (see *charge of nature* and the way in which Proudhon thinks the problem of the relation between the inorganic, the living, and the human). As a synonym for *force* and the differences between forces, from this point of view, the anarchist conception of life can be related to the concept of "potential energy" as

---

in two, scalped a giant bandit who preyed on travelers and made his hair into a flyswatter, and dashed out the brains of Lichas, one of the many envious people who mocked him, against a rock.

1   For a complete version of this narrative, which Proudhon freely translates from a Latin textbook for college students, see Proudhon, *La Guerre et la paix*, 14 et passim.

understood by Gilbert Simondon. In a usage even closer to the libertarian vocabulary, it can also be related to Gabriel Tarde's concept of "energy," in which, in the form of an "élan" – something "irresistible," "anarchic, demiurgic, protean" – life always exceeds any order, even that of living beings, and any ordered and stable "types."[1] As Tarde writes, "Types are only brakes and laws are only dykes erected in vain against the overflowing of revolutionary differences and civil dissensions, in which the laws and forms of tomorrow secretly take shape [see *intimacy*], and which, in spite of the yokes upon yokes they bear, *in spite of chemical and vital discipline*, in spite of reason, in spite of celestial mechanics, will one distant day, like the people of a nation, sweep away all barriers and from their very wreckage construct the instrument of a still higher diversity [emphasis my own]."[2]

Voluntarism (see *will*, with which voluntarism should not be confused). An idealistic and (thus) authoritarian conception of an oppressive order in which beings are supposed to subject their desires to external prescriptions issued by others (God, the State, and their many priests and servants), according to the principle that we can do what we must do, that we are capable of performing all of our moral obligations. On the contrary, following the philosopher Jean-Marie Guyau, anarchism proposes a social logic without duties or obligations, in which one must do only what one can do.[3] This proposition is only seemingly restrictive because the power specific to each being is infinitely richer in *possibilities*, for *good* or for *bad* (see these terms), than any law, moral principle, or normative precept.

Voluntary servitude (see *exterior/interior*).

---

1   Milet, *Gabriel Tarde et la philosophie de l'histoire*, 180.

2   Tarde, *Monadology and Sociology* 46-47, modifications my own. It is regrettable in this sense that Maurizio Lazzarato, in an otherwise very interesting essay (postscript to *Monadologie et sociologie*, Gabriel Tarde), reduces the Tardean conceptions of force and energy, contrary to the thesis of the texts themselves, to a narrowly vitalist dimension (in the current sense of the term), titling his text "Gabriel Tarde: un vitalisme politique" (Gabriel Tarde: A Political Vitalism), thus interning the political and revolutionary implications of Tarde's analyses within the framework of questions of biopower – a framework that is certainly interesting, but limited and deceptive compared with the libertarian dimension of Tarde's analyses.

3   Jean-Marie Guyau, *A Sketch of Morality Independent of Obligation or Sanction*, trans. Gertrude Kapteyn (London: Watts, 1898).

W

War (warlike) (see *tools/weapons, insurrection, violence,* and *labor*). Because it emerged in the 19ᵗʰ century and accumulated most of its experiences before the collective trauma of the war of 1914-1918,[1] anarchism is closely related to a form of heroism the importance of which should not be obscured by the military and totalitarian horrors of the 20ᵗʰ century. If the pacifist *reaction* to World War I could lead to the aberrations of *integral pacifism* during World War II, it is by no means certain that some of the versions of *nonviolence* that tend to prevail in some currents of the libertarian movement do not also contain forces and wills radically incompatible with libertarian emancipation. *Revolt, insurrection,* and thus a particular form of pride, violence, and relation to death are, in various forms, at the center of the anarchist imaginary and its project: the black flag of the Lyon silk workers of 1831 ("better to die on our feet than to live on our knees!"), the cavalry and the light *tachanki*[2] of the Makhnovist insurrectionary army, or, in a rather different context and in a very different sense, in Ascaso's death in battle on the Ramblas of Barcelona in July 1936. We would be wrong to interpret the way in which, historically, the anarchist movement integrated death into its project – whether in the explicit symbolism of its flag, the often desperate character of its battles, or, in yet another sense, the *attentats* of the years 1880-1890 (see *anarchist chemistry*) – in terms of morbidity or nihilism. The libertarian movement is not unaware of the horrors of war nor, on another register, of the repugnant character of

---

1 Although the Spanish revolution comes later, it is clear from a historical perspective that, in a country spared from World War I, this revolution formed part of the final manifestation of the 19th century libertarian workers' movements.

2 Translator's note: *Tachanki* were machine guns mounted on peasant carts, a tactical innovation of Makhno's forces.

the military institutions that make them possible, which it has never ceased to denounce and to combat in word and deed, through *insubordination* and the consistent refusal of any form of militarization and military institution.[1] But this resistance and this denunciation (individual or collective) are not to be confounded with a refusal of struggle as such, even in its most explicitly and cruelly warlike dimension: when it is a question "of taking up arms," of taking them back from the adversary and from the military institutions, or of transforming *tools* into *weapons* (see *tools/weapons*), making them serve purposes altogether different from their primary function, placing them within an entirely different dynamic, a radically new movement that is nonetheless deeply rooted in the origins and history of humanity. The particular egoism and care for the self that are frequently imputed to anarchism are in no way incompatible with an unfolding [*déploiement*] of the self that frequently pushes one to *risk one's life*, to go beyond one's own *limits* (see this term), insofar as this life consists precisely in going to the limits of one's capacities, discovering this *power of the outside* that one contains (see this term and also *more than oneself, implication*), where, perhaps, life and death merge.[2]

It is undoubtedly Bakunin who best and most frequently expresses this warlike and cruel dimension of libertarian revolt and insurrection, particularly when he appeals to "the action of the people," to "a mass uprising of all the French people," an uprising "organized from the bottom upward" for a "war of destruction," a "merciless war to the death."[3] But we also find it in Louise Michel, who was revolted by the ill treatment to which children subject animals, but who nonetheless engaged in all the battles of the Paris Commune, rifle at her shoulder, and who was congratulated by the *Journal officiel de la Commune* on April 10th for having "killed several gendarmes and policemen." As she explains in her memoirs, "Barbarian that I am, I love cannons, the smell of powder, machine-gun bullets in the air."[4] Even Proudhon, that impassioned singer of *labor*, was impelled to celebrate the virtues of combat and war in terms for which one would be wrong to reproach him too quickly:

"War, we greet you! It was war that enabled man to assert majesty and valor

---

1   See the beautiful Spanish text, *A Day Mournful and Overcast: By an "Uncontrollable" From the Iron Column* (London: Kate Sharpley Library, 2003), originally published in *Nosotros* in March 1937, or the methods of organization and action of the Makhnovist army of 1918-1921.

2   On "a life that is the power of the outside" and on its bond with death, cf. Deleuze, *Foucault*, 94 et passim.

3   Mikhail Bakunin, "Letters to a Frenchman on the Present Crisis," in *Bakunin on Anarchism*, 184.

4   Louise Michel, *The Red Virgin: Memoirs of Louise Michel*, ed. and trans. Bullitt Lowry and Elizabeth Ellington Gunter (University, AL: U. of Alabama Press, 1981), 66.

when he had scarcely emerged from the primeval slime which served him as a womb. He first dreamed of glory and immortality as he stood over the body of an enemy he had slain. Our philanthropic souls are horrified by blood that is spilled so freely and by fratricidal carnage. I am afraid that this squeamishness may indicate that our virtue is failing in strength…Wolves and lions do not make war on each other any more than sheep and beavers. This fact has for a long time been used to satirize our species. Why do people not see that, on the contrary, this is the sign of our greatness; that if, to imagine the impossible, nature had made man as an exclusively industrious, sociable being, and not at all warlike, he would from the first moment have sunk to the level of the beasts whose destiny is limited to a purely collective existence? Why can they not see that he would have lost his faculties for revolution along with his proud heroism, that most marvelous and most fertile of all his faculties?"[1]

One finds this positive perception of war and the warlike in contemporary expressions of libertarian thought: in Pierre Clastres's analyses of stateless societies, for example,[2] and especially in Deleuze and Guattari, when, following Nietzsche,[3] they distinguish the "warrior" from the "soldier," the "nomadic war machine" (of which the Makhnovshchina is undoubtedly one of the best examples in recent history) from "the State apparatus."[4] Indeed, alongside the two great divinities of the Indo-European tradition, Varuna and Mitra (the magician-king and the priest-judge, the bond and the pact, the despot and the legislator, the founding couple of the State and domination), stands the warlike and rebellious god Indra, the god of "pure and immeasurable multiplicity, the pack, an irruption of the ephemeral and the power of metamorphosis," the god who "*unties the bond just as he betrays the pact,*" the god who "brings a *furor* to bear against measurement, a celerity against gravity, secrecy against the public, a power against sovereignty, a machine against the apparatus." He is the warrior god who "bears witness to another kind of justice, one of incomprehensible cruelty at times, but at others of unequaled pity as well," the god who "bears witness, above all, to other relationships with women, with animals, because he sees all things in relations of becoming, rather than implementing binary distributions between 'states': a veritable becoming-animal of

---

1   Proudhon, *Selected Writings of P.J. Proudhon*, 203-4.

2   Pierre Clastres, *Society Against the State: Essays in Political Anthropology*, trans. Robert Hurley and Abe Stein (New York: Zone Books, 1987), and *Archeology of Violence*, trans. Jeanine Herman (Los Angeles: Semiotext(e), 2010).

3   "I see many soldiers: if only I saw many warriors!" (Nietzsche, *Thus Spoke Zarathustra*, 33).

4   It is precisely in this sense that insurrectionists, as the "constant rebels" and "passionate lovers of self-cultivation" of whom Fernand Pelloutier speaks, are opposed to "militants," obedient soldiers devoted to humanitarian causes (Pelloutier, "Lettre aux anarchistes," in *Le Congrès général du parti socialiste français, 3-8 décembre 1899* [Paris: P.-V. Stock, 1900], vii.).

the warrior, a becoming-woman, which lies outside dualities of terms as well as correspondences between relations. In every respect, the war machine is of another species, another nature, another origin than the State apparatus."[1] Quite logically, beginning with a critique of *work* (see *labor/work*), Deleuze and Guattari can emphasize the radical character of "the opposition between the socialist and anarchist currents of the nineteenth century," between the *will* of the former to take power and to transform the State apparatus – "the point of view of labor power" – and the will of the latter to destroy the State apparatus, which is "the point of view of a nomadization power." This opposition justifies anarchism's references to "nomadic themes originating in the East," its will to make the proletarian "the heir to the nomad in the Western world" (see *nomad, power of the outside*).[2]

Weapons (see *tools/weapons*).

Will (see *collective force* and *arrangement*). An important concept in revolutionary syndicalist and anarcho-syndicalist discourse, but especially in the thought of Malatesta, one of the principal theorists of libertarian communism (see *subjectivity*). Contrary to the schemas of Cartesian dualism, the libertarian conception of will has nothing to do with the so-called freedom of choice or decision always presupposed and required by oppressive orders from those it subjugates, as exemplified by when one asks a child to demonstrate his or her "willpower" to subject himself to demands external to his own desires (to do his duty, to love his little sister, to respect sexual morality) or, more ethereally, when one asks a citizen to express his or her "will" at the ballot box or when he or she signs a contract (of employment, marriage, rental, etc.). In the libertarian sense of the term, the will of a collective being is always the more or less conscious expression of the *force*, the *desire*, or the *power* of this being, the singular arrangement and the quality of the forces and situations that constitute it at a *given moment*. In this sense, the libertarian conception of will has much more in common with Nietzsche's *will to power* than with so-called free will. A "pure" will, separated from any determination intrinsic to the being that is supposed to be its subject and of which the only manifest demonstration lies in the constraint that this being imposes on itself, always indicates a relation of domination, the submission of this being to another being external to itself. This is the sole origin (quite real this time) of the will that it imposes on itself and that separates it from its own power, from its own will (see *self-discipline*).

Will to power. Nietzschean concept (see *plastic force*, *power*, and *desire*).

---

1   Deleuze and Guattari, *A Thousand Plateaus*, 352.
2   Deleuze and Guattari, *A Thousand Plateaus*, 558n61.

Worker (workerism) (see *labor/work*).

Worker separatism (see *master/slave*).

Worlds (plurality of worlds) (see *plane of immanence*).

MINOR COMPOSITIONS

Other titles in the series:

Occupation Culture – Alan W. Moore
Crisis to Insurrection – Mikkel Bolt Rasmussen
Gee Vaucher. Introspective – Ed. Stevphen Shukaitis
The Aesthetic of Our Anger – Ed. Mike Dines & Matthew Worley
The Way Out – Kasper Opstrup
Situating Ourselves in Displacement – Ed. Marc Herbst et al.
Organization after Social Media – Geert Lovink and Ned Rossiter
Don't Network – Marc James Léger
Neurocapitalism. Technological mediation and Vanishing Lines –
    Giorgio Griziotti